DIGITAL FAMILY JUSTICE

The editors' earlier book *Delivering Family Justice in the 21st Century* (2016) described a period of turbulence in family justice arising from financial austerity. Governments across the world have sought to reduce public spending on private quarrels by promoting mediation (ADR) and by beginning to look at digital justice (ODR) as alternatives to courts and lawyers.

But this book describes how mediation has failed to take the place of courts and lawyers, even where public funding for legal help has been removed. Instead ODR has developed rapidly, led by the Dutch Rechtwijzer. The authors question the speed of this development, and stress the need for careful evaluation of how far these services can meet the needs of divorcing families.

In this book, experts from Canada, Australia, Turkey, Spain, Germany, France, Poland, Scotland, and England and Wales explore how ADR has fallen behind, and how we have learned from the rise and fall of ODR in the Rechtwijzer about what digital justice can and cannot achieve. Managing procedure and process? Yes. Dispute resolution? Not yet.

The authors end by raising broader questions about the role of a family justice system: is it dispute resolution? Or dispute prevention, management, and above all legal protection of the vulnerable?

Oñati International Series in Law and Society

A SERIES PUBLISHED FOR THE OÑATI INSTITUTE
FOR THE SOCIOLOGY OF LAW

Recent titles in this series

Trust in International Police and Justice Cooperation
Edited by Saskia Hufnagel and Carole McCartney

Human Rights Encounter Legal Pluralism
Edited by Eva Brems, Giselle Corradi and Mark Goodale

Transitional Justice and the Public Sphere: Engagement, Legitimacy and Contestation
Edited by Chrisje Brants and Susanne Karstedt

Law and the Precarious Home: Socio Legal Perspectives on the Home in Insecure Times
Edited by Helen Carr, Brendan Edgeworth and Caroline Hunter

Criminologies of the Military: Militarism, National Security and Justice
Edited by Andrew Goldsmith and Ben Wadham

Law and the Precarious Home: Socio Legal Perspectives on the Home in Insecure Times
Edited by Helen Carr, Brendan Edgeworth and Caroline Hunter

Collective Bargaining and Collective Action: Labour Agency
and Governance in the 21st Century?
Edited by Julia López López

Fundamental Rights and Legal Consequences of Criminal Conviction
Edited Sonja Meijer, Harry Annison and Ailbhe O'Loughlin

For the complete list of titles in this series, see
'Oñati International Series in Law and Society' link at
www.bloomsburyprofessional.com/uk/series/
onati-international-series-in-law-and-society

Digital Family Justice

From Alternative Dispute Resolution to Online Dispute Resolution?

Edited by
Mavis Maclean
and
Bregje Dijksterhuis

Oñati International Series in Law and Society

A SERIES PUBLISHED FOR THE OÑATI INSTITUTE FOR THE SOCIOLOGY OF LAW

•HART•
OXFORD • LONDON • NEW YORK • NEW DELHI • SYDNEY

HART PUBLISHING

Bloomsbury Publishing Plc

Kemp House, Chawley Park, Cumnor Hill, Oxford, OX2 9PH, UK

HART PUBLISHING, the Hart/Stag logo, BLOOMSBURY and the Diana logo are trademarks of Bloomsbury Publishing Plc

First published in Great Britain 2019

A catalogue record for this book is available from the British Library.

Library of Congress Cataloging-in-Publication data

Names: Maclean, Mavis, editor. | Dijksterhuis, Bregje Monique, 1975- editor.

Title: Digital family justice : from alternative dispute resolution to online dispute resolution? / edited by Mavis Maclean and Bregje Dijksterhuis.

Description: Oxford ; New York : Hart, 2019. | Series: Oñati international series in law and society | Includes bibliographical references and index.

Identifiers: LCCN 2019031422 (print) | LCCN 2019031423 (ebook) | ISBN 9781509928521 (hardback) | ISBN 9781509928538 (Epub)

Subjects: LCSH: Domestic relations courts. | Matrimonial actions. | Online dispute resolution.

Classification: LCC K672 .D54 2019 (print) | LCC K672 (ebook) | DDC 346.01/50269—dc23

LC record available at https://lccn.loc.gov/2019031422

LC ebook record available at https://lccn.loc.gov/2019031423

ISBN: HB: 978-1-50992-852-1
ePDF: 978-1-50992-854-5
ePub: 978-1-50992-853-8

Typeset by Compuscript Ltd, Shannon

Acknowledgements

We wish, as always, to thank the Oñati Institute for hosting the workshop which gave rise to this publication. For the participants it made possible the stimulating and constructive exchange of experience and ideas which can only take place in such a supportive environment.

Mavis Maclean
and
Bregje Dijksterhuis
May 2019

Contents

Acknowledgements .... *v*
List of Contributors .... *ix*

Introduction *1*
Mavis Maclean and Bregje Dijksterhuis

PART A
DIGITAL FAMILY JUSTICE: POLITICAL AND PROFESSIONAL CONTEXTS FOR CHANGE

(1) **The Political Landscape**

1. *'My Problem, My Solution'? Private Ordering and Self-help in British Columbia, Canada* *17*
Rachel Treloar

2. *Choosing Paths to Dispute Resolution in Post-Communist Poland* *43*
Małgorzata Fuszara and Jacek Kurczewski

3. *Competing Logics, Norms and World Visions: The Family Justice System in Turkey* *59*
Verda Irtis

(2) **The Professional Landscape**

4. *Legal Help by Student Lawyers: Harnessing the Thinking Behind Digital Expert Systems* *75*
Lisa Webley

5. *Mediation in Germany – The Possibilities for and Limits of Mediation* *87*
Adelheid Kühne and Barbara Willenbacher

6. *Different Forms of Alternative Dispute Resolution: The Framework for Family Mediation in Spain* *103*
Teresa Picontó Novales, Elena Lauroba, Cristina Merino and Marcos Loredo Colunga

PART B
THE DEVELOPMENT OF DIGITAL FAMILY JUSTICE

7. *Family Justice in France: Two Dimensions of Digitisation* *127*
Benoit Bastard

8. *From ADR to ODR in Scots Family Justice: No Clear Direction of Travel* *139*
Jane Mair

9. *Representations of Family Justice in Online Communities* *157*
Leanne Smith

10. *Digital Pathways in Australian Family Law: An Initial Snapshot* *179*
Belinda Fehlberg and Bruce Smyth

PART C
THE WAY AHEAD

11. *The Online Divorce Resolution Tool 'Rechtwijzer uit Elkaar' Examined* *193*
Bregje Dijksterhuis

12. *The Digital Contribution to Reforming the Traditional Family Justice System in England and Wales: Reaching for the Best of Both Worlds?* *215*
Mavis Maclean

13. *A Short Case Study: A Considered and Collaborative Approach to Digital Delivery in England and Wales* *231*
Alexy Buck, Alejandra Diaz and Kate Gregory-Smith

Index *237*

List of Contributors

Dr Benoit Bastard is a senior researcher at CNRS-ENS – Universite Paris Saclay France

Alexy Buck is Chief Social Researcher and Head of Family Justice Research, Ministry of Justice, London, England

Alejandra Diaz is a member of the Digital Unit, Ministry of Justice, London, England

Bregje Dijksterhuis is Assistant Professor, University of Utrecht, Netherlands

Belinda Fehlberg is Professor of Law, University of Melbourne Australia

Malgorzata Fuszara is Professor in the Institute for Applied Social Sciences, University of Warsaw

Kate Gregory Smith, formerly Ministry of Justice, now Ministry of Housing, Communities and Local Government

Dr Verda Irtis is Assistant Professor, Department of Sociology, Galatasaray University, Istanbul, Turkey

Adelheid Kuhne is Professor at the Institute of Sociology, Leibniz University, Hannover, Germany

Jacek Kurczewski is Professor of Sociology and Anthropology of Custom and Law, University of Warsaw

Marcos Laredo Colunga is Professor of Law, University of Oviedo, Spain

Mavis Maclean is Senior Research Fellow, University of Oxford, UK

Jane Mair is Professor of Private Law, University of Glasgow, Scotland

Cristina Merino is Professor at the Universidad del Pais Vasco, Spain

Elena Nauroba is Professor of Law, University of Barcelona, Spain

Teresa Picontó Novales is Professor of Law, University of Zaragoza, Spain

Dr Leanne Smith is Reader in Law, University of Cardiff, Wales

Bruce Smyth is Professor of Family Studies, ANU Australia

Dr Rachel Treloar is Lecturer in Law, School of Law, Keele University, England

Lisa Webley is Professor of Law, University of Birmingham, England

Dr Barbara Willenbacher is a member of the Institute of Sociology, Leibniz University, Hannover, Germany

Introduction

MAVIS MACLEAN AND BREGJE DIJKSTERHUIS

THIS INTRODUCTION WILL set out the aim and scope of this book, and identify the structure and analytical framework employed in the chapters which follow from Canada, Poland, Turkey, Spain, France, Scotland, Germany and Australia, ending with a look to the future from the editors who draw on analysis of the problems arising from ambitious projects in the Netherlands and the slower developments in England and Wales. We present as our final chapter a short case study from the Ministry of Justice in London, which makes clear the complexity of the task, and the potential for contributing to access to family justice in hard times.

I. AIM AND SCOPE

We begin by exploring the policy and professional context for recent developments.

A. Digital Family Justice: Exploring the Policy Context

The continuing period of financial austerity has led governments in a number of jurisdictions to seek ways of limiting public expenditure and seeking value for money in many areas of activity, not least in the provision of family justice. The support traditionally supplied by lawyers, with varying levels of public funding, was expected in some jurisdictions to be replaced by the less costly provision of help through mediation. This policy, however, appears to have met with limited success. Instead, governments are showing increasing interest in the development of IT in many areas of activity, digital pathways being seen as a route to self help in resolving family problems, offering information and sometimes advice and dispute resolution. In jurisdictions where the policy context can be described as neo-liberal, this policy approach has the attraction of offering not only cost savings but also the prospect of increasing individual responsibilisation, rather than continuing dependence on the state. Access to family justice appears to be moving away from the traditional pathway of access to the services of courts and lawyers and towards new digital systems for support with legal matters.

In this book we present observations and analysis of these developments in a number of jurisdictions in Europe, Canada and Australia as well as the UK (Scotland and England and Wales). Digital procedures which reduce or bypass the role of lawyers and attendance in court may work well. But following the limited success of the previous investment in other alternative methods of dispute resolution (ADR), particularly mediation, we wish to look with caution at the ongoing experience of help by vulnerable parties who are seeking settlement of financial and children issues after divorce without access to the individualised services of courts and lawyers. We aim to address the question of the nature and impact of these changes in a number of settings, which we suggest may represent the continuing search for a 'silver bullet' if we are expecting IT to provide a solution for all problems. We hope to draw attention to the additional need for a careful consideration of the different kinds of pathways through family problems which are likely to need a range of different forms of information and advice, and hopefully conflict avoidance, as well as support with problem solving and dispute resolution.

B. The Professional Landscape: The Observed and Potential Impact on Access to Family Justice of Digital Developments in Relation to Other Recent Innovations in the Family Justice System

Family justice systems in many jurisdictions are finding themselves under increasing pressure as both public and private resources diminish, and the policy context remains dominated by the rolling back of state responsibility for legal help. Parties in family disputes are becoming more likely to turn to the help of volunteers, including both professional lawyers and law students, and also lay advisers, or to public legal education provision through advice services and websites. Where cases still go to court, there are pressures for them to be dealt with more effectively with online filing of documents and video conferencing with witnesses.

We note also how the legal profession is changing its ways of working. A narrower range of casework is being carried out by lawyers in several jurisdictions, and new forms of more specific task-focused activity (known as unbundling or limited brief work) are being carried out in law firms, and also by new occupational groups in an attempt to cut costs. Professional boundaries are becoming more permeable. Lawyers may find themselves arbitrating or mediating for clients to avoid court costs rather than advising or representing. Non-lawyers are being drawn in to give low-cost advice in legal matters, though there is considerable discussion about what constitutes legal advice and what activities may be carried out by lawyers and non-lawyers. For example, a new group of 'decision makers' whose background was not specified appeared in the interactive divorce website Rechtwijzer in the Netherlands, adding a decision-making option when agreement could not be reached.

However, this service recently ceased activity, as it was unable to achieve commercial viability.

The distinction between legal advice and legal information is becoming increasingly blurred. For example, in England non-lawyer volunteers are present in some courts to support unrepresented parties in family cases (known as litigants in person or LiPs) and may be drawn into giving specific legal information which comes close to being advice. The distinction is hard to draw, and is often dependent on the context. For example, the line between helping an unrepresented party fill in a form, and advising on what to say on a form is hard to draw in the heat of the moment with distressed men and women about to walk into a court hearing about access to their children. Similar developments are reported in other professions, particularly in medicine, where nurses are now undertaking work formerly done by doctors, such as prescribing drugs and even carrying out surgical procedures. And the patient also is expected to do more, as clinical decisions are being made jointly by the medical experts together with the patients aided by diagnostic websites.

Such changes are exciting, but when driven primarily by economic constraints, we need to be cautious. The policy maker usually seeks an option which will be quicker, better and cheaper. But usually only two of these three aims can be achieved. If an option is better and quicker it is unlikely to be cheaper … and if cheaper it is unlikely to be both better and quicker. We are concerned that the vulnerable men, women and children involved in family difficulties which are serious enough to lead to family separation, and cannot be resolved by the parties alone or with informal help from friends and family, should be able to access appropriate support in finding fair and informed settlement. Public levels of education have risen, deference in the legal system has decreased, and the internet gives most people access to unlimited information. But information alone, however skilfully provided, is not enough. Parties need advice on how to use information when making decisions. And the information needs to be clear and reliable, and not spread over a multiplicity of websites.

There is a need for caution and careful evaluation as we turn to the rapid development of digital process in family cases. The Rechtwijzer in the Netherlands has now been followed by a private commercial venture called Justice42. There have been rapid developments in civil matters in British Columbia, and an Out of Court Digital Pathway for family matters is being developed in the UK. These changes are accompanied by the development of online information management and support, mediation, and court hearings using electronic paper management and video conferencing in many jurisdictions.

We note a common direction of travel towards acceptance of increased personal responsibility, and privatisation in decision making. Instead of the traditional end-to-end legal service, a lawyer may offer a defined element of work for a fixed fee. While this option is cheaper for the client who may take over some parts of the work for himself, there are risks associated with the lawyer not knowing what he does not know about a matter, and with the client failing to understand the limits of the lawyer's intervention. The lawyer may no longer take on the central role of the traditional lawyer working face-to-face with the client on the totality of their case. There may be gains in terms of increased personal responsibility and wider acquisition of dispute resolution skills in a community. But there are also risks to the client if the system fails to address the impact of power imbalance between parties, and there may be limited access to optimum results where there is no skilled advice to help in securing the best possible outcome for all concerned, including the children. We must also consider the impact of any reduction in the visibility of clear social norms as embedded in an enforceable legal framework, which may be of even greater importance in more diverse societies.

Digitisation is becoming the policy of choice for a number of reasons. There are clearly substantial benefits to be gained from developing the use of IT in administering legal procedures and in the running of court business. The more sophisticated websites have made great strides in other areas of government activity, such as enabling clients to apply for social security benefits online, thereby cutting administrative costs, though personal support in using the system may be necessary. But there remains a serious difficulty in trying to facilitate online interaction when it is not between client and government but between two parties in dispute. A computer cannot interrogate evidence, or challenge disclosure, as a court can do. And while a website can provide accurate and relevant information, it cannot help the user decide how to respond to it. Recent research in London (Denvir, 2014) involved a controlled experiment using students with good computer skills to test an interactive website designed to help with legal problems. They were given a landlord and tenant problem, familiar to students in many jurisdictions. The students were easily able to find the information they needed on the website. But when it came to making a decision on how to proceed, what to do next, the computer could not help them. The most common outcome was that the students telephoned their parents to ask for advice, that is, they need a trusted intermediary.

II. STRUCTURE AND ORGANISATION OF THIS BOOK

A. An Analytical framework

The starting point for this group of scholars is a shared interest in supporting the Rule of Law through Access to Justice, and the part played by courts and lawyers in making this possible for those with family matters. We come from different starting points, with different issues and concerns. But we are all experiencing a period of rapid change. Following our earlier title in the Oñati Series, *Delivering Family Justice in the 21st Century*, which identified the gradual withdrawal of the state from the private sphere when dealing with couples but maintaining control when dealing with children and parenting (Maclean,

Eekelaar and Bastard (eds) (2015)), in this book we are better able to place the different jurisdictions at different points along this complex multi-route journey, looking carefully at who is doing what and how. For some of us, the court is the place of last resort for dealing with serious conflict, offering both decisions and mechanisms for enforcement. For others, the court is the hub where information on helping services is available, making decisions not about individual behaviour but about how to access the help needed by families in difficulty. For example, in the UK we face the recent restriction of access to justice in the traditional form of courts and lawyers to those who have the resources to pay. In Canada there is a strong focus on community-based private ordering, and in Poland there is interest in the increasing levels of confidence in courts with an independent judiciary after so many years of alienation from state values and policies, but a concern to protect the privacy of the family. In France family matters are moving away from courts into a more private but still legalised sphere, while in Australia lawyers who were previously excluded have begun to work with counsellors in Family Relationship Centres.

The common factor remains the lack of resources, which results in delay, reduction of public funding for various services, the reduced availability of lawyers for those without resources, and the continuing search for alternative and hopefully cheaper methods of dispute resolution. Mediation, as we have noted, has had limited success. The great hope of policy makers now lies in increased use of digital technology.

The chapters which follow are set out in three parts: Part A – Digital Family Justice: Political and Professional Contexts for Change; Part B – The Development of Digital Family Justice; and Part C – The Way Ahead.

Part A starts by looking at the political context, with chapters from Canada, Poland and Turkey which demonstrate the impact of different political settings on ways of approaching the place of the courts in access to family justice.

In chapter one, from British Columbia, Canada, Rachel Treloar describes an extreme form of withdrawal by a neo-liberal state from ensuring access to justice in family matters, even those with complex parenting problems where there will be direct consequences for the children. She describes how, in the context of cutbacks to publicly funded legal aid and other services, parents are now expected to take responsibility for resolving their legal problems without recourse to the courts. In such a context, parents with complex family law problems have few places to which to turn. She presents evidence from her qualitative study of mothers and fathers who experienced high conflict divorce, describing how they interpret and navigate the experience. The chapter first describes how parents experienced ADR, and how they used the internet for self help purposes. The author then goes on to describe MyLawBC, an interactive digital platform introduced in 2016 with the aim of empowering individuals to act on their legal problems. The platform is new, and not fully evaluated, but the author draws on detailed knowledge from her study to reflect on whether it would have helped the parents in her study, noting also that a three-day trial would cost around

40,000 dollars while a mediation costs usually only 3,000 dollars. She suggests that while the platform could provide basic information, those with complex needs will require access to court and social support services. Practitioners and policy makers need to know more about parental needs.

By contrast, in chapter two, from Warsaw, Poland, Jacek Kurczewski and Malgorzata Fuszara present data from their long-term quantitative study of preference for different methods of dispute resolution in Poland in the context of changing political circumstances. In discussing how and if courts are used, they found in earlier work that the current strength of the courts as an institution of justice had been underestimated. They suggest that ADR, or mediation, was not the first method to be considered by the majority of those with justiciable disputes. Although neighbourhood informal justice was regarded positively by those who had used it, these respondents did not advocate using it in future disputes. The authors were concerned to identify why and how the various procedures (mediation, conciliation, arbitration) which offer an alternative to courts for dispute resolution are perhaps leading to simplification and softening of the adjudicative model of justice.

They present data on the general patterns of dispute resolution in Polish popular culture, looking at different types of court experience, according to religiosity and to socio demographic profiles, and in particular look at the effect of regime change on these patterns. Free elections began in 1989, and the position of the judiciary changed to become free from party political control. Surprisingly, in their first study, they did not find that economic freedom had led to more court cases arising from property disputes, but rather the contrary, in that the sense of an increase in private rights seemed to have been accompanied by an increase in the wish for private forms of settlement, particularly in family matters. In this chapter they describe the development of digital procedures to provide, as in other jurisdictions, for speedier and less costly resolution of minor civil disputes, particularly small debts of recent origin. But they note an ongoing reluctance to deal with family matters outside the family circle, and that if it becomes necessary to approach a court, it would not be appropriate for parties to be dealt with by digital procedures but only by a judge who has personally interviewed and formed a view of the people concerned. In earlier work, they also found that those higher up the social scale were more likely to use the courts. And by 2014, when compared with data from 1974, there was more interest in official settlement strictly according to the law among younger people living in towns, while informal mediation remained popular among older people in the country. In family matters, however, there remains a firm preference for a dispute with an individual to be settled informally, though if the dispute was with an institution, the preference would be for court.

Chapter three is by Verda Irtis, who begins by analysing the different norms that govern family justice in Turkey, where the system, despite its local dynamics, is very open to what is transferred or imported from the external world. She describes the unsuccessful short history of family mediation, and considers the

Irsat Offices and Centres for Women's Solidarity as 'alternatives' to mediation. She then describes the Turkish response to the digital environment in public services, including the judicial function, illustrated by interviews with practising lawyers on the impact on their work and more generally on the impact of competing logic, norms and world vision in practice for those working in the family justice system. The author explains how Turkey was awarded the UN public service award largely as a recognition of the development of digital public services. There is a national electronic service covering all court functions: citizens and lawyers can examine files, pay fees, submit documents and claims, and file cases electronically in any court in the country. This process began in the eCourt for Commercial and Labour Law, but it is planned that the Ministry of Justice should extend this to services concerning family matters, including divorce and children cases.

Part A then moves to look at changing professional roles and boundaries in family justice. In chapter four, Lisa Webley describes the part increasingly played by students with the development of Clinical Legal Education (CLE). The role of the student is limited to support and supervised advice in family matters without ongoing assistance or representation, and with referrals to specialist advisers. Sadly, it can do little to fill the gap left by the cuts to legal aid in England and Wales. It is, however, having an important impact on developing the future ability of these students to work with clients, and on their understanding of the political context of family justice. It has also led to the development of new ways of teaching family law. Lisa Webley describes how, as the supervising faculty member, she developed flow charts to demonstrate the demographics of family clients, and the need for binary questions to be interrogated. She also notes the students' need for support in coping with the emotional impact of being unable to solve the problems being brought to them. The level of supervision makes the process labour intensive and costly to the providing college. But the service is highly valued by local courts dealing with unrepresented litigants, and by clients and students.

Chapters five and six look at the situation in Germany and Spain where, although the earlier forms of ADR, including family mediation, have not been widely taken up, there is not yet a major policy interest in developing Online Dispute Resolution (ODR). In chapter five, Barbara Willenbacher and Adelheid Kuhne describe the relatively successful impact of mediation in criminal cases as a form of restorative justice, and within peer groups of school children, where it remains popular, though use is declining. But mediation is not thought to have developed a useful role in interpersonal family conflicts (it is used in only 1% of family cases). In family matters, legal problem solving is preferred. In children hearings, the aim is now to impose joint legal custody. They report that only 3% of cases recently observed resulted in sole custody. A third of cases are contested, and all the relevant professionals, including mediators, attend. But as mediation has been so unsuccessful, the mediators who have little work are now asking for state funding and for mediation to be compulsory, though this is not likely to happen.

For Spain, a wide range of experience across three autonomias is described in chapter six. Professor Piconto begins by setting out the national picture, with independent training and accreditation for mediators on registers within autonomias. Her colleagues follow with short accounts of similar events in three autonomias. The process from Mediation to Collaborative Law in Catalonia is described by Professor Lauroba; for the Basque Country, Cristina Merino describes pre-court extrajudicial mediation organised by social services, with a comment on the intra judicial mediation organised by the department; and finally Professor Loredo describes the absence of mediation but the development of collaborative practice across Spain. There is little interest so far in ODR.

Part B covers the development of digital family justice, and the impact of some examples of digital activity in family justice on the legal profession, the courts and the substantive law. Chapter seven describes the use of digital techniques in managing family cases by courts and lawyers in France, followed by chapters eight and nine which compare developments in England and Scotland.

In Chapter seven, Benoit Bastard describes how from the 1970s until 2017 the pressure on the courts in divorce and family matters led to a speeding up of the process by the judges, who were making twice as many decisions a month (80) as their colleagues in other civil cases. Benoit Bastard describes how the digital initiative came first from the courts. When a digital network was created in 2005, linking court and advocates in civil cases, it was welcomed and was successful. However, it still gives rise to questions, for example about the impact of the decline in personal interaction between lawyers in the courts, and about the future of the profession. In 2017 the law was changed to remove judges from the divorce process where the matter was agreed. The two lawyers now prepare agreements which are lodged with a notary, though a child may request to be heard and represented by a lawyer free of charge, and for the matter to be reviewed by a judge. There are questions about the relationship between these digital developments which Benoit Bastard describes as an aspect of the ongoing managerialisation of judicial process, and this new, so far unevaluated, procedure.

In chapter eight, by contrast, Jane Mair describes how and suggests why Scotland has been slow to turn to digital process, citing the importance of the lawyer's role. The Scottish system presents an ideal framework for the development of ODR, as each element of the process, the divorce itself and the arrangements for children and property division, is relatively discrete. The legal rules are clear, and there is a well-established preference for client autonomy. A simplified divorce procedure is already online, and it is used by the majority of couples. It can only be used where there are no ancillary disputes, which adds an inbuilt incentive for couples to reach agreement. But while there seems to be a good fit and the technology is clear, there is a danger that, by focusing on simplification, what is lost is an understanding of the overarching framework. The rules are easy to explain and therefore digitise. What requires more thought is how to replicate artificially the intelligence of the family lawyer who sees how these simple steps fit together.

In chapter nine Leanne Smith adds to the digital impact picture her account of the discussion taking place online in chat forums among people sharing their experiences of family disputes, enabling us to examine previously invisible approaches to dispute resolution. Analysis of these conversations has the potential to provide rich insights into the extent to which people bargain in the shadow of the law, and why conceptualisations of family justice vary.

This section closes with an account in chapter ten of rapidly growing digital developments in family justice in Australia from Belinda Fehlberg and Bruce Smyth. Their consideration of the extent to which Australia has seen increasing interest in and commitment to the development and use of online family law resources finds that most work, often originating in America, has been done in the area of providing information online. There has been much less emphasis (although some early work) on online advice and dispute resolution options. However, recent moves to online divorce and online court orders suggest that the position is changing, raising concerns regarding access to justice for those who do not have ready access to the internet and digital technology. The authors describe increasing use of smartphone apps in Australia for parents to manage post separation parenting, These post separation apps for parents are also used in Canada (see chapter one) and in the Netherlands.

Part C, looking to the future, describes two very different ways in which governments have supported digital developments in the Netherlands and England and Wales. We have a cautionary tale from the Netherlands, where government enthusiastically supported an interactive website which tried to embrace conflict resolution as well as divorce process. And in England and Wales, we describe a more cautious approach, with constant reference to the needs of the potential users. We end with a proposal for including the best of both worlds … asking digital systems to do what they do well, but inserting the contribution of the experienced lawyer … putting the lawyer into the website.

In chapter eleven, Bregje Dijksterhuis describes the rise and fall of the most famous of all digital developments, the Rechtwijzer, an innovative tool developed by the research centre HIIL and supported by the Dutch Legal Aid Board. The aim was to enable divorcing parties to do more for themselves and work towards a harmonious divorce. The project received a great deal of attention internationally, and an adapted version was implemented in Canada and considered in England. However, the Rechtwijzer was used by only a small number of divorcing couples and was not received with enthusiasm by the majority of the legal profession, including the judiciary. The digital technical expertise in preparation was not fully matched by an understanding of the legal context and the experience of separating couples and their children. It was not commercially viable, and HIIL withdrew. There is now a successor to this scheme Justice42, endorsed but not funded by government which tries to attract more users than before, but faces competition from other services and does not yet have public confidence.

In chapter twelve, Mavis Maclean describes how the Ministry of Justice digital team from London presented their work at a showcasing event in August 2016, describing how work on the role of digital development in the family justice space was being organised and carried out in England and Wales. The value of an interdisciplinary and collaborative approach, drawing on policy, digital and analytical expertise, was highlighted. These digital developments were taking place against the background of the long established policy goal of helping separating parents to avoid court hearings, *where appropriate*, in order to help families resolve disputes in environments which do not exacerbate conflict and lead to poorer outcomes for children. Importantly, however, there was also recognition that there is a real need for some cases to be in court. Policy thinking has been informed by evidence, limited by financial constraints and excited by digital possibilities. The overall aim is to develop user-centred digital and non-digital products to help support separating parents through their journey of making arrangements for their children. Continuous feedback contributes to wider policy work, and facilitates a more nuanced response when a new digital product is not yet fulfilling user needs. The book ends with chapter thirteen, a case study by Buck and Diaz of one specific example of the successful development and implementation of a digital tool, the 'C100' application form for a child arrangements order.

When the Workshop which gave rise to this book was first discussed in 2016, the Rechtwijzer was widely regarded as the path to take, and digital developments were moving ahead with the speed of an Express Train. We were nervous about the speed and direction of travel. The Express appeared likely to bypass traditional courts and lawyers, and to have only one stop at the destination of Digital Dispute Resolution. We have now developed a clearer picture of what digital technology can and cannot provide. Assistance with court management and procedure is clearly able to cut costs and time taken. It may require digital support services for those with limited literacy, language issues or technological skills, but provided that a system is user-centred and legally expert in its development, there is much to be gained. The role of the lawyer, however, becomes less clearly defined if expert systems are able to provide informative websites which may offer advice on the options available and the next step to take. At the same time the lawyers themselves are using IT to develop their own working practices, for example in Australia using a 'Lawbot' to carry out the 'on boarding' process with new clients which takes time but does not require a high level of legal expertise. Digital Justice needs to find a place for the legal and non-legal experience-based expertise of the lawyer. In London, the major advice agency, Citizens Advice, developed a system that does incorporate both in the website 'CourtNav' for divorce application which uses simple questions drawing on practical experience to collect the information needed for a petition. For example, several pages of legally technical questions in the petition about domicile are replaced with the single question 'do you usually live in the UK?'. The information is then checked and used to populate the petitions which can then be submitted to the court. The process includes a number of pop-up boxes giving the applicant the benefit of the experience of the lawyers who worked on its design by indicating the potential consequences of some of the choices to be made.

While welcoming the recent more nuanced-user centred approaches to digital family justice, we nevertheless suspect that what we are seeing is one more stage in the continuing search for an instant 'fix' to the problems of providing conflict resolution for those with family legal problems. Divorce has been a key focus for both ADR and ODR, partly as a result of two widespread but questionable assumptions; first, that parties can be enabled to achieve self-reliance and, secondly, that experts, particularly lawyers, escalate conflict. Further research is needed to evidence both these ideas. The journey from ADR to ODR has taken us so far … but this is unlikely to be the last stop on the Express journey. Indeed, a single train is unlikely to enable everyone to reach their individual destination.

The chapters in this book, like all the best research, provide more questions than answers. We suggest it is time to learn more about the various pathways through family life before problems arise in order to develop at least some variation in the paths which can best lead separating couples, particularly parents, through the difficult period of change which inevitably accompanies family change. In doing so we need to keep in mind that conflict resolution is not the only goal. We are also concerned with preventing conflict, and with solving problems and post-decision management. If conflict cannot be avoided and must be managed, we then seek not only conflict resolution, which may simply be the victory of the strongest. We seek access to justice. The Ministry of Justice in London has used different 'straplines' to describe the goals for family justice over the years. In 1990 the message was clear and simple and set out a needs-based goal: 'Protecting the Vulnerable'. By 2012 attention had moved to improving delivery and value for money, and spoke of systems for 'promoting fair and informed settlement'. Now the line has become rather abstract and calls quite properly for 'promoting and advancing the principles of justice', but there is no reference to the needs of users. This wide spectrum of goals makes it hardly surprising that one system, whether ADR or ODR, cannot achieve them all.

REFERENCES

Maclean, M, Eekelaar, J and Bastard, B (eds) (2015) *Delivering Family Justice in the 21st Century* (Oxford, Hart Publishing).

Denvir, C (2014) *What is the Net Worth?* PhD Thesis, University College, London.

Part A

Digital Family Justice: Political and Professional Contexts for Change

(1) The Political Landscape

1

'My Problem, My Solution'? Private Ordering and Self-help in British Columbia, Canada

RACHEL TRELOAR

I. INTRODUCTION

THIS CHAPTER EXPLORES private ordering and self-help in the contemporary British Columbia (BC) family law and justice context, which involves both significant cutbacks to legal aid and other services and the expectation that parents will take responsibility for resolving their legal problems, in most cases without recourse to the courts. In such a context, parents with complex family law problems have few places to turn. Drawing on the socio-legal literature and from my doctoral research which explored how mothers and fathers who experienced a high-conflict divorce process make meaning of and navigate the experience, the chapter first provides a critical review of the literature on Alternative Dispute Resolution (ADR), discusses the privatisation of family law disputes, and summarises participants' experiences of ADR. Secondly, the chapter discusses participants' use of the Internet for self-help purposes. Thirdly, the chapter describes MyLawBC, an interactive digital platform introduced in mid-2016 with the aim of empowering people to act on their legal problems, and reflects on whether it would have helped these parents. Finally, the chapter considers the shift to digital self-help, especially given the shrinking role of the state in family justice.

The empirical study on which this chapter draws was undertaken from a critical and feminist perspective and employed a qualitative research design. The study sought to answer the following research questions: (1) How do individual mothers and fathers come to make meaning of and know themselves through the process of a high-conflict divorce? Subquestions included: How are individual interpretations influenced by social relations and discourses? How do collective meanings drawn from extra-legal discourses shape personal meanings and experiences of conflict in such situations and influence the take-up of legal norms? (2) How does high-conflict divorce become transformed into a positive experience? What personal and social relations/processes facilitate this? What challenges are encountered and how are they overcome? The research method involved in-depth face-to-face interviews with 25 parents[1] residing in British Columbia, who at one time experienced a high-conflict divorce and later identified surviving or navigating the experience as transformative. Participants were recruited through newspaper advertisements, community agencies, legal and health practitioners, ADR practitioners and chain referrals by previous participants.

Three key themes emerged from thematic analysis of participant interviews: the interrelationship of financial and child-related issues; the construction of expert knowledge and implications for justice and voice; and that positive personal change occurs over time when supported with personal, social, and material resources that address a parent's particular needs and challenges. While each of these themes links to the focus of this workshop, this chapter focuses on what participants said about their use of out of court dispute resolution (ADR) and how they used the Internet for self-help purposes.

Canada has both federal and provincial/territorial laws that play a role post-separation. The federal Divorce Act[2] regulates divorce for married spouses and also applies in situations when child custody, access, child support, and spousal support are aspects of a divorce application. Outside of the context of a divorce application, provincial or territorial laws regulate child custody, access, child support and spousal support. The division of family property is regulated by provincial and territorial statutes, even when divorce is involved.

BC's Family Law Act (FLA)[3] came into full force in March 2013. This statute is intended to reflect social change, to put children first and to keep families safe (Bond, 2013). The Act emphasises out of court dispute resolution,[4] which was promoted as cheaper, faster, and as having fewer emotional consequences for all involved (Bond, 2013). However, no new funding was provided to fund the services and programmes that families require as they go through the emotional and legal process of divorce. In line with a broader shift from welfare state provision toward a neoliberal approach to governance, family justice in BC is now largely privatised (Treloar, 2015; Treloar and Boyd, 2014).

In Canada, legal aid plans prioritise constitutionally guaranteed legal aid services, with the remaining funding going to civil legal aid. Beginning with significant cuts in 2002, family law legal aid has largely been eliminated in BC. Nevertheless, the provincial government, the legal aid service provider (Legal

[1] Study participants (18 mothers and 7 fathers aged between 42 and 72 years) were 4–23 years post-separation. At separation, the age of participants' youngest child ranged from unborn to 14 years and 18 of 25 participants had a child less than five years of age. Interviews took place between 2012 and 2014.

[2] Divorce Act, RSC 1985, c 3 (2nd Supp), s 2(1).

[3] British Columbia Family Law Act, SBC 2011, c 25.

[4] British Columbia Family Law Act, SBC 2011, c 25, s 4.

Services Society (LSS)), and other academic and professional groups are trying to broaden the scope of legal services within existing funding and new initiatives are being piloted. For example, between 2013 and 2015 a pilot project allowed designated paralegals to appear in family law proceedings in certain courts, with legal supervision. However, the project was discontinued[5] before it could be determined whether paralegals could effectively perform specific procedural applications in court and whether the service provided a benefit. More recently, LSS launched two new pilot programmes. The first expands the scope of family duty counsel services[6] at the Justice Access Centre (JAC) in Victoria. The second provides callers to the Family LawLINE[7] up to six hours with the same lawyer. Furthermore, Family LawLINE now offers those who qualify additional unbundled services, such as the preparation of documents and settlements. Virtual initial needs determination (VIND), a telephone triage system operated by the provincial Family Justice Services, is also now part of the legal self-help landscape in BC.[8]

In 2016, MyLawBC,[9] an interactive digital platform modelled on the Dutch Rechtwijzer, was introduced in BC. The inevitable shift to online service provision for family dispute resolution not only responds to the high cost of legal services but also reflects a broader trend for people to conduct business, seek information and communicate online. British Columbia is a vast province of 944,735 square kilometers (364,764 sq mi),[10] almost four times the size of the UK. The majority of BC residents live near the southern border, where most services and transportation connections are located. Residents of northern, rural, and remote communities, many of whom are Aboriginal, have limited access to legal and other professional services. Internet access is not available in all communities.

An understanding of how privatisation is implicated in parents' experiences of, and responses to, the family justice system is central to this chapter. While the state has largely withdrawn from support and intervention in family matters, the remaining funding has been redeployed both to ADR and to the development of online informational resources, neither of which are sufficient to assist parents with complex or high-conflict disputes. Yet, as my study demonstrates,

[5] Apparently, the pilot project was discontinued due to low participation by lawyers: http://vancouversun.com/news/local-news/ian-mulgrew-b-c-law-society-sidelines-paralegal-access-to-justice-initiative.

[6] Family duty counsel (FDC) is available to provide 'brief advice services' to 'eligible' clients. The pilot programme provides more continuity of advice (up to six hours with the same lawyer, rather than the usual three) and expanded coaching for Litigants in Person (LiP). Besides limited advice, information and referrals may be provided and eligible persons may also obtain assistance with preparing documents and preparing for a court appearance.

[7] LSS's province-wide phone advice line: www.lss.bc.ca/legal_aid/FamilyLawLINE.php.

[8] A VIND interviewer provides the client with basic programme/service information, conducts an initial evaluation of whether their needs may be served by Family Justice Services or those of an external agency, and then makes referrals as appropriate. However, VIND is a triage system only.

[9] http://mylawbc.com.

[10] www.britannica.com/place/British-Columbia.

parents involved in a high-conflict divorce process do engage in self-help, exercising their agency and parental responsibilities. They do so even though they are not always able to resolve their disputes out of court or fulfil contemporary social and legal norms for divorcing parents.

II. ADR: ISSUES AND CRITIQUES

Mediation is perhaps the best known, used and researched form of ADR. In BC, mediation emerged in the late 1970s, largely in response to the legal profession's struggle to effectively deal with interpersonal conflicts and a search for alternatives (Boyle, 2013). Although mediation may vary in terms of how it is practised and funded, and the extent to which it is genuinely voluntary, generally it is a voluntary process in which a trained third party attempts to bring parties in conflict to a consensual agreement (ie, a 'win-win' solution). The third party is said to be neutral in the dispute, although this has been a matter of debate in the sense that mediation is settlement driven. Recent research conducted in the province of Ontario (Saini et al, 2016) found that mediation was associated with the outcome of more overall contact hours per month with the non-primary parent.[11] This result may be associated with the particular characteristics of those who opted for mediation (eg, domestic violence cases may have been screened out and/or parents opting for mediation in the first place may have been more inclined to cooperation) or even a mediator's approach or values, making it an interesting finding that requires further study.

Collaborative Family Law (CFL) is a newer approach that involves both parties and their lawyers (and sometimes a multidisciplinary team that includes divorce coaches and financial and child specialists) meeting face to face to negotiate a settlement. The parties sign a participation agreement committing to the process and to negotiation in good faith. A defining feature of this comprehensive approach is a 'disqualification agreement' by which both lawyers must withdraw if the case does not settle. Although proponents of this approach claim that it is effective and results in high client satisfaction (Tesler and Thompson, 2006), there have been few empirical studies to date and only one Canadian study that includes the experiences of clients (Macfarlane, 2005). To my knowledge, no empirical studies specifically examine the use of CFL in high-conflict family disputes. Like mediation, it is often promoted as a better alternative to litigation, with benefits including improved communication and more creative and harmonious solutions. However, participants select into the process and

[11] This finding is similar to that of Trinder and Kellett (2007) regarding in-court conciliation in the UK. Trinder and Kellett found that it resulted in contact for more children as well as an increase in contact (compared to previously). Nevertheless, parents remained in conflict (with 40% returning to court within two years) and some agreements broke down. Accordingly, simply knowing the path of resolution and initial outcome does not mean these agreements are sustained. Further, little is known about the usefulness of ADR in cases of high conflict.

are normally those with higher incomes, and many claims concerning outcomes lack empirical evidence (Zylstra, 2011).

Claims by mediators and policymakers that mediation results in better and faster outcomes at lower expense (see eg Salem, 2009) and is generally better than a litigated outcome remain a matter of debate. Nevertheless, ADR is heavily promoted on the basis of its 'promise' for reaching agreement (Kaganas, 2010). However, there are diverse views as to the effectiveness of ADR approaches, which are also based on a different philosophy from litigation (Genn et al, 2007). Litigation is also used far less often than ADR to resolve family law disputes. Attempting to evaluate studies on mediation outcomes has been described as comparing apples with oranges (Shaw, 2010) while comparing mediation to other forms of dispute resolution could be considered as 'apples vs lemons' (Parkinson, 2013: 213).

According to Semple (2012), three feminist critiques that are often directed at ADR are that it may disadvantage the party with lesser economic power (often mothers), that women are more likely to feel pressured to compromise because of social conditioning, and that it is usually inappropriate when there is a history of domestic violence. Gutman (2010) raises ethical issues in this regard, particularly concerning power imbalance between the parties, mediator use of power, pressures to settle, and cost. Therefore, although ADR may on the surface appear to fit with a relational approach because it is based on values of consensus and autonomy, Gutman (2010) points out that mediation may, in fact, contain coercive elements. There may be an imbalance of power between the parties as well as between the parties and the mediator. Semple (2012: 236) also highlights feminist concerns about the privacy of the process, pointing out that mediation can be seen as a form of privatisation in the sense that it is no longer open to public or legal oversight and therefore may lead to the wealthier party having an advantage and power imbalances becoming further entrenched. The confidential nature of such processes can make it very difficult to revisit the agreement later if one party discovers that the other did not fully disclose their assets or income. A final feminist concern summarised by Semple (2012: 236) is that of mediator neutrality and bias. He notes that mediators may hold gender stereotypes and that because of what he describes as the 'almost clandestine nature of the settlement mission', there is insufficient oversight and few safeguards. Nevertheless, drawing on the argument of Rhoades (2010) that mediators are now required to undertake training with respect to domestic violence whereas judges and lawyers are not, Semple (2012: 239) suggests that, paradoxically, the feminist critique may actually favour mandatory mediation in cases of domestic violence where the alternative is the 'informal and unregulated settlement mission'. At present, those who have experienced domestic violence may be screened out[12] and are not required to participate in mediation. This

[12] The existing FLA appears to leave this screening out to the discretion of mediators rather than creating a rule.

interesting and provocative argument suggests that debates about the value and appropriateness of mediation are likely to carry on for some time yet.

Turning to CFL, a significant critique concerns its cost. First, this form of ADR is expensive, largely due to the number of professionals involved. It must be financed by the parties, typically on a 50-50 cost sharing basis, even if their incomes are quite disparate. Also, there may be considerable pressure to settle, and settlement is not always in a party's interests. Further, if the parties do not settle then they will incur far greater expense than if they had gone to court in the first place. For some, it may deplete the resources they could otherwise have used for litigation. Non-settlement also lengthens the time involved to resolve the disputes because the parties must begin with new lawyers as a result of the disqualification agreement (Zylstra, 2011). The significant cost of CFL also means that those in family law disputes have very different access to services based on their income level (Treloar and Boyd, 2013).

A second broad concern raised in the literature is that the client-led process of CFL may mean that lawyers may be slow to identify (or acknowledge) when the process is not working or a party is either not ready or unsuitable (Healey, 2015). Nevertheless, among those who did use the process, satisfaction was high. Barlow, Hunter, Smithson, and Ewing's[13] *Mapping Paths to Family Justice* project undertaken in England and Wales involved similar findings in terms of satisfaction, outcomes, and sense of control over the CFL process. This suggests that in spite of the concerns previously raised, parties who use CFL generally find it to be of benefit, although more needs to be done to determine whether the many benefits that are claimed are symbolic or are reflected in outcomes (Zylstra, 2011).

Additional concerns involve issues of informed consent and the potential for one party to use the process as a stalling tactic (Macfarlane, 2005; Zylstra, 2011), and whether CFL could contribute to power imbalances (Wiegers and Keet, 2008). Although mostly positive about the potential for CFL practice, MacFarlane (2005) suggests that four key values should guide its development:

> Commitment (carefully balancing commitment to the process, to one's client and to one's colleagues); transparency (being frank with one's clients regarding core values and what might go wrong); flexibility and responsiveness (developing different styles of CFL practice and adjusting one's own practice to client needs); and a recognition of the limitations of the CFL model and practice (realising that not every case is suitable for CFL and not every lawyer has the necessary skills for every potential CFL case).

As for whether or not ADR increases access to justice, Genn (2009) argues that it does not increase access to the courts because it is not court based. It also involves 'putting aside' thoughts of legal rights in order to focus on common ground. Further, it is often seen by policymakers as a way to reduce government

[13] See Barlow et al (2017).

costs, and, since its primary aim is to settle a dispute, it should be evaluated against doing nothing rather than against litigated outcomes (ibid). Parkinson (2013) also emphasises that the parties need legal advice during and after the process and that they bargain 'in the shadow of the law' (ie, each party is likely influenced by the knowledge of their entitlements and likely outcomes in court). Indeed, as Kaganas (2013) points out concerning the introduction of a presumption of joint parental involvement post-separation in the 2013 UK Children and Families Bill, in ADR parents would likely be expected to agree to arrangements that involve both parents being responsible and involved. In some circumstances this expectation may actually contribute to the vulnerability of mothers and children. The next section builds on these critiques and indicates that there remain a number of concerns about the shift to private ordering, especially when so little is known about the experiences of parents in a high-conflict divorce process who use ADR. Further, there is little research on the success of ADR in such situations and no research on the long-term outcomes. It is important to know whether or not agreements were made, and if they were, whether those agreements were sustainable.

III. THE PRIVATISATION OF FAMILY DISPUTES

My earlier work[14] raised concerns about ADR and the fact that such processes are now framed as the best way to resolve family law disputes, noting that they also shift costs back to families and that they may not always be appropriate means of resolving disputes in more high-conflict situations. This chapter continues to focus on the trend towards the privatisation of family law disputes and to highlight the shift in political discourse in that regard,[15] while building on my earlier work by including material from my recently completed study of how parents navigate and make sense of a high-conflict divorce.

To begin, however, I must briefly revisit an earlier point. I noted that the BC Ministry of the Attorney General's Working Group on Family Justice Reform[16] proposed that 'families should have primary responsibility for making their own arrangements, even if their legal relationships are changing',[17] while also declaring that their recommendations were 'designed to change the way people think about resolving family disputes'.[18] The Working Group concluded that a 'reversal of long held assumptions must be reflected in public spending priorities.

[14] eg Treloar (2015); Treloar and Boyd (2014); Treloar and Funk (2011).

[15] A similar shift in political discourse concerning 'expenditure of public money on private quarrels' has been noted in England and Wales. See eg Maclean and Eekelaar (2016) 5.

[16] British Columbia Ministry of the Attorney General, 'A New Justice System for Families and Children (Victoria, BC, Author, 2005): www2.gov.bc.ca/assets/gov/law-crime-and-justice/about-bc-justice-system/justice-reform-initiatives/final_05_05.pdf.

[17] ibid 39.

[18] ibid 40.

Subsidies should be shifted so that the fee for taking a family matter to court more closely reflects its true cost'.[19] Despite a lack of clear evidence about ADR costs and outcomes, as discussed above, the Working Group believed that mandatory mediation was not only less costly in terms of relationships but also to the public purse. They recommended that the government cover the cost of a single session and that there be a sliding scale for those who wished to continue thereafter. Further, those who could afford to do so should be 'free to use, and pay for, the services of a CDR professional who charges more, if they so choose'.[20] Given the significant cost of CFL, particularly when a multidisciplinary team of professionals is involved, the Working Group showed little concern about the shift of ADR services to the market and the downstream implications, including a lack of access for those without financial resources. This discourse reflects a clear trend towards the privatisation of family law disputes in BC, including during the period in which some of my study participants were attempting to resolve their disputes.

Parents whose divorce processes are categorised as high-conflict receive little assistance or research attention, despite what are often complex circumstances and the fact that their disputes consume considerable court time. A possible explanation for this gap is that family law disputes are seen to arise as a consequence of individual choices (Eekelaar, 2011). Nevertheless, this position fails to consider the interdependencies that exist between family members, such that the 'choices' one family member makes has consequences for others, with the potential for their vulnerability (ibid). Moreover, it does not take into account that some high-conflict divorces involve complex and unanticipated circumstances (eg, medical issues), or the implications for justice (whether real or perceived). Perceptions of injustice may be significant either when the parties' financial resources are extremely dissimilar or when both parents have lower incomes. Therefore, promoting ADR to the parties for its stated advantages without ensuring that it is a real 'choice' seems rather harsh, especially given cuts to legal aid and other support programmes, most of which hurt low-income women and their children (See eg Kaganas, 2017; Track, 2014; Trebilcock, Duggan and Sossin, 2012; Treloar, 2015). Overall, the result of shifting the costs of ADR and other legal services back to families alongside a downgrading of public funding has implications for social justice, and especially for gender equality.

Considerable research suggests that a prudent approach would ensure that families receive sufficient assistance to successfully navigate difficult family changes, especially given the many financial, health and social costs of protracted conflict and litigation. (See eg, Currie, 2009; Balmer et al, 2004; Treloar and Funk, 2011; Wickrama et al, 2006). An increasing number of self-represented litigants (LiPs), both in Canada (Macfarlane, 2013) and elsewhere (the UK, for example: Trinder, 2015) has placed additional strain on the courts.

[19] ibid 39.
[20] ibid 50.

If parents cannot afford to access the legal system, this provides further reason to use limited public funds for alternatives, even if some situations still require adjudication. The court's role has shifted to handling only the most complex cases. With this refocus, costs are shifted to individuals, families, and communities (Treloar, 2015). That ADR processes are settlement driven (Fiss, 1984; Semple, 2012) raises concerns about whether settlement and cost cutting are now prioritised over just outcomes. Since mothers still do more of the care work and earn less money overall,[21] individualising the costs of ADR, as well as litigation and other family supports if necessary, will most likely result in unequal and gendered access to justice.

IV. PARTICIPANTS' EXPERIENCES OF ADR

This section summarises the study participants' use of and perceptions regarding ADR. I use the term ADR narrowly to refer to any out-of-court dispute resolution mechanism. More precisely, ADR includes mediation, Collaborative Family Law (CFL), lawyer-assisted negotiation, arbitration, or the use of a parenting coordinator (PC). However, in-court settlement conferences such as Judicial Case Conferences (JCC) or other in-court negotiations could be included in a looser definition of any settlement prior to trial (ie, outside a court-decided case). ADR was important in the legislative and policy context in which the former statute operated,[22] and it remains so under the FLA. ADR has long been touted as the preferred alternative for couples to negotiate their divorce on the basis that it is less adversarial and cheaper than litigation through the courts, and that it provides parents with more autonomy in decision-making. Indeed, the ability to resolve child-related disputes out of court is central to contemporary norms of divorcing 'responsibly' (Reece, 2003). Yet most disputes are negotiated informally or formally, as was the case even before ADR was promoted in a formal sense. Although ADR may well have benefits for some parents post-separation, its implementation by governments, both in BC and elsewhere, is associated both directly and indirectly with a shift in costs and responsibilities for resolving family law disputes to individuals and families (Eekelaar, 2011; Treloar, 2015; Treloar, 2016; Treloar and Boyd, 2014; Treloar and Funk, 2011).

As noted earlier, a key theme that arose from study participants' narratives was the interrelationship of financial and child-related issues. Within that theme, a subtheme concerned the significant costs of justice and access to justice (including ADR), and the implications for those who must use the legal process in terms of power and choice. Access to money largely determined participants'

[21] Statistics Canada *Women in Canada: A Gender Based Statistical Report* (2015). *89-503-X*: www.statcan.gc.ca/pub/89-503-x/89-503-x2010001-eng.htm.

[22] All of the participants who went to court had their cases heard under the former Family Relations Act 1996.

access to justice (whether formally or informally as ADR) as well as to other forms of support. Furthermore, access to money was significant in the choices participants made in pursuing that justice. The costs of justice, responsibility, and care for children under difficult material conditions, the marital division of labour within households (and expectations thereof) and financial autonomy are all interlinked. Notably, all but two participants (both fathers, minimal litigation) mentioned the cost of justice, with most linking the cost of lawyers and litigation to their ability to access the legal system and/or ADR. They understood this had implications in terms of their power and choice in the legal process, with many also noting that with less money than the other parent[23] they were at a disadvantage. Participants seemed to regard this disadvantage as the consequence of an inequity of power and social class, with wealthier parties able to 'play the system' and/or exhaust the resources of the other party. Money was understood as a tool of power, used and wielded by those with more of it, largely determining the ability to get a fair outcome. Even when participants came up with the money for legal services, in the end most felt that it had not been worth the enormous expense and they were no further ahead. Thus there is a contradiction that on the one hand, money is necessary to participate in the legal process, but on the other hand, few were able to secure a satisfactory outcome even with it. As Cindy, a mother who had ongoing issues with child support, said:

> There was no way of doing it differently because there was no one to help. I mean, yes, you could go and see a lawyer again and he would take your money, and there would be no solutions even if he said oh, it will be like this, or oh, I think … after you've paid him for every minute you sat in his office. It was like ka-ching – another twenty-five dollars, another hundred dollars, another two hundred dollars, and eventually you just get to the point like I can't do that. There's no money for this.

While Cindy's narrative clearly articulates her frustration at the cost of legal services, it also suggests that she sought assistance in the hope that someone would help her to finally resolve her disputes. This suggests a somewhat passive help-seeking approach that is in line with gender norms. However, despite her perception of injustice, in the end she exercised her agency by giving up on the legal system and money owing to her and putting extra hours into her business. Unfortunately, this meant less time with her children, which she perceived as unfair, especially as she had already agreed to shared parenting (defaulted to parallel parenting[24]) in the CFL process, against her better judgement.

[23] In some cases, the parent and his or her extended family. Interestingly, the fathers I interviewed considered their ex-wife's parents' and new partner's resources as part of the wife's resources (whereas they saw their own resources as individual in making the same determination).

[24] In this form of post-divorce parenting, parents share parenting time but each has the authority to parent independently without the requirement to communicate with the other or reach consensus.

Another participant, this time a father (Doug), flagged money as a significant factor in all processes and outcomes:

> If you try and mediate everything, [there are] a lot of vindictive smart people out there. They will push it right to the limit, because you can get away with falsehoods in family law forever, if you don't go to trial. If you don't have that option, sorry. I don't see that there is much you can do about it if somebody is that determined, and particularly if you have no money.

He also pointed out that after spending a considerable amount of money and expending much effort, the other party can just walk out.

> So you get no agreement, in fact, it's a complete waste of money. You are worse off than you were in the beginning and you're going to go right back into the full blown court process. You know, they trumpet how wonderful cooperative law is, but you can use [it] as a weapon too.

Finally, he recommended against 'naively' following the advice of collaborative lawyers, saying 'they are business people, they are interested in revenues too, billable hours, and so are psychologists'. Overall, he highlighted the importance of understanding how the system works and of self-advocacy. His narrative draws attention to the fundamental tension between experts and lawyers as business people, on one hand, and as neutral guides through the divorce process who will advocate on the client's (and/or children's) behalf as necessary, on the other hand. Doug divorced prior to the introduction of CFL, so in this instance he is not speaking from personal experience. He did, however, mention that others turned to him for advice.

Thus, although out of court dispute resolution processes are currently favoured by family law policymakers in BC (Treloar and Boyd, 2014) and elsewhere (eg England: see Genn, 2009, 2012), many participants who had used ADR[25] felt that it had not been especially helpful. Rather, it had depleted limited resources that they would later need for litigation (in some cases making litigation no longer an option), leaving them frustrated and feeling that they had been misled. Furthermore, ADR had prolonged the process, leaving them with the stress and the cost of the process but without resolution of their issues. Although ADR may be helpful for some parties (especially those with low levels of conflict), it does not always result in resolution and can delay resolution and increase overall costs. One mother (Anne) said that an attempt to divide family assets through collaborative family law (CFL)

[25] 23 of 25 participants mentioned using one or more forms of ADR (lawyer negotiation, mediation, CFL, parenting coordinator). However, it is important to note that: (a) I did not specifically ask about ADR, (b) some participants separated before ADR was developed in a formal sense, and (c) the two participants (both over 60 years of age) who did not attempt ADR had experienced domestic violence and there were also other complex issues involved. Had they separated more recently, it is difficult to know whether they would have been screened out as inappropriate for ADR. It is possible that lawyer assisted negotiation was involved but this was not mentioned.

> was not a very good process. He just wasn't cooperative or collaborative at all and he threatened to take me to court and sue my ass off, like just really awful things. So try as I might to continue to pursue some kind of collaboration, you can't collaborate if there is only one person.

Consequently, she advised others who do not have a cooperative partner to 'get a lawyer and get on with it because it will save you money in the end. Because whatever you think you spend now you'll spend five times it later.' Unfortunately, parents are not always told early enough that their case is inappropriate for ADR.

A lack of empathy and support for parents involved in litigation is often justified by notions of choice. That is, if people make poor choices of partners, they should face the consequences of those decisions, including paying for the services they need, rather than relying on the 'public purse'. However, notions of choice are socially constructed and tend to ignore social contexts, power relations, and other factors (Boyd, 2011) that may position parents differentially in the ADR process. ADR typically assumes that both parties have approximately equal bargaining power, yet parenting generally imposes greater limitations on mothers' autonomy than on men's autonomy as fathers (Ibid).

A related assumption is that parents who are in conflict are equally unreasonable people who would rather fight with each other than focus on their children's needs and interests. However, my research provided ample evidence that such assumptions are often mistaken. For example, a participant whose former spouse had suddenly developed a medical condition that impacted his ability to care for their children attempted to resolve their issues 'fairly' through the collaborative family law (CFL) process. However, because of the challenges involved, it was unsuccessful, both in terms of bargaining and in terms of their differing abilities to understand the children's interests and meet their needs. From this mother's perspective, the lawyers and other experts (such as psychologists) involved in the collaborative process were unable to accept or acknowledge that the issues were not going to get resolved through the CFL process, which resulted in extra costs and delays. Once it failed, she not only had to pay the outstanding bills but also had to come up with a retainer and pay bills for a new lawyer. As well, she was required to share the cost of a number of expensive assessments, find and pay for counselling for their children, and was left to assume complete responsibility for the costs of raising their children – all on a moderate salary and outside of her paid work time. By the time she finished with litigation, she had spent more than $100,000 and had yet to 'see a dime' of child support. In contrast with the view that parents should 'take responsibility' for their choices and that instead of going to court they should just resolve their disputes in a reasonable manner, this woman had emptied her own purse to try to resolve her disputes and address her concerns. Moreover, she has yet to find a professional who has the skills to assist her children *and* the willingness to assist them, given the complex nature of her family law dispute.

Although lawyers often point out the disadvantages of litigation and try to encourage out of court settlement, honesty and full disclosure are essential to the success of ADR. Significantly, while participants who tried Collaborative Family Law (CFL) believed in the *ideal* of collaboration and saw its promise, ultimately none found it helpful. Some felt there was no accountability or enforcement beyond the process, while others complained that their former partner refused to produce financial records that were integral to resolution and/or believed the other party used CFL as a stalling tactic.

Even though CFL is but one form of ADR, participants raised a number of issues that apply across these approaches. Problems with enforcement and lack of accountability were raised most often. Participants who tried a number of approaches without success, or who used up their funds to make an agreement that was not honoured, described significant difficulty with accessing the courts once their resources were depleted. For example, even though she had a separation agreement made through lawyers, Leanne, a mother of three children, described being unable to get the agreed child support from her former husband, a physician who lived in a different city. Despite simultaneously experiencing a number of difficulties, including the recent death of her father, and juggling a full-time job and the needs of her children, she decided to go to court to enforce the terms of their agreement. On top of the other challenges she faced and the demands on her time, she found the process extremely difficult:

> Super, super stressful because he delayed a bunch of times. Eventually I had no more money to do it and I had to represent myself, but of course he hired some lawyer. Anyway, it went on, I had to take time off work; I didn't get paid for the time I took off work. I went to court, sometimes he would cancel, say he couldn't make this date or that date or whatever, I lost a lot of time on it. And in the end I lost because they said that the separation agreement didn't apply.

Leanne said that she was informed that the agreement was not enforceable on the basis of her former husband's claim that he had no money, and that he was working less while she was working more (as was necessary to cover family and household expenses). She was aware that he did private work and was not declaring all of his income, but could not prove it. She added:

> (Leanne) At the end of that I was so angry. As I came out of the court I can remember walking away from the courthouse and going, I will never do this again! I will never go here again! The justice system is not fair, there is no way of resolving any of this stuff, it's just he said, she said, goes back and forth and it doesn't go anywhere. So I just kind of came home from that and said, never again. I will never go there again. I just concluded the only people who are making money on this are the lawyers.
>
> (Rachel) *At the end of the day they didn't produce an outcome for you that was worth all that.*
>
> (Leanne) No. I have been divorced for fifteen years, I have not had one dollar of child support increment during that time. One of my children has [documented] special

> needs; he was supposed to pay for those extra things. He has never paid one cent. He was supposed to pay for half or all post-secondary expenses. He has not given me one cent. Not one penny. And whenever I call him to talk to him about it, 'Oh, I have no money. I have no money. I have no money.' And could I go back to court? I suppose. Hire a lawyer, pay a lawyer, pay a private investigator, do all that kind of stuff. But I'm not convinced that the system has changed and I'm not convinced I will get anything. Over the course of the years as I've kind of come to that conclusion, I've just basically said, I'll live my life, do my own thing. Do I feel bitter? Of course. Do I feel angry? Yes. But I didn't see that I had a chance of winning anything. Really, what's the point?

Again, in this example, we hear the frustration and sense of injustice felt by those who cannot enforce their child support claims, even when child support was negotiated through ADR. This participant found herself alone in bearing responsibility for the children, whereas the lawyers who represented her did not deliver but had to be paid regardless. People in her situation, often mothers, have all of the responsibility and far too little support.

Although norms of good post-divorce parenting involve the expectation that parents will resolve their disputes through ADR and cooperate for the sake of the children, ADR does not always live up to its promise. Research also suggests that in the context of post-separation disputes mothers more often draw on normative ideals of cooperation and contact with both parents as central to a child's well-being (welfare discourse), whereas fathers tend to argue more on the basis of individual rights (rights discourse).[26] 'Stubbornly gendered' (Boyd, 2010: 140) parenting arrangements and social expectations that mothers will be selfless in facilitating their children's well-being and autonomy, while also accepting significant constraints on their own autonomy (Boyd, 2010), may place mothers at a disadvantage in the negotiation process. Gendered differences that disadvantage mothers may also be apparent in financial disputes. Barlow, Hunter, Smithson and Ewing's *Mapping Paths to Family Justice* study (Barlow et al, 2017) found that women were more likely than men to bring 'normative considerations into their financial disputes, including feelings of guilt, pragmatism, sacrifice or self-preservation, concerns about compensation or a desire for reasonableness, which were rarely put forward by men' (ibid: 178).

Mothers in my study were more likely to feel pressured to agree, to be aware of power imbalances (especially in the context of domestic violence), and to feel that their former partners agreed to things on a strategic basis and were not held accountable for agreements. Put simply, when the mothers and fathers in this research engaged in ADR, it was with different understandings of collaboration. Although mothers sought collaboration in general, when they agreed (or conceded) on shared parenting what they 'got' was more likely to be a division of time without the ability to discuss or cooperate on child-related issues.

[26] Day Sclater (1999). However, Kaganas and Day Sclater (2004) suggest that both mothers and fathers use the welfare discourse strategically. That is, they resist and reinterpret it in ways that enable them to maintain themselves as good parents.

Examples of gendered expectations described by mothers included being 'nice' (ie, accommodating) and putting up with 'bullying,' including during ADR. Krista, for example, perceived both the mediator and her former partner as bullying her during a mediation session. Although only one other mother used the term bullying to describe the behaviour of a mediator and former spouse in combination, five mothers in total described experiencing intense pressure tactics during ADR sessions. This suggests that they were conscious of the gendered expectations described above, in combination with an imbalance of power.

While there was little difference between mothers and fathers in terms of their satisfaction with public family law procedures, in general, fathers who participated in the study seemed to be more satisfied with the ADR process than were mothers. In order for ADR to live up to its promise, both parties must be genuinely committed to full disclosure and resolution, and follow through on their agreements. Furthermore, there needs to be greater understanding of power imbalances and the appropriateness of ADR for all cases. Indeed, ADR may not be the best option for those in high-conflict disputes as a result of complex circumstances, such as that of the mother whose former spouse developed medical issues affecting his ability to parent. A better understanding of which cases are suitable and which are not would spare those for whom the approach is not suitable from wasting resources and enable faster resolution of their disputes. However, even those who poured all their resources into litigation were no more satisfied with the process or outcome, even after years of struggle. As often as not, it was a struggle to enforce the terms of the order. Hence, going to trial may not be a viable solution.

Money affects not only access to legal services (including ADR) and expert opinions, but also access to other services and supports that parents and families need and depend on in difficult times. Some parents also described depleting their resources on ADR and being left without money for a lawyer when it proved necessary. In a small number of these cases, practitioners appear to have been overly optimistic about their ability to assist, while in other cases more careful screening could have enabled faster resolution at lower expense to the parties.[27] Recent research conducted in England (Barlow et al, 2017) found considerable evidence of improper screening and varying beliefs among ADR professionals about which cases are appropriate for mediation. Given the state of development of the field, similar issues may well exist in BC. Nor does going to trial, which entails significant expense, always provide the finality desired and in some cases, as with ADR, it was left to the receiving party to attempt to enforce payments or to return to court. Consequently, I argue that greater attention to financial and social support needs, alongside a fundamental shift in how we think about and respond to post-separation parenting disputes, is needed.

[27] FLA, s 8 introduces some screening provisions, primarily for domestic abuse and power imbalance. However, it is likely those provisions would have 'screened out' only one of the 25 cases in this study.

Based on their lived experiences, the majority of study participants felt that family law does not belong in the legal system (alongside criminal law, for example). Further, they felt that ADR should be taken out of the free market. The latter point is thought-provoking; indeed, it is contrary to trends in family law in Canada and most other common law jurisdictions, where the responsibility for resolving issues that arise as a result of 'family breakdown' (alongside the cost) is increasingly regarded as that of the family or individuals involved rather than a public responsibility (See eg Maclean and Eekelaar, 2016; Treloar, 2015; Treloar and Boyd, 2014; Treloar and Funk, 2011; Trinder, 2015).

V. PARTICIPANTS' USE OF THE INTERNET FOR SELF-HELP

When parents are in a high-conflict dispute, they turn to a variety of sources beyond family lawyers for help, including health professionals, advocacy groups, community agencies, family and friends, academic literature, and the Internet. While they seek information and support, few have the skills or the time to critically evaluate these sources, especially at an already overwhelmingly emotional and busy time. However, what became clear from listening to the diversity and complexity of participants' experiences is that they sought information and advice that was specific to the particular challenges they faced, rather than generic information.

While the information they obtained was a source of their meanings, it was not always suitable for their circumstances and at times it fuelled legal disputes, which indicates that there is a need for improved support from, and access to, knowledgeable and skilled professionals. A key implication here is that if this support is not available, people are likely to fend for themselves by seeking out whatever help is available. Elsewhere, I described how when participants found themselves unable to fully resolve their disputes through litigation or ADR, all sought support outside the family legal system (Treloar, 2018). 17 participants turned to some form of personal development as the best available solution to assist them in moving forward despite the difficulties they faced. The other six turned to research, advocacy, and political strategies that would help to reform the system and assist others facing similar circumstances. While participants usually leaned towards one or the other of these approaches in response to the frustration and sense of disempowerment and injustice they felt, many engaged in both strategies.

Although one father (separated in the early 1990s) was an early adopter of Internet self-help and active in the fathers' rights movement, few of those who grew up prior to the 'digital age' used the Internet for self-help or peer-to-peer support. However, those who did, did so in an environment where the available help largely came from organised advocacy groups, often directly from individuals with personal experience of a conflicted divorce (ie, email list serve or through a blog or website). Often, those who sought out online information had already sought assistance from local services, or had exhausted all other sources of support. Two of the participants described their difficulties as well beyond the scope of what local resources could assist with (child abduction, complex situations involving professional ethics and unequal resources). The manner in which those parents used the Internet was similar to the way in which individuals now seek out medical information and advice online, including peer-to-peer sharing and support.

Having attempted to be 'collaborative' without success, Emily described finding an online support 'community' as being extremely helpful. However, the group folded due to privacy issues. She later found other groups online, including an American group comprised of women involved in 'acrimonious divorces'. Some of the women, like her, were being accused of 'this alienation syndrome. I was learning everything I could about it'. In commenting on the shift to ADR and online information, she said:

> It doesn't work when you're dealing with a … sociopathic partner who is very wealthy and [of high professional status]. It doesn't work. As a matter of fact, it puts you at more risk and I do not use the word risk lightly because I think I'm quite a resilient personality and um, I was left with very little to hang onto. I felt a lot of the time that I was on a precipice, I felt there was nobody I could really lean into.

Despite contemporary norms that direct parents toward cooperation and respectful behaviour so that they could still 'work together as parents' (a goal she shared), now almost two decades later, Emily wonders '[whether] I should have been more angry and assertive. I wonder how I could have protected myself and my children from all that pain and suffering'. Unfortunately, such norms, especially when accompanied by a shrinking state, may contribute to an imbalance of power and leave parents and children without adequate support. In such a situation, some parents now turn to peer-to-peer support from strangers with personal experience of high-conflict divorce. Although this support may meet certain needs, there is no guarantee that the support provided will help them in a legal sense.

Participants varied in the extent to which they used online resources. However, those that did so were often seeking information specific to their circumstances. Some sought neutral information and advice, whereas others sought information that they hoped would enable them to win their case. Three of the fathers mentioned using the Internet to research psychiatric disorders. Greg explained:

> I had always tried to understand their mum's behaviour and how she approached situations, how she emotionally reacted to, you know, major situations or approached stuff and I came up with borderline disorder, and narcissism and you know, all these different traits that all seemed to fit, uh, but wasn't educated enough to be able to be able to portray them. And then as I started reading more about the parental alienation a lot of it started making sense and really twigged and you know, hearing other stories and you go, wow, you know what? That is me!
>
> (Rachel) *So you read about it on the Internet.*

> (Greg) Yup. I would just sit down and start googling *(laughs)*. Searching and coming up with what I could. You just keep grasping at every bit you can. It's almost obsessive compulsive.

Other parents, however, sought 'unbiased' and user-friendly information. One father described much of the information online as contradictory. Another father found a lawyer's blog to be informative and accessible. Shelly described her difficulty in finding resources that provided the information she needed, including answers to her questions:

> [It] seems to be the only way people are successful in it is if they … if they self advocate, because there's nobody else, like there was nobody to answer my questions. I read all the brochures. They didn't really help. Stuff online might have been helpful if it had been … less legal jargon. I would rather have a website that had case studies and … what would I have wanted? Oh, if you have gone through this then you are not alone *(laughs)*. This many people have gone through this and these are some of their stories, you know what I mean, just to know that other people have gone through it. I could have done an online discussion forum, that would have worked. I want ideas of how to … like how the heck do you co-parent? I read a book on co-parenting but the problem is that you need two people to do that whole thing so I can't co-parent. When I got divorced I looked online and I went to the courthouse and I googled divorce and separation and BC. And I tried to look. … I do like looking for official sites because they are more reliable than Wikipedia, so I came up with the stuff that's really awful like the boring codes and laws.

Since Shelly does not live in one of the larger cities in British Columbia, 'services' in her area are limited to family duty counsel (four hours each week), and to the court itself.

Next, the chapter describes MyLawBC, an interactive digital platform inspired by the Dutch Rechtwijzer platform, and reflects on whether it would have helped study participants. While the online platform does address some of the concerns described by Shelly, it is unlikely to help most parents to navigate a high-conflict and/or complex divorce.

A. MyLawBC

Recent digital dispute resolution developments promise to change the way family disputes are resolved. While these developments are likely still in their infancy, there is little doubt that policymakers see the potential for online dispute resolution (ODR) to reduce costs and resolve disputes in an accessible and expedient manner. MyLawBC was introduced in mid-2016 with the aim of empowering people to act on their legal problems. Subtitled 'My Problem, My Solution', the platform offers to assist viewers to 'find a solution to your family law matters in 15-20 minutes'.[28] MyLawBC enables parties who *can* negotiate with their former

[28] http://mylawbc.com/paths/family/#.

spouse to work on their legal problems from their own homes and at their own pace, without exorbitant costs. The parties can also access online mediators and lawyers to assist them. This is similar to the Rechtwijzer which, according to Hiil, who developed the platform with the Dutch Legal Aid Board, 'costs a couple on average 400€ to go through the entire divorce process [...] compared to traditional costs of upwards of 3000€'.[29] MyLawBC explicitly informs users that the average cost of paid mediation is $3044, whereas the cost of an average two day trial is $39,900 and a five day trial is $66,850.[30] Like ADR, ODR is 'marketed' as relational, interest based, low cost, and user friendly. However, while MyLawBC is likely to be helpful to those with simple disputes, the extent to which parents in the midst of a complex or high-conflict family law dispute will find it to be a useful tool remains unstudied.

In reflecting on whether MyLawBC would have been helpful to the study participants, given their particular circumstances and needs, I think it is unlikely to have significantly changed either the experiences of parents or the outcomes of their cases, whether or not they ultimately went to court. Nevertheless, as illustrated by the excerpt from Shelly's interview above, the platform could now provide some of the basic information that parents then sought. In addition, it would help parents at an overwhelming and emotional time to focus on legal issues, and to understand their obligations and the legal process. Participants for whom health or mental health issues (parent and/or child) also existed would likely find the platform of little assistance. Parents in my study found these issues as, and in some cases more, challenging than the divorce related issues. Similarly, those dealing with child abduction, domestic violence, immigration status, etc, would still need to obtain information and advice elsewhere. Most of the women who participated in my study also had difficulty obtaining full financial disclosure or collecting child support. Even in situations where some matters had been agreed on using ADR (sometimes at considerable cost and after using more than one approach) the other party did not always honour the agreement. Simply knowing that children are entitled to be supported by both parents (as detailed on MyLawBC) does not help if child support cannot be collected. Nevertheless, self-help was a common theme in participant interviews. Even when support was unavailable for their particular issues, most parents continued seeking resources and actively engaged in self-help. This finding is consistent with research conducted at the Canadian Forum for Civil Justice (Currie, 2016), which found that a considerable proportion of people with legal problems prefer to engage in self-help out of a sense of personal responsibility. Arguably, people in a variety of difficult circumstances do seek solutions for their problems, thereby exercising their agency.

[29] www.hiil.org/project/?itemID=2641.

[30] Sources: *Canadian Lawyer Magazine* (The going rate, July 2015) and mediatebc.com. Of course trials can go on for 10 days or more, and may not resolve the issues in a final sense.

VI. DISCUSSION

Next, I consider the shift to digital self-help, especially given the shrinking role of the state in family justice. As described in the previous section, while some participants sought online resources and found them helpful, it can be difficult for litigants to critically evaluate the reliability of the information. Participants also noted that available information was rather piecemeal and could be contradictory.[31] In line with the findings of Macfarlane's (2013) study of litigants in person, online resources were not always helpful and some participants needed legal advice rather than information.

Overall, participants in my study did seek support online or by telephone, but most needed a personal guide through the process and face-to-face support that was tailored to their particular needs and circumstances, which were in most cases far too complex to be addressed through ODR. Recent research conducted in England and Wales found that face-to-face social welfare legal aid had considerable advantages over older technologies such as telephone advice (Burton, 2018). Moreover, as noted by Smith and Paterson (2014), evaluation research indicates that hotlines are least helpful for vulnerable clients with complex problems, especially those who are separated from a partner or afraid of a former partner, are not white, and have lower levels of income and education. Smith and Paterson (2014) point to similar results in a 2012 evaluation of family law services in BC (Legal Services Society, 2012), which also found that while people used services such as the Family LawLine for initial legal advice, issues tended to re-emerge even though some issues had (supposedly) been settled. While this finding is consistent with my research with parents who had experienced a high-conflict divorce, it is unclear whether issues re-emerged because of the services used or because of the complex nature of the disputes. Parents in such circumstances expressed considerable frustration not at a lack of information, but at their difficulty settling issues in the first place, followed by their lack of ability to enforce orders once they were made.

Although ADR is frequently portrayed as the respectful and healthy alternative to adversarial approaches and as facilitating improved relationships among the parties, participants' narratives and significant research demonstrate that such a dichotomous view is inaccurate. Given the findings concerning ADR, an initial question arises about whether mediation and CFL processes can be refined to better address the difficulties described by study participants. A further question is whether early access to ODR would have provided adequate help and changed the outcomes for parents in this study. Although early indications

[31] Certainly that was the case in the early days of the Internet, although a participant interviewed in 2014 expressed similar sentiments. However, in the past few years there has been much more information available and I suspect that those now in similar circumstances might find the amount of information quite overwhelming.

are that ODR, like ADR, is helpful to some parents (generally those with less contentious or complex disputes who are more likely to be able to agree on arrangements for their children), based on the overall findings of my study, I do not think it is likely that ODR will assist parents involved in a high-conflict or complex divorce process. It would be far better to screen out cases that are unsuitable early on, and ensure that these disputes can be resolved sooner and with less emotional and financial cost.

A better option would be a state funded hybrid model that ensures parents receive needed support while also advancing the legal resolution of their disputes, if and when it is possible to do so. In contrast to CFL, such a model would likely involve legal case management as well as an interdisciplinary team that includes medical, mental health, domestic violence and/or addictions professionals as required. However, such a model would need to be non-adversarial in order to be effective. Removing such cases from regular courts would go some distance toward changing the mindset of both parents and professionals. Parents in the study often mentioned features of the criminal justice system that structure courthouse procedures and practices (eg, the presence of sheriffs with guns and the physical layout) as problematic. Perhaps, therefore, appearance via video link (whether from a lawyer's office or home) would be a way of incorporating positive aspects of ODR. Rather than displacing lawyers from the delivery of family justice and replacing them with mediators and online information, such an arrangement would ensure that participants can access legal information and advice, including 'real-time' representation as needed.

The sweeping reconfiguration of the legal profession predicted by Susskind (2013), with services delivered and disputes resolved online by global legal businesses, now seems to be well underway and is unlikely to change course. However, while these changes are largely accepted as inevitable (and perhaps even to be celebrated), what remains to be seen is whether technology can match, or even outperform, professionals' ability to solve complex human problems that have personal, interpersonal, social, and structural dimensions. Arguably, high-conflict divorce involving child-related matters cannot be properly addressed through drop down menus. While my research shows that parents do indeed engage in online self-help, most parents said they needed a skilled and well-informed guide to assist them in navigating through the process and in accessing appropriate resources. What would be most helpful is a properly funded 'one stop shop' (similar to Australia's Family Relationship Centres) which is staffed by multidisciplinary professionals and other support staff.

It is likely that in the future, those in need of legal information and advice will increasingly turn to the Internet. However, while study participants sought legal information and advice online, as well as peer support, many found the information available to be too general, contradictory, and variable in quality. Nevertheless, my research interviews preceded recent online innovations in BC. While those currently in the process of divorcing may find the volume of online information overwhelming, especially if they are already feeling stressed and short of time, it is likely that they will find at least some information that is useful to them in resolving their disputes.

VII. CONCLUSION

In BC, as in many other jurisdictions, there is an increased reliance on online or telephone legal information and self-help services, with or without limited legal assistance (eg, MyLawBC, FamilyLawLine, duty counsel, and public legal education programmes). Although these resources may indeed help those with straightforward issues to resolve them entirely and at little cost, I do not think the trend to ODR will be helpful for parents with high-conflict and complex disputes. Since ODR is in many respects the same as ADR, it shares similar strengths and weaknesses in the context of high-conflict disputes. ODR also shares similarities to telephone advice and referral hotlines (eg, FamilyLawLine and BC's new VIND system), services that previous research (described above) suggests are inadequate for complex matters.

While it remains important that parents in the midst of a high-conflict divorce can access legal advice, legal representation, and the courts as necessary, online and low-cost services may provide useful information and meet the needs of some parties. Nevertheless, it is unlikely that any single profession, delivery format, or service will adequately serve parents in the midst of a high-conflict divorce, nor alleviate inequities between parties where they exist. Rather, strong working relationships and interdisciplinary programmes are needed. Parents in the midst of a high-conflict divorce are not currently well served, perhaps in part because of the tendency to understand divorce in a simplistic and polarised way. On the one hand, with the shift to digital approaches, especially in the context of privatised justice, there is a risk of greater polarisation and simplification of divorce. ADR should not be framed and marketed as the better, cheaper, and more lasting way to address the issues of family dissolution; rather, researchers, policymakers and practitioners must dig deeper and come up with innovative and interdisciplinary approaches to meet the complex needs of parents in the midst of a high-conflict divorce. On the other hand, with a strong commitment from policymakers, researchers, practitioners and digital developers, there is an excellent opportunity to address the distinct needs and challenges faced by parents in complex and high-conflict disputes.

ODR may indeed put more legal information and self-help tools in the hands of disputing parties, and it may initially come at a lower cost both to individuals and to the state. However, in the context of austerity and a lack of will on the part of government to provide a broader safety net for families in crisis at times of change, expecting families to 'help themselves' is also problematic. ODR is likely to be helpful to some parties with simple disputes who perhaps could not afford legal advice and really only need basic information. However, the development of ODR services uses limited funds to provide additional service to the majority while doing nothing to improve services to the most complex (and potentially costly[32]) cases. While ODR provides still another tool for divorcing parties and may assist in advancing access to justice, it is no substitute for quality personalised advice and support services.

REFERENCES

Balmer, P, Buck, N, O'Grady, A and Genn, H (2004) 'Civil Law Problem and Morbidity', *Journal of Epidemiology and Community Health* 58(7), 552.

Barlow, A, Hunter, R, Smithson, J and Ewing, J (2017) *Mapping Paths to Family Justice: Resolving Family Disputes in Neoliberal Times* (London, Palgrave).

Bond, S (2013) 'BC's New Family Law Reflects Modern Society (Op-ed)' *Vancouver Sun*, 27 March 2013: www.vancouversun.com/news/familyþreflectsþmodernþsociety/8161327/story.html.

Boyd, SB (2010) 'Autonomy for mothers? Relational Theory and Parenting Apart', *Feminist Legal Studies* 18(2), 137.

Boyd, SB (2011) 'Motherhood and Autonomy in a Shared Parenting Climate' in J Jones, A Grear, R Fenton and K Stevenson (eds), *Gender, Sexualities and Law* (New York, Routledge).

Boyle, K (2013) *A Short History of Family Mediation in British Columbia* (Victoria, BC, Mediate BC Society).

Burton, M (2018) 'Justice on the Line? A Comparison of Telephone and Face-to-Face Advice in Social Welfare Legal Aid', *Journal of Social Welfare and Family Law* 40(2), 195.

Currie, A (2009) *The Legal Problems of Everyday Life: The Nature, Extent and Consequences of Justiciable Problems Experienced by Canadians* (Ottawa, Department of Justice): www.justice.gc.ca/eng/rp-pr/csj-sjc/jsp-sjp/rr07_la1-rr07_aj1/rr07_la1.pdf.

Currie, A (2016) *Nudging the Paradigm Shift, Everyday Legal Problems in Canada* (Toronto, Canadian Forum on Civil Justice).

Day Sclater, S (1999) *Divorce: A Psychosocial Study* (Aldershot, UK, Ashgate).

Eekelaar, J (2011) '"Not of the Highest Importance": Family Justice under Threat', *Journal of Social Welfare and Family Law* 33(4), 311.

Fiss, O (1984) 'Against Settlement', *The Yale Law Journal* 93(6), 1073.

Genn, H (2009) 'ADR and Civil Justice: What's Justice Got to Do With It?' in *Judging Civil Justice* (New York, Cambridge University Press).

Genn, H (2012) 'What is Civil Justice For? Reform, ADR, and Access to Justice', *Yale Journal of Law & the Humanities* 24(1), 397.

Genn, H, Fenn, P, Mason, M, Lane, A, Bechai, N, Gray, L and Vencappa, D (2007), *Twisting Arms: Court Referred and Court Linked Mediation Under Judicial Pressure.* Ministry of Justice Research Series 1/07 (London, Ministry of Justice).

[32] Considerable research has documented the significant financial and social costs of legal problems, especially when they are moved downstream to individuals and communities. See eg Currie (2009) and Pleasence et al (2008).

Gutman, J (2010) 'Legal Ethics in ADR Practice: Has Coercion Become the Norm?', *Australasian Dispute Resolution Journal* 21(4), 218.

Healy, C (2015) 'Dispute Resolution through Collaborative Practice: A Comparative Analysis', *Child and Family Law Quarterly* 27(2), 173.

Kaganas, F (2010) 'When it Comes to Contact Disputes, What are Family Courts For?', *Current Legal Problems* 63(1), 235.

Kaganas, F (2013) 'A Presumption that 'Involvement' of Both Parents is Best: Deciphering Law's Messages', *Child and Family Law Quarterly* 25(3), 270.

Kaganas, F (2017) 'Justifying the LASPO Act: Authenticity, Necessity, Suitability, Responsibility and Autonomy', *Journal of Social Welfare and Family Law* 39(2), 168.

Kaganas, F and Day Sclater, S (2004) 'Contact Disputes: Narrative Constructions of "Good" Parents', *Feminist Legal Studies* 12(1), 1.

Legal Services Society (2012) *Evaluation of the Family Law Services of the Legal Services Society: Final Report* (Vancouver, BC, Legal Services Society).

Macfarlane, J (2005) *The Emerging Phenomenon of Collaborative Family Law (CFL): A Qualitative Study of CFL Cases* (Ottawa, ON: Department of Justice Canada, Family, Children and Youth Section): http://justice.gc.ca/eng/rp-pr/fl-lf/famil/2005_1/pdf/2005_1.pdf.

Macfarlane, J (2013) *The National Self-represented Litigants Project: Identifying and Meeting the Needs of Self-represented Litigants. Final Report* (May 2013): http://representingyourselfcanada.files.wordpress.com/2014/02/reportm15-2.pdf.

Maclean, M and Eekelaar, J (2016) *Lawyers and Mediators: The Brave New World of Services for Separating Families* (Oxford, Hart-Bloomsbury).

Parkinson, P (2013) 'The Place of Mediation in the Family Justice System', *Child and Family Law Quarterly* 25(2), 200.

Pleasence, P, Balmer, N and Buck, A (2008) 'The Health Cost of Civil Law Problems: Further Evidence of Links Between Civil Law Problems and Morbidity and the Consequential Use of Health Services', *Journal of Empirical Legal Studies* 5(2), 351.

Reece, H (233) *Divorcing Responsibly* (Oxford, Hart).

Rhoades, H (2010) 'Mandatory Mediation of Family Disputes: Reflections from Australia', *Journal of Social Welfare and Family Law* 32(2), 183.

Saini, M, Birnbaum, R, Bala, N and McLarty, B (2016) 'Understanding Pathways to Family Dispute Resolution and Justice Reforms: Ontario Court File Analysis and Survey of Professionals', *Family Court Review* 54(3), 382.

Salem, P (2009) 'The Emergence of Triage in Family Court Services: The Beginning of the End for Mandatory Mediation?', *Family Court Review* 47(3), 373.

Semple, N (2012) 'Mandatory Family Mediation and the Settlement Mission: A Feminist Critique', *Canadian Journal of Women and the Law*' 24(1), 207.

Shaw, LA (2010) 'Divorce Mediation Outcome Research: A Meta-Analysis', *Conflict Resolution Quarterly* 27(4), 447.

Smith, R and Paterson, A (2014) *Face to Face Legal Services and their Alternatives: Global Lessons from the Digital Revolution* (Glasgow, CPLS Centre for Professional Legal Studies, University of Strathclyde): https://strathprints.strath.ac.uk/56496/1/Smith_Paterson_CPLS_Face_to_face_legal_services_and_their_alternatives.pdf.

Susskind, R (2013) *Tomorrow's Lawyers: An Introduction to Your Future* (Oxford, Oxford University Press).

Tesler, P and Thompson, P (2006), *Collaborative Divorce: The Revolutionary New Way to Restructure Your Family, Resolve Legal Issues, and Move on With Your Life* (New York, Harper Collins).

Track, L (2014) *Putting Justice Back on the Map: The Route to Equal and Accessible Family Justice* (Vancouver, BC, West Coast LEAF): www.westcoastleaf.org/2014/02/28/putting-justice-back-on-the-map/.

Trebilcock, M, Duggan, A and Sossin, L (2012), *Middle Income Access to Justice* (Toronto, University of Toronto Press).

Treloar, R and Funk, L (2011) 'Mothers' Health, Responsibilization, and Choice in Family Care Work after Separation/Divorce' in C Benoit and H Hallgrimsdottir (eds), *Valuing Care Work: Comparative Perspectives on Canada, Finland and Iceland* (Toronto, University of Toronto Press).

Treloar, R and Boyd, SB (2014) 'Family Law Reform in (Neoliberal) Context: British Columbia's New Family Law Act', *International Journal of Law, Policy and the Family* 28(1), 77.

Treloar, R (2015) 'The Neoliberal Context of Family Law Reform in British Columbia, Canada: Implications for Access to (Family) Justice' in M Maclean, J Eekelaar and B Bastard (eds), *Delivering Family Justice in the 21st Century* (Oxford, Hart Bloomsbury).

Treloar, R (2016) 'High Conflict Post-separation Disputes Involving Family Violence in a Neoliberal Context: British Columbia, Canada', *Child and Family Law Quarterly* 28(2), 111.

Treloar, R (2018) 'High-Conflict Divorce Involving Children: Parents' Meaning-Making and Agency', *Journal of Social Welfare and Family Law* 40(2), 340.

Trinder, L (2015) 'Taking Responsibility? Legal Aid Reform and Litigants in Person in England' in M Maclean, J Eekelaar and B Bastard (eds), *Delivering Family Justice in the 21st Century* (Oxford, Hart Bloomsbury).

Trinder, L and Kellett, J (2007) 'Fairness, Efficiency and Effectiveness in Court-based Dispute Resolution Schemes in England', *International Journal of Law, Policy and the Family* 21(3), 323–40.

Wickrama, K, Lorenz, F, Conger, R, Elder, G, Abraham, W and Fang, S (2006) 'Changes in Family Financial Circumstances and the Physical Health of Married and Recently Divorced Mothers', *Social Science & Medicine* 63(1), 123.

Wiegers, W and Keet, M (2008) 'Collaborative Family Law and Gender Inequalities: Balancing Risks and Opportunities', *Osgoode Hall Law Journal* 46(4), 733.

Zylstra, A (2011) 'A Call to Action: A Client-Centered Evaluation of Collaborative Law', *Pepperdine Dispute Resolution Law Journal* 11, 547.

2

Choosing Paths to Dispute Resolution in Post-Communist Poland

MAŁGORZATA FUSZARA AND JACEK KURCZEWSKI

I. INTRODUCTION

THE ADMINISTRATION OF justice in Poland has recently been subject to turbulence of fundamental importance. It began with the election victory of the Law and Justice party in 2015, who were calling for reform of the administration of justice as part of their 'Good Change' electoral manifesto. Since then controversies concerning the principles for nominating common court judges, controversies resulting from the attempt to shorten the term of service for judges in the Supreme Court, and controversies concerning nominations for the Constitutional Tribunal have led to protests and street demonstrations by thousands of people over several months, as well as to cases seeking judgment at the Court of Justice of the European Union. The 'Good Change' programme had been supported by many of those who had been party to movement towards 'illiberal democracy' as advocated by Hungarian allies of the Polish government.

Despite all these sharp controversies involving judiciary, government, opposition parties and ordinary citizens, the everyday life of the courts continues without major changes. Some procedural innovations are being introduced aiming at accelerating, simplifying and shortening proceedings, which are in many ways similar to the solutions being adopted in other countries. On the other hand, there are some other areas of justice, including divorce law, where government reforms are going in a different direction as a result of the traditionalist ideology which the government is considering, rather than whether access to justice is becoming easier or more difficult.

II. DIVORCE IN POLAND

Statistical data show the incidence of divorce to be relatively stable in Poland (Table 1):

Table 1 Divorce and separation in the period 2005–17 (in thousands)

	2005	2010	2015	2018
Divorce	67.6	61.3	67.2	65.3

Source: Statistical Yearbook of GUS (Central Statistical Office).

Divorce is more frequent in cities. In 2017 there were over 17,000 cases in cities with over 46,000 inhabitants. The disparity between urban and rural social milieux is clearly visible when one compares the relative frequency of divorce – 20.3 divorces per 10,000 inhabitants in the cities and 14.4 in the rural areas. The divorce rates follow the same pattern as marriages. In cities there are 410 divorces for each thousand new weddings but in rural areas only 223, while in the whole of Poland last year there were 337 divorces per thousand weddings.

One reads also that while the number of weddings falls each year falls, the relative frequency of divorce has increased. On the other hand, Poland remains one of the few European countries where the occurrence of divorce remains comparatively low. While overall about every second European marriage ends in divorce, in Poland the figure is about one third of marriages, similar to the incidence in countries like Italy, Ireland or Romania where religion strongly influences behaviour (Szukalski, 2016: 86). However, religion and the related emphasis on the indissolubility of marriage are not the only possible explanations. Earlier research showed the difference is also related to access to justice both in terms of the cost of court fees and physical distance from a court. Until 1990, divorce cases were handled by family courts, which were sections of local courts (*rejonowy*). In 1991, the jurisdiction of courts changed. The district courts (*okręgowy*) are now the first-instance courts in divorce cases. This has made the procedure less accessible, since there are 310 local courts in Poland and only 45 district courts. Clearly after this change the pathway to court, especially for residents of smaller towns, is now much longer, and as a consequence the procedure becomes more expensive. The outcome is manifested in the statistics. In 1990, that is before the organisational change, 50,300 divorce proceedings were started in the Polish courts while in 1995 the figure had fallen to 41,900 cases.

This difference was reflected in the statistics: in the 1980s, the increase in divorce cases was faster in rural than in urban areas, though the number of divorces in rural areas has always been much smaller than in urban ones. In the 1990s, however, divorce rates in rural areas fell more rapidly. On analysing the court statistics on divorce cases, the impact of 'distance to court' on the number of cases can be clearly seen. In some provinces, the divorce rates dropped rapidly after the change: the number of divorce suits filed in 1993 amounted to a mere 49% of the 1991 figures. A fall of this extent was found mainly in provinces where no provincial court had been set up, and the inhabitants' distance from the divorce court was therefore particularly great (Fuszara and Łaciak, 2000: 120).

III. THE SCOPE OF E-JUSTICE IN POLAND

Let us begin with the changes already introduced. Following the development of technological change in Poland, as in many other countries, electronic proceedings in some cases had been introduced before the legal reforms commenced by the present government. E-justice was introduced into the Polish justice system on 1 January 2010[1] as part of the amended code of civil procedure (see the chapter on Electronic Proceeding).[2] For this purpose a special court had been set up (Sixth Branch of the Regional Court in the city of Lublin) to deal with all e-cases brought in from the whole country, centralising e-justice in an unusual way.

Generally speaking cases dealt with by the e-court stand out as not demanding any evidence. At present the plaintiff has a right to demand payment of a debt incurred not more than three years before bringing the case to the court. All relevant actions – entering the suit, issuing a court order for payment and communicating with the defendant – are carried out electronically. The law says that bringing a suit in any way other than electronically will not lead to a debt summons. The procedure is simple as the plaintiff puts in the claim and identifies the supporting evidence which does not need to be attached. The e-court will send the case on to a proper regional court if any further evidence is needed. If a case is self-evident, the order of payment is simply issued. The defendant when receiving such an order may reply with an objection which does not need to be justified. Once the objection has been made the e-court order for payment is nullified and the case follows conventional procedure before the proper court (Rylski, 2015).

Since the first year of functioning, the e-court has attracted wide interest, much more than was expected, and more than 650,000 cases[3] have been entered against the 400,000 predicted by the drafters (Rylski, 2015:155 n 9). In recent years a large increase in the volume of these cases can be observed. This is due, among other things, to the adding in of new categories of cases that may be dealt with electronically. For instance, mortgage payments have recently been put under the e-procedure. In general terms, e-justice is being gradually extended to

[1] Ustawa z dnia 9 stycznia 2009 r.o zmianie ustawy – Kodeks postpowania cywilnego oraz niektórych innych ustaw, Dziennik Ustaw Nr 26, poz 156.

[2] Arts 50528–50537 of the Code of Civil Procedure.

[3] EPU-elektroniczne postępowanie upominawcze (e-sąd) w latach 2010 – 2017: https://isws.ms.gov.pl/pl/baza-statystyczna/opracowania-wieloletnie/; Podstawowa informacja statystyczna o działalności sądów powszechnych – I półrocze 2017 roku na tle poprzednich okresów statystycznych: https://isws.ms.gov.pl/pl/baza-statystyczna/publikacje/, accessed 17 March 2019.

include all simple, self-evidential cases, especially those that are more and more often related to obligations and other legal actions which themselves have arisen from electronic transactions.

This rise in the volume of cases dealt with electronically may be illustrated with figures for the period 2013–17. The Ministry of Justice reports that 1,724,533 cases started in the first half of 2013, while in the first half of 2017 there were 2,192,001 new cases, that is about 400,000 more. Before the mortgage cases were added in 2017, the volume of e-cases from 2014 to 2016 had been decreasing, with slightly more than 900,000 cases in the first half of 2014. The decrease was also partly related to changes in legal regulations. At first there had been no time limits as to the availability of the e-procedure for money claims. However, it soon became the case that many cases were being entered after the time limit had already expired. This involved the activities of a recovery/bailiff business that had been buying up debts and had entered all related claims under the e-procedure including also those that were already beyond the expiry date. This practice led the government to introduce an amendment in 2013 limiting the availability of e-procedure explicitly to claims arising from obligations made no more than three years before the summons. This is the main reason for the drastic decrease in the volume of cases.

Cases before the e-court now constitute a large proportion of the total cases dealt with by the common courts in Poland. The Ministry of Justice reports that in the first half of 2017 the e-court dealt with about 28% of all cases. The reasons for the popularity of the new procedure are, above all, its speed and the cheapness. The court fees amount to one quarter of the standard court fee. Not only are the plaintiffs satisfied with the new procedure, but so are those involved in the administration of justice. The major reason behind the innovation may indeed have been the wish to relieve the courts of the burden of dealing with petty cases.

But if we look at the plaintiffs, it would be rather difficult to claim that the e-procedure is widely used by society at large. Despite popularity and increasing use, the e-procedure is currently used mainly by the enforcement business, where there has been a failure to pay institutions such as banks, and telecommunication and transportation businesses (regarding travel without tickets or without proper tickets). These businesses are getting court orders for payment in cases of pecuniary obligation simply, quickly and cheaply without the need to provide further evidence.

There is indeed little to praise about the new procedure from the perspective of the defendants. The e-court is sending out writs to the email address given by the plaintiff in the summons. If the email address is incorrect the message does not reach the addressee. This is why the defendant often learns about an order for payment only when executive action is undertaken by a bailiff. It is still possible at that stage to make an objection despite the date for payment having expired, but the defendant must now substantiate the claim that the address entered by a plaintiff was wrong. Fortunately, the objection itself needs to be made not only electronically but on paper as well. The court might then affirm the objection and the case would be directed to the common court following the common procedure.

The exclusive character of the initial e-procedure should also be checked against the availability of access to the internet. This is obviously related to the socio-economic position of a potential user of justice. The businesses that dominate the applicant side are almost always (95.6% in 2018 according to the General Statistical Office data) e-empowered, while the proportion of the population using the internet was 77.5%.[4] Amongst households with at least one person aged between 16 and 74 years, 82.7% had access to the internet. Childless and rural households often had less access. Those who are remaining 'offline' explain this often as being due to 'lack of need' (65.7%) or lack of skills (51.3%). Smaller groups refer to lack of money (22.6%), lack of access (17.4%) or general dislike of the internet (11.7%).[5] It is clear that despite the permanent increase in the availability of online communication, the fact is that some underprivileged sectors (the elderly, the poor, the isolated rural population) are effectively excluded from access to e-justice. This puts the socially disadvantaged at risk of losing their legitimate interests not only as defendants against the more powerful businesses but also as potential plaintiffs.

The approaches to the e-court with cases that had expired or had already settled eventually led the court to be more cautious in ordering payment. In 2018 the issue of an order was refused in 40% of cases. Still, the simplicity, speed and low cost of the e-proceedings encourages the extension of the procedure. In Poland it has been emphasised until now, however, that such proceedings may be used only in the area of simple money cases. Matters such as protection of personal rights or family matters are excluded, and it has never been proposed to extend the e-procedure into such areas. On the contrary, in 2018 the Ministry of Justice began working on draft legislation that would extend and complicate divorce proceedings. This included a proposal to raise the fees as well as introduce a mandatory mediation attempt before a legal divorce could be granted. Such a mediation process should be at least one month long. All these planned divorce-preventing measures are based upon the ideological stance of the present government. But we should remember that immediately after the political transformation of Poland from a Communist system of party state and law, the resurgent Catholic philosophy of marriage and the family had already led

[4] https://stat.gov.pl/obszary-tematyczne/nauka-i-technika-spoleczenstwo-informacyjne/spoleczenstwo-informacyjne/spoleczenstwo-informacyjne-w-polsce-w-2018-roku,2,8.html, accessed 17 March 2019.

[5] www.benchmark.pl/aktualnosci/ile-procent-polakow-ma-dostep-do-internetu-2018.html, accessed 17 March 2019.

in the early 1990s to the re-introduction of separation into state law, to putting church and civil marriage on a par, and also increasing the distance between the public and the divorce courts by elevating the divorce procedure to higher level courts.

IV. USE OF COURTS IN POLAND

Public willingness to use the courts and the way they are used in Poland has been studied by the authors since the 1970s when – under Communist rule – interest in the settlement of civil disputes led Jacek Kurczewski and Kazimierz Frieske to study the Social Concilliatory Commissions, which were a voluntary informal but official alternative to courts in the case of petty disputes between neighbours. The study was published as part of the Florence Access-to-Justice Project headed by Mauro Cappelletti (Kurczewski and Frieske, 1977). In the 1970s Jacek Kurczewski (Kurczewski, 1982: 1993) directed local surveys on the experience of disputes and dispute settlement patterns, while Małgorzata Fuszara (Fuszara, 1989) investigated disputes brought before local courts in the form of private criminal prosecutions (these are allowed by Polish law in cases of a breach of physical or moral integrity such as insult, slander, or minor physical injury). This long-term research makes it possible for the authors to compare the use and perception of the courts or other options during the communist period with attitudes to dispute settlement in the post-1989 period of democracy and a market economy. Such historical comparisons have already been made elsewhere (Kurczewski and Orzechowski, 2016; Kurczewski and Fuszara, 2017a).

In the present chapter we limit ourselves to data collected in 2014, just a year before the so-called 'Good Change' reform of the administration of justice and judiciary began under the Law and Justice government. Several factors had been listed to support the claim that such reform was needed, but the greatest importance was attached by party politicians and the Minister of Justice to the dissatisfaction of the people with the courts and the judiciary. In a way, therefore, our findings record the supposedly worst possible state of public opinion concerning the administration of justice in democratic Poland.

The 2014 research on 'Patterns of Dispute and Dispute Settlement in Popular Legal Culture' was undertaken by a team directed by Jacek Kurczewski and financed by the National Science Center Poland (NCN DEC2012/07/B/HS6/02496). Using the CAPI method, face-to-face interviews were conducted with a random sample of 1,036 people living in Poland by CBOS (Public Opinion Research Center). The questionnaire included closed and open-ended questions on general patterns of dispute settlement, as well as on ways out of a conflict, on the basis of several specific examples of types of conflict between an individual and other private persons, or between an individual and public bodies such as the local government, police, or health service.

The preference for compromise in private disputes with people from outside the family is significantly related to being female, in average or below living conditions, and living in the cities. The preference for compromise in public disputes (with the police, the municipal administration, or a hospital administration) is significantly related to being older, currently unemployed, and living in the countryside. The preference for use of the courts in private disputes is significantly related to younger age, living conditions assessed as being above average, and living in the cities. In the case of public disputes the pattern is repeated except that living conditions are less important than being currently employed, either permanently or temporarily.

When referral to all official bodies, including the courts, is taken into account, the pattern changes slightly in comparison to preference for the courts considered in isolation.

Again, the younger urban group is significantly more prone to advocate the use of authoritative dispute-settlement bodies in both types of disputes – private and public – but this applies also to the better educated and those living in better than average conditions in regard to private disputes, and to employed persons in regard to public disputes. Withdrawal was significantly related to being older and female, while men and younger people were more likely to prefer the ambiguous category of 'self-help' or 'private dealing with the matter on one's own', which could involve the arbitrary action of taking compensation for a loan as described in case script no 3, or slapping someone's face as in case script no 2, or any type of revenge or compensatory action without official legitimacy. These findings made us look again at the aggregate Social Position Index (based on Johan Galtung's theory of Center-Periphery) as a predictor of dispute settlement patterns (Kurczewski and Fuszara 2017b: 513, 516).

The final results of our analysis are as follows. There seems to be a social-structure filter in the pathway from a dispute to the court. We note that Petrażycki's image of judicialised disputes as the tip of the iceberg of everyday interactions has been confirmed in our data, along with the image of double icebergs, or better yet, pyramids standing on top of each other. Among all those interviewed, 347 (26.2%) declared that they had experienced at least one such dispute, and of these 43 (13.2%) declared that they had taken the case to court. If all the reported disputes are taken into account, then below the visible tip of 49 cases that were reportedly brought to court, 91% of the disputes reported (546 in total) remained outside. But of primary importance seems to be the institutional context of the dispute – whether it is a dispute with an institution (where going to court prevails) or with an individual (where direct negotiations are the preferred option). Still, the sociological external variables seem to matter little; resort to the court is either an institutional formal necessity or due to the specific intrinsic traits of the dispute – its substance and context (Kurczewski and Fuszara 2017b:519).

One of the questions in our 2014 poll asked whether respondents agreed with the following statement: 'Some people say that taking one's own matter to Court is always unpleasant, even if you are completely in the right'. The answers were as follows (see Figure 1):

Figure 1 Some people say that taking one's own matter to court is always unpleasant, even if you are completely in the right (n = 1,036)

Yes, involving a court in a matter is always unpleasant: 713 (68.8%).
No, involving a court in a matter does not always have to be unpleasant: 231 (22.3%).
No, involving a court in the matter is not unpleasant at all: 47 (4.5%).

The traumatic association of taking a case to court is dominant in Polish society and should be included in all discussion of access to and use of the court. Our further open questioning about the reasons for such an association rarely elicited a detailed explanation. The risk mentioned most often (n = 69) was of making public matters that are usually confidential and private. 55 people in our national representative survey pointed at the waste of time in courts and 21 at the costs of initiating the court action. It is very difficult to diagnose more specifically what lies behind the pervading sense of unease about courts explicitly mentioned by at least 62 of our respondents, as the other reasons need to be categorised at a more general psychological level. This applies even to those who refer seemingly to costs or loss of time. Our conjecture is that contact with court is unpleasant as it removes us from our daily routine and makes our life dependent upon strangers, above all the judge. The effects of interaction with courts are unpredictable and the proceedings make us the potential victim of unforeseeable forces. Such a perspective is significantly more widespread among older people, but in general is popular in all sectors of the society (Fuszara and Kurczewski, 2017: 98/99).

V. FAMILY DISPUTES: WHAT PEOPLE DO

Family disputes, the most intimate and thus amongst the most secret matters, are difficult to study. In previous research we hesitated to ask anything about family disputes in mass surveys. One of us focused on such disputes in her detailed studies (Fuszara 1994, Fuszara 2011). In our 2014 national Polish representative public opinion survey on dispute settlement, when a question was included asking whether the subject had experienced any family (ie, intra household) dispute in the last three years, only 51 people out of 1,035 sampled reported such an experience. As the frequency of such disputes in psychosocial reality is beyond a doubt higher than this, we focus on the typology of the conflicts that were – hopefully – randomly revealed and briefly recorded by the interviewer. What follows is the full list of the types, quoting the self-reported description of the cases. This is inevitably short, given the lengthy questionnaire used in the survey.

- Conflicts between parents and children: these could often be characterised as concerning life style and conduct, for example: 'I was not been allowed to leave home to attend a party'; 'a conflict with mum concerning daughter's pregnancy'; 'my brother's fiancée was at the core of the conflict, she was staying with us, not doing anything, not contributing to daily life and full of requests'; father rejecting the daughter's partner; children not coming home at a specified time; 'taking the garbage out'; 'doing the housework'.
- Disputes between marriage partners including divorce: this group included a husband who said his wife was critical of his conduct saying 'I have entered [the house] with dirty shoes on and similar trifles': and 'for guaranteeing a loan on our apartment for 200,000 zlotys'; and 'about the say in bringing up our children'.
- Financial disputes, examples were related to the sharing of living expenses among those living together, or about leaving the property in a will to a family member and then expecting lifelong reciprocal services. There was also conflict about 'paying the rent by the agreed deadline'; dividing the property: 'I wanted a fair share while the second party arranged for too low an evaluation.' Other parent child conflicts included 'my parents are wanting me to contribute more to the household and be at home more often'; 'I transferred land to my son and he left to go to the US and leased out the land. The lessee was paying in kind, with potatoes, corn for the hens, and meat once a year, but after my son left the lessee gave us nothing so I wanted my share to be paid back'; 'lowering the apartment rent'; 'a dispute about money'.
- Disputes related to co-residence and joint property: for example, dispute about the distribution of rooms in a new house; different ideas about restoration of the house; and; 'joint investment in a piece of land'.
- Abuse, battery; 'stepson attempted to beat me'.
- Alcoholism of a family member.
- Care for a family member: the dispute concerned care for a sick grandmother, about who was to take care and who was to meet the financial obligations.
- Disputes were sometimes described as everyday life and trifling cases: 'these were trifling cases and I don't want to speak about it'; 'everyday life cases'; 'everyday life'.

As we see the list includes everything from serious property disputes to apparent trifles, but many of those interviewed had been reluctant to give details about intimate matters, such as conjugal deception about sexual matters which were at the heart of the conflict. The family conflicts were often inter-generational (eight cases), more rarely between spouses and siblings (four cases), and sometimes with people from outside who endangered the existing union (three cases) or had attempted to set up a household with someone from the family (two cases).

Family disputes are most heterogeneous when participants are asked to choose between the emotions felt towards the opponent. Emotions varied from fear (four cases) to benevolence (five cases). In no other type of disputes – with neighbours, with colleagues, with strangers does 'ambivalence' appear as the way to describe the emotion felt towards an opponent in a dispute. Such emotional ambivalence seems to lead towards the drastic solutions so vividly described in therapy, media and art, solutions such as escape, suicide, murder or another way of annihilating the emotional dissonance felt in the conflict situation.

Where such conflicts had not been referred to the court, this was explained by the respondents as due to the 'trifling' nature of the problem or – if the underlying conflict was very grave – precisely because it is intra-family conflict. One of our female respondents said that 'if I were to be attacked with an axe then certainly I would go to the court' and this illustrates well the problem of judicialisation of family disputes.

But returning to previously reported findings concerning willingness to use the courts by the Polish public, we refer now to two particular questions from our 2014 survey that deal with intra-family conflicts. These are two vignette-based questions starting with brief descriptions of hypothetical cases: first, of a financial dispute between spouses, secondly, of a physical assault of a woman by her husband. Both questions were followed by a list of possible reactions, from withdrawal (or avoidance (Felstiner, 1975)) to bringing the case to the court. The results are shown in Figures 2 and 3.

Figure 2 Preferred ways to manage the financial marriage dispute case (n = 1,036)

Case Script 7: A dispute arose between spouses when the wife inherited 10,000 euros and placed these funds in her own account, rather than contributing it to the family budget. In your opinion, what should her husband do?

1. Don't react, do nothing: 234 (22.6%).
2. Reach agreement and compromise with wife 741 (71.5%).
3. Use self-help to achieve in private what one considers due: 18 (1.7%).
4. Go to court: 20 (2.0%).
5. Go to another agency: (0.3%).

In the case of a financial dispute in which Polish law in principle recognises as a default option the right of a woman to decide on her own acquired wealth, the dominant opinion was to advise the male spouse wishing to get his share to negotiate a compromise agreement with his partner. The next, though much less often chosen approach, is simply to give up making further demands.

One would expect the opposite in the battery case. However, as the results presented in Figure 3 below show, here also there is a dominant preference for private compromise, supported by the majority, even if referral of the case to the police and/or the court is fully available to the wronged woman. The publicisation of the conflict in any case outside the family inner circle is advised by about a quarter of the respondents, almost equal to the frequency of advocacy of giving up the matter in the financial dispute (22%).

Figure 3 Preferred ways to manage an intra-marriage physical assault case (n = 1,036)

Case Script 8: A husband battered a wife suspecting her of secretly meeting with another man. In your opinion, what should the woman do?
1. Don't react, do nothing: 49 (4.7%).
2. Reach agreement and compromise with husband: 574 (55.4%).
3. Use self-help to achieve in private what you consider as due: 69 (6.7%).
4. Go to court: 138 (13.3%).
5. Go to another agency (WHICH?): 128 (12.4%).

It is noteworthy that on this point we were able to observe an unexpected change from communist times when there had been more reasons to suspect the courts and keep authorities in general away from knowledge about personal matters. We had a unique opportunity to compare the public opinion data we had collected in the 1970s in a small town in South East Poland with the local polls we conducted there in 2002 and 2014. While the mean percentage of those advocating use of the court and other official agencies in three hypothetical cases of domestic conflict (including the two described above as asked in the 2014 national survey) remained similar (20%, 16% and 21%), the preference for private compromise increased (30%, 52% and 56%) at the expense of withdrawal and private pursuit of presumed wrongs. This also applies to the other private disputes with neighbours and friends but contrasts with disputes involving public institutions like local government, police or hospitals in which there was an evident rise in the declared willingness to use the courts.

VI. THE SECRET OF FAMILY DISPUTES

In Catholic teaching the family is sacred, and it is not surprising that family disputes are therefore secret. The above data gain in strength if one takes into consideration the degree of secretiveness surrounding intra-family disputes, a factor prohibiting the use of judicial and other public agencies as well as self-reporting to the researcher. One of the questions in our 2014 questionnaire dealt with this issue directly (see Figure 4):

Figure 4 Do you agree or disagree with the opinion that in the case of a dispute, there are different approaches for people we are close to from approaches for other people. Please tell us which of the opinions is closest to how you feel? (n = 1,059)

1. If a dispute takes place within a family, you can never take it to an institution, but if the opponent is not a family member, it is OK to go to an institution, eg a court. Agreed: 172 (16.2%).
2. It does not matter whether a dispute is within a family or not. If your interest is at risk, you have to go to an institution (eg, a court), even if the other person is a family member. Agreed: 228 (21.5%).
3. Generally when there is a dispute in a family, you shouldn't go to court or another institution, but sometimes if a dispute is about something very important (eg, assault, reputation, major assets) you have to go to court or another appropriate institution. Agreed: 615 (58.0%).

The dominant response to our question was thus one of moderate familism. One should restrain oneself in conflict with other family members and keep it within the family unless one's basic rights had been abused. Such a response was chosen by 58.0% of the national sample. Of course, this is an ambiguous position, as many cases of physical or psychological abuse and assault are considered as not serious, and the individual level of tolerance might also differ very much between individuals in the same society, or even in the same family. Two clearly consistently opposing views on the issue of family privacy – one that supports unconditional secrecy and the other that puts no restraint on a family member as to making a conflict public – are quite close in numerical terms. Family loyalists comprise 16.2% of the sample while those wholly independent from concern about the family unity were 21.5%.

We looked more closely at these attitudes, dividing people into full individualists and moderates as opposed to absolute familists. Logistic regression analysis using this dichotomy as the dependent variable and a set of dichotomised social-demographic variables is shown in Table 2:

Table 2 Summary of Logistic Regression Analysis for Socio-Demographic Variables Predicting The Approval of Approaching of the Court in a Family Dispute (n = 1,059)

1- The use of court in a family dispute allowed as a reference category

	Beta	Standard error	Chi2	df	Significance	Exp(B)
GENDER_R (1 – men)	0.078	0.180	0.187	1	0.665	1.081
AGE_RR (1 – up to 50 yrs)	0.138	0.189	0.532	1	0.466	1.148

(continued)

Table 2 *(Continued)*

	Beta	Standard error	Chi2	df	Significance	Exp(B)
EDUCATION_R (1 – higher)	0.493	0.236	0.366	1	0.037	0.611
EMPLOYMENT_R (1 – employed)	0.080	0.221	0.132	1	0.716	1.084
LIVING STANDARD_R (1 – good and very good)	0.071	0.193	0.136	1	0.02	0.931
URBANISATION (1 – above 20,000 inhabitants)	0.077	0.178	0.190	1	0.663	1.081
const	−1.773	0.367	23.392	1	0.000	0.170

$Chi^2(6) = 7{,}51$ **, R^2 Nagelkerke = 0.013.

Of the socio-demographic variables included in the multivariate logistic regression analysis – gender, age, education, employment, self-assessment of living standard and level of urbanisation of the place of residence – only one, education, was significantly ($p<0.01$) associated with family privacy. Higher education increases the likelihood of bringing a family conflict to the court. Other components of social position (as well as the summary index of social position) are not significantly related (at $p<0.01$ level) with attitudes towards family privacy. These details are important as we had also discovered that when all legal consciousness variables available in the questionnaire were used, and these include family secretiveness, the latter came out as significantly associated (Exp(B)=0.49, $p<0.01$) in general with choice of the court against the choice of friendly mediation as a means to satisfy one's claims. Even more importantly, familistic secretiveness is a better predictor (to a small degree) of the choice of the court than personal experience of a court, knowledge of unjust verdicts, and the general sense of uneasiness related to presence in a court described above (Kurczewski and Fuszara, 2017: 110/111).

VII. CONCLUSIONS

In Poland, e-court procedure has been widely used since 2010, though it remains deliberately limited to the area of financial cases considered as simple and self-evident, even though willingness to use the procedure exceeds this limitation as shown by the recent rejection of about 40% of such submissions by the e-court. The development of e-justice under present conditions seems to prejudice the chance of getting justice for underprivileged people at the social periphery (Johan Galtung's concept, see Wiberg, H et al, 2009). But the interests of the mostly institutionalised repeat players (Gallanter, 1974) are in alignment with both the state administration of justice worrying about the budget, and the judiciary who are tired of almost menial legal labour. All these factors are pushing e-justice further, and this therefore needs to be carefully monitored so that the obvious merits of the new procedure, its relative speed, low cost and simplicity, will not be outweighed by the social exclusion effect. The ideological reluctance to ease the access to divorce has until now excluded intra-marriage disputes from the reach of e-justice.

In Poland – especially when the rightwing party is in government – legal regulation hindering divorce rather than facilitating it has been introduced since the fall of communism: 'The measures introduced are simply legal regulations with the hidden aim of increasing the permanence of marriage. Various methods are employed to this end: physical distance to the court in divorce cases is increased; separation is reintroduced as an alternative to divorce; the programmes that had offered the chance of escape to victims of family violence have been stopped; and campaigns to reveal family violence are criticized' (Fuszara and Łaciak, 2000: 136). In spite of introducing these limits to accessibility, the frequency of divorce in Poland is on the rise. It is feared that if the aura of intimacy and resulting secretiveness of internal family issues is considered, the relative anonymity of e-justice would relax the parties in conflicted marriage enough to seek for formal recognition of the break-up of their union much more often than nowadays. The decision is ideological in character but independently of that – as the example of pecuniary 'simple and self-evident' cases shows – the potential social effects should be considered as well.

The ideological tendency to limit and prevent divorce is not the only reason why it is difficult in Poland to advocate e-divorce proceedings. There is a strong tendency also to maintain direct contact between the judge and parties to a dispute. E-proceedings clearly contradict such a principle. One may add also that all procedural mechanisms introducing a degree of automatism at the expense of individual judicial decision-making arouse suspicion. This is best illustrated by the attitudes to the maintenance cases. It has been suggested several times that Poland might follow the example of other countries and use tables setting the level of child support due according to the age of the children and the income of the liable parent. However, the discussion has always ended by upholding the idea that individual judicial decision after learning the details of the case and situation of the parties is much more reliable than any general scheme predetermining the decision on the alimonies (Chełstowska, 2018). Our conjecture is that such a belief in the better quality of particularistic and inductive individual judicial decision as against 'automatism' militates against predicting any extension of online justice in family cases in the near future. Our research into the patterns of court use in Poland clearly shows that the basic differentiating factor is the nature of the parties – with more action by private person versus the public body or private corporation. This could be explained by the increased belief in the independence of the courts after the end of communism in 1989. After turning to democracy the willingness to go to court against the public bodies increased, while private disputes tend to be settled between the interested parties themselves. We think that a considerable part of the population believes strongly that personal matters such as divorce if publicised as the last resort should be dealt with in a traditional personalised procedure allowing for direct face-to-face contact with the judge who listens to the arguments put forward by the parties to a family dispute and conflict.

REFERENCES

Alina, P, Tassig, T, Reinert, T, KiriŞci, J, Sloat, A, Kirchik, J, Hoope, M, Eisen, N, and Kenealy, A (2019) *The Anatomy of Illiberal States: Assessing and Responding to Democratic Decline in Turkey and Central Europe*: www.brookings.edu/wp-content/uploads/2019/02/illiberal-states-web.pdf, accessed 23 March 2019.

Chełstowska, A (2018) 'Praktyki nie płacenia alimentów na dzieci w systemie instytucjonalnym i dyskursie publicznym'. Unpublished Ph D dissertation, ISNS University of Warsaw.

Felstiner, W (1975) 'Avoidance as Dispute Processing; An Elaboration', *Law and Society Review* 4(9), 695–704.

Fuszara, M (1989) *Codzienne konflikty i odświętna sprawiedliwość*. (Warsaw, IPSiR UW).

Fuszara, M (1994) *Rodzina w sądzie* (Warsaw, ISNS UW).

Fuszara, M (2011) 'Divorce in Poland', *Societas/Communitas* 2(12), 211–27.

Fuszara, M and Łaciak, B (2000) 'Pro-family Policy in Poland in the Nineties', in M Maclean (ed) *Making Law for Families* (Oxford, Hart Publishing) 117–36.

Fuszara, M, and Kurczewski, J (2009) 'Disputes and Courts in Poland 25 Years Later', *Societas/Communitas* 7(1), 101–34.

Fuszara, M, and Kurczewski, J (2017) *Spory i ich rozwiązywanie* (Cracow, Nomos).

Galanter, M (1974) 'Why the "Haves" Come out Ahead: Speculations on the Limits of Legal Change', *Law & Society Review* 1(9), 95–160.

Kurczewski, J (1982) *Spór i sądy* (Warszawa, IPSiR UW).

Kurczewski, J (1993) *Resurrection of Rights* (Oxford, Oxford University Press).

Kurczewski, J and Frieske, K (1978) 'The Social Conciliatory Commissions in Poland: a Case Study of Nonauthoritative and Conciliatory Dispute Resolution as an Approach to Access to Justice' in M Cappelletti and J Weisner (eds) *Access to Justice: Promising Institutions* (Milan, A Giuffrè; Alphenaandenrijn: Sijthoff & Noordhoff) 2(1), 156–427.

Kurczewski, J and Fuszara, M (2017a) *How People Use the Courts* (Frankfurt a/M, Peter Lang).

Kurczewski J, and Fuszara, M (2017b) 'Patterns of Preference for Dispute Resolution in Poland', *Polish Sociological Review* 4(200), 505–22.

Kurczewski, J and Orzechowski, P (2016) 'Dispute Settlement Patterns in Public Opinion. Four Local Studies of Transformation', *Societas/Communitas* 17(2), 253–280.

Rylski, P (2015) 'Funkcjonowanie w praktyce przepisów o elektronicznym postępowaniu upominawczym na etapie po wniesieniu sprzeciwu lub po przekazaniu sprawy sądowi właściwości ogólnej' in *Prawo w działaniu. Postępowanie cywilne* 24, 153–220.

Szukalski, P (2016) 'Małżeństwa i rozwody' in *Sytuacja demograficzna Polski. Raport 2015–216* (Warszawa, Rządowa Rada Ludnościowa).

Wiberg, H, van der Vee r, CG, van den Berg, H, Hartmann, A, Galtung, J and Diez-Nicolas, J (2009) 'The Centre-periphery Theory Revisited: A Holistic Multidimensional Approach of Social Behaviour, Social Change and Social Conflicts' in K van der Veer, A Hartmann, H van der Berg, J Diez-Nicolas, J Galtung and H Wiberg (eds) *Multidimensional Social Science. An Inclusive Approach to Social Position and Inequality* (Amsterdam, Rozenberg) 161–66.

Internet Sources

www.benchmark.pl/aktualnosci/ile-procent-polakow-ma-dostep-do-internetu-2018.html, accessed 17 March 2019.

https://stat.gov.pl/obszary-tematyczne/nauka-i-technika-spoleczenstwo-informacyjne/spoleczenstwo-informacyjne/spoleczenstwo-informacyjne-w-polsce-w-2018-roku,2,8.html, accessed 17 March 2019.

EPU-elektroniczne postępowanie upominawcze (e-sąd) w latach 2010 – 2017 https://isws.ms.gov.pl/pl/baza-statystyczna/opracowania-wieloletnie/; Podstawowa informacja statystyczna o działalności sądów powszechnych – I półrocze 2017 roku na tle poprzednich okresów statystycznych, accessed 17 March 2019.

https://isws.ms.gov.pl/pl/baza-statystyczna/publikacje/, accessed 17 March 2019.

3

Competing Logics, Norms and World Visions: The Family Justice System in Turkey

VERDA IRTIS

I. INTRODUCTION

THE FAMILY IS not only a scientific object of study in different disciplines, but also a space for social and political intervention. It is a means for controlling and regulating society. It can serve to defend a way of life, or a way of organising society. Since the family is mainly seen in the public sphere as a 'natural' phenomenon, this controlling and regulating is not always detectable.

In the case of today's Turkey, if we want to analyse family justice, we cannot overestimate the importance of the changing political structure. In other words, now more than ever before we need to be careful with using names for the phenomena, and with an assumption that things are not exactly as they appear. Thus, in these circumstances, 'family' becomes even more of a 'hot' issue and an ideological device. Consider the following:

> (…) The family is the basis of society. A family which is based on mutual love and respect, self-sacrifice, understanding, empathy, and on warm relations gives to the society happy and spiritually healthy individuals. The unhappy family that lacks love and respect, in clash, struggle, conflict, violence, gives unhappy individuals to society. For the marriages which cannot continue, divorce is envisaged as a right for couples in our legal system. (…) Although spouses have been granted divorce in our legal system, the policies aimed at protecting the integrity of the family have been put into force by the state and followed closely (…). Divorce shows an increasing trend in our country. According to the data of the Ministry of Interior General Directorate of Population and Citizenship Affairs, divorce has increased in number and ratio in the 2000s. The number of divorces increased from 91,994 in 2001 to 95,895 in 2005, 118,568 in 2010 and to 128,411 in 2017. The crude divorce rate was found to be 1.6 per thousand in 2017, while the rate of divorce was 1.4 per thousand in 2001. According to

> the data published by EUROSTAT, the crude divorce rate in the European Union countries is 2.1 per thousand. Turkey's divorce rate is approaching the EU average. (…) The main purpose of this call is to identify the multi-faceted economic, social, cultural and psychological reasons and results of divorce, and to develop solutions and models for strengthening family structure, inter-family relations and union of marriage.[1]

This excerpt from a 'scientific call' from the Research Support Programs Presidency under the Scientific and Technological Research Council of Turkey offers one example among several others (some of which will be mentioned later) illustrating how the family (and divorce) are increasingly conceived.

This chapter will describe the different aspects of family justice in Turkey, starting with the Family Courts and ending with Online Dispute Resolution. This will show how the system is fragmented and how difficult it is to predict the long-term consequences of all these policies and legislative initiatives. In conclusion, besides furnishing some interpretative hypotheses, the chapter will try to reflect upon the impact of these interlinked transformations on the professionals involved.

II. FROM FAMILY COURTS TO MEDIATION

It is through Law No. 4787 on the Foundation of Family Courts, their Function and the Proceedings of the Judgment that the first Family Court appeared in Turkey in 2003. These courts are designated to deal with cases arising in Family Law, which is part of the Civil Code modified in 2001. It is expected that there will be one judge to create a court in every province and also in districts having more than 100,000 inhabitants.

Considered as equal in degree to a court of First Instance, each court is supposed to have an adequate number of staff. As for the judge, it is expected that he/she comes from the ordinary courts, is qualified for the appointment, is aged over 30 years, preferably married, with a child, and having a postgraduate degree in the field of family law. In accordance with the Civil Code, these courts are charged with the issues related to marriage, divorce, property regime, establishment of paternity, adoption, and custody as well as (in accordance with International Private Law) with the recognition and enforcement of the decisions of foreign courts. Each court is expected to have a pedagogue, a psychologist and a social worker as experts with an investigative role and taking part in the trial if necessary. The preferred characteristics show similarities with those of the judges.

The measures taken by these courts are protective, social and educational. For 'adults', they are supposed to encourage spouses to respect the obligations

[1] TÜBİTAK-ARDEB Family Call Program-1003-SBB-AILE-2018-1 Divorce, available at www.tubitak.gov.tr/sites/default/files/281/1003-sbb-aile-2018-1.pdf, accessed 19 February 2019.

of the marital union, and if it is necessary to reconcile, to take the measures necessary for the protection of the economic assets of the family or the fulfilment of financial obligations arising from the marital union, to use public or private health or social service agencies, nursing homes or other places, or an educational institution or appropriate vocational courses. For 'minors', they take the necessary measures for the supervision, maintenance and alimony obligation, place a minor whose physical and mental development is endangered or who is spiritually abandoned in the family in a public or private health institution or in a specialised training institution, take measures concerning the management and protection of children's property placed with local authorities, state based economic enterprises and banks, etc. All these measures are supposed to be followed up by one or more of the experts.

Concerning the procedural provisions, according to the characteristics of the cases, before proceeding with a case, courts should encourage a 'friendly settlement' (*sulh bulmak*) in order to protect respect and tolerance and mutual love within the family by identifying the problems faced by the spouses and children. In the case of necessity, the court seeks the experts' opinion. If 'peace' cannot be achieved, the judicial process continues.

I have described above is what is written in the law.[2] When we look at what happens in practice, we see that, contrary to the Law, in 2008, there were only 157 Family Courts for the whole country. In 2016, there were 257.[3] Today, in some cities there is still no Family Court. In 2017 (the latest data available), a significant number of divorce cases were still dealt with in the Civil Court of First Instance (Adalet Bakanligi: 150).

Since their establishment, there has been a quite tense public and academic debate around the duties and judgments of these Family Courts, especially between 2002–12. This has been reinforced by Law No. 5636 on Modification of the Protection of the Family (2007), former Law No. 4320 Law on Protection of the Family (1998) ending with Law No. 6284 on Protection of the Family and the Prevention of Violence against Women in 2012. In their research 'Law on Protection of the Family Protects Who and What? Judges, Prosecutors and Lawyers' Narratives' conducted during just before the coming into force of Law No. 6284, Ayata and colleagues point out how, particularly as a result of lack of expertise in this field, Law No. 4320 was 'understood and interpreted by practitioners in different ways, the Law itself providing a basis for different interpretations about whether the family or the victim should be protected' (Ayata, Eryilmaz and Kalem, 2011: 171). This debate is not over. My observations within the Family Courts showed a tendency to protect the family. The 'pressure' towards achieving a 'friendly settlement' was in some cases putting the litigants in a more uncomfortable situation.

[2] Law No. 4787 on the Foundation of Family Courts, their Function and the Proceedings of the Judgment, 2003.

[3] High Commission of Judges and Prosecutors: www.hsk.gov.tr/, accessed 30 June 2016.

Following the Family Courts, mediation entered the landscape very recently. In 2012 Law No. 6325 came into force with the purpose of regulating the procedures and principles to be applied in the mediation of legal disputes. It applies to the resolution of private law disputes not only in family matters but also arising out of employment or commercial transactions, including those with foreign/international elements. However, disputes involving a claim of domestic violence are not thought conducive to mediation.[4] According to the Law, mediation involves bringing the parties together to implement systematic techniques, to negotiate and to encourage negotiations, to establish the communication process between them in order to enable the parties to understand each other and to produce their solutions themselves. If the parties cannot produce a solution, the third person/mediator, being well-trained and specialised, can propose a solution to resolve the dispute. This third person should be impartial and independent, and the process should be voluntary for the parties.[5] The Law specifies that the parties may agree to apply to the mediator before the legal proceedings or during the trial. The judge may also encourage the parties to apply to the mediator.[6] In 2017, it was added that a party in need of legal assistance to meet the mediation fee may benefit from legal aid by the decision of the Court of Peace,[7] and the parties themselves can participate in mediation negotiations through their legal representatives or their lawyers. Specialists who can contribute to the resolution of the dispute can also be present in the negotiations.[8] It is envisaged that the mediation will terminate when: (a) the parties have reached an agreement, (b) the mediator identifies that there is no need for further efforts to mediate after the parties have been consulted, (c) one of the parties notifies the other party or the mediator that he/she will withdraw from the mediation activity, (d) the parties have agreed to terminate their mediation activities, and (e) it is determined that the dispute is not suitable for mediation.[9]

In 2018, a new Article 20 was added to the Law under the heading 'Mediation as a condition of the case'. This article defines the conditions for registration as a mediator, including that it is necessary to be a Turkish citizen, to be a law school graduate with at least five years' experience in the legal profession.[10] A list of crimes (starting with crimes against the security of the state and ending with perjury) was added, and conviction for any of these would disqualify a mediator.[11] Law faculties, the Bar Association of Turkey and Turkey's Justice Academy are given the authority to organise mediation training with the condition that they obtain the permission of the Ministry of Justice. The list of

[4] Law No. 6325, Art 1.
[5] ibid, Art 2.
[6] ibid, Art 13(1).
[7] ibid, Art 13(3).
[8] ibid, Art 6.
[9] ibid, Art 17.
[10] ibid, Art 20.
[11] ibid.

permitted educational institutions is published electronically.[12] When we looked at the mediation statistics for the period of 2 January to 27 May 2018,[13] we noted 15,655 applications. In 97% of the cases agreement was achieved. 14,140 applications concerned employment disputes. 24 applications in family law are recorded, of which 19 disputes were resolved, with an agreement reached.[14] For the same period, 127,845 applications were registered for mediation as a compulsory step to begin a law suit of which 65% ended with a resolution.[15]

As the data over the years shows (Adalet Bakanligi, 2017: 207) today it is hard to say that institutionalised family mediation exists. But it is emerging. Nevertheless, when we consider how it has become visible as a form of alternative dispute resolution, especially in matters related to commercial and employment law, and when we take into account the tendency to introduce new laws to make mediation *an obligatory step* before going to the court, we may easily think that mediation as an ADR will gain importance in family matters. At the same time, it is quite clear that, despite all the efforts, mediation has not 'enthused' the (potential) litigants in general. In fact, the policy debate around mediation in civil disputes started in 1998. The process of legislative deliberation took several years during which lawyers argued that they were the only professional group capable of being mediators. Through this, we see again as Kalem's (2010) work illustrates very well, the ideological role of law and legal professionals in Turkey's modernisation history.[16] As the content of the 2012 Law proves, lawyers win, and even if they must have an additional training[17] after their graduation from the Law faculties, they become the only persons who are permitted to mediate.

After 2012, we can say that the debate was over. Through its General Directorate of Law Works, and the Presidency of the Mediation Department website in the Ministry of Justice (which includes 'templates' as well as explaining its organisation, offices, training, accreditation, related laws, and statistics, etc),[18] the system/structure for mediation was in place. But 'where were the clients'?[19]

[12] Law No. 6325, Art 23. Note that in this Law alone four modifications were made in 18 months. Is Law really 'in action'?

[13] The most recent ones.

[14] www.adb.adalet.gov.tr/Sayfalar/istatistikler/istatistikler/ihtiyari.pdf, accessed 8 February 2019.

[15] ibid.

[16] The role and the ideological role of law is still in operation. At the same time as this operation, ruling with laws has a more complex face today.

[17] This mediation training includes the basic information about mediation activities, communication techniques, negotiation and dispute resolution methods, behavioural psychology and other theoretical and practical information to be shown in the regulation (Art 22(1)).

[18] During my research in different courthouses in the country, between 2012 and 2018 I observed how mediation was promoted through advertising, public spots, conferences, recruitment, etc.

[19] 'In fact, in choosing to control entrance into the profession in order to give guarantees of quality, they [family mediators] probably undermined what has been the main reason for their own success – the attractiveness and accessibility of the training programmes they used to offer to a wider group of social workers, who constituted, indeed, the real "clients" of family mediation.' (Bastard, 2010: 142.) It seems that this excessive appropriation by the lawyers in Turkey prior to the Law has provided a similar consequence, at least for the moment.

We cannot say that nobody was interested in ADR. As the data shows, in disputes related to commercial and employment law, mediation has been used. But, it was widely below expectations. However, making it obligatory in some cases brought some success.

Thus, it would be interesting to see how litigants will or will not react if mediation becomes obligatory for conflicts in the family law domain. But even the existence of such a stage demonstrates that '(…) mediation has something unclassifiable' (Bastard, 2005: 66) in raising awareness of the cultural, social and psychological dimensions of both the family sphere and private life. In the context of Turkey, it seems that people do not want the presence of a third person, a stranger or 'external third person' where family and friends can often play (directly or indirectly) the role of mediator. In a sense, since in reality private life is still a very collective/communal one in Turkey, when there is a conflict it seems more appropriate, and more secure for the parties, not to make (consciously or unconsciously) this a part of public sphere. I first witnessed this argument when I was interviewing Children Courts Judges on the subject of reconciliation which was available, but not used, or only exceptionally. From their point of view, 'these kinds of device were not fitting to the characteristics of the culture'. For many of them, people tend to think that (for instance) 'an older man respected in the mahalle [a neighbourhood unit] could play the role of the mediator'.[20]

III. FAMILY AND RELIGIOUS GUIDANCE OFFICES

In this context it is important to mention another agency concerned with family matters which has been institutionalised since 2002: *Aile Irsat ve Rehberlik Burolari*. It is already interesting to note that these offices were opened in 2003 which was also the year during which the first Family Court opened. These offices were first known as *Aile Irsat ve Rehberlik Burolari*, and later, in 2015, the name was modified and became *Aile ve Dini Rehberlik Burolari*. *Irsat* (the word that was dropped) comes from Arabic, meaning 'showing the correct way', 'illuminate', and also 'warning'.[21] This was not a word applied in daily life. When the modification had been made and *Aile Irsat ve Rehberlik Burolari* had turned into 'Family and Religious Guidance Offices', the word *Irsat* was kept for *Irsat Hizmetleri Daire Baskanligi*, a unit with the duty to 'enlighten society on religion'.[22]

[20] It was not the only argument, but the most recurrent.

[21] www.tdk.gov.tr.

[22] According to Law No. 633 On the Foundation of the Law on Establishment and Duties of the Presidency of Religious Affairs, this unit has the duty 'to enlighten society on religion'. For this, it organises sermons in the mosques and masjids as well as conferences, seminars, panels, symposia, religious programmes in the medias, etc. Source: https://dinhizmetleri.diyanet.gov.tr/sayfa/50/, accessed 19 February 2019.

In 2002, the Directorate of Religious Affairs decided to open Family and Religion Guidance Offices with the aim 'to preserve and strengthen the family institution'. 15 were opened in six provinces in 2003, then 18 in 2006, 11 in 2007, 14 in 2008, three in 2009, and in 15 provinces and in some large districts in 2010. Since then, their number has steadily increased (Ozdemir, 2013: iii). In 2017, Family and Religious Guidance Offices were open in 81 provinces and 293 districts (depending on the Mufti's Office). A total of 2,178 personnel, 1,457 women and 721 men, work in these offices.[23]

As we observed, although there have been some modifications since their emergence, when we examine the website of the Presidency of Religious Affairs, we notice that there is a continuity in their implementation and the objectives assigned to these offices. The maintenance and strengthening of the family institution is now expressed as '... to bring religious services to all segments of the society and to increase its effectiveness'.[24] It is noted that 'in our society religion is a strong source of reference. Religious officials who have a reputable place in the society are confronted with many applications to be consulted (...), since they have a close relationship (...)'.[25]

When we look at the distribution of office personnel by title, we record 772 preachers, 48 religious services and education experts, 925 Koran course instructors, 314 imams and muezzins. The number of office staff (such as branch manager, auditor, data preparation and control operator) is 54. Office services are generally provided by preachers and Koran course instructors.[26]

As one of the very rare studies of the Family and Religious Guidance Office demonstrates, in the city of Adana,[27] 97.4% of the people who apply to the Office are women. The people who received religious and guidance services are mostly between 20 and 59 years old. The majority of them (nearly 61%) are housewives. In 80% of the cases they are married. When we take into account the educational background of applicants, we see that nearly 36% of them graduated from primary school. If the questions/demands are classified by subject, the most recurrent ones (as grouped by the researcher) are in the domains of Islamic Law, family problems, worship, marriage and wedding, social problems and divorce (Ozdemir, 2013: ii, 48).

When we put together different pieces of information (including others I do not mention here), we realise that children and women constitute the main target of these offices. Religious guidance is introduced as 'the best way to happiness'. 'For a healthy society, healthy families are needed.' In this sense, divorce is considered as a 'real danger to avoid'. By following Sirman's (2013) comment, we may think that this situation creates a kind of double exclusion. On one hand,

[23] Republic of Turkey Presidency of Religious Affaires. General Directorate of Religious Services.
[24] ibid.
[25] ibid.
[26] ibid.
[27] An important city in South-Central Anatolia.

institutionalisation of these Offices by the state leaves an important segment of the population with a single solution by removing them from alternative structures, and on the other hand, it makes more fragile other sections of society, including social services and feminist organisations. 'In a sense, it is a blow to the pluralism of society. It is difficult for women to evaluate information according to their own life conditions and to make choices' (Sirman 2013). When we take into account also other facts, such as the attribution in December 2017 to the imams after muftis the capacity to perform the marriage ceremony,[28] which was formerly done only by marriage officials in the municipalities, we see that this politico-juridical inclusion of religion in family affairs should be analysed through separate research.

IV. DIGITAL PATHWAYS

At the same time, Turkey responds also to the 'digitising environment' which becomes more and more present on a global scale. In this regard, we see that recent years are marked by a kind of 'mobilisation' to digitise nearly all the public services. This includes judicial functions. It seems important to note, just to give some idea about the extent of this 'mobilisation', that in 2012 the UN's public service award was given to Turkey. In *The Guardian* newspaper it was stated that

> Turkey, which won the UN's public service award (…), now has a national electronic service across all its judicial functions. Lawyers and citizens can examine files, pay application fees, submit their documents and claims and file cases electronically to any court in the land. As a case progresses, they can access all relevant information and learn the day fixed for the trial without checking with court staff by phone or in person.[29]

Thus, websites, social media, public view terminals, emails, intranets, audioconferencing and videoconferencing are increasingly used. Judges, prosecutors and lawyers have their common UYAP[30] system. Besides, e-Bars are under discussion. I-Bar exists already.[31] Growing numbers of lawyers are working with their iPhones. 'If these new technologies did not exist, I do not know how these divorce cases would be' was expressed by one of the judges in reaction to the physical absence of the lawyers which seems to have become quite frequent. The lawyer with whom I had conducted an exploratory interview indicated that 'We do not need to be present in the court all the time. Some of my colleagues go only for the end of the case'.

[28] But they do not marry if one of the persons is a foreigner or not a Muslim.
[29] *The Guardian*, 16 January 2017.
[30] System of National Justice Network.
[31] I-Bar is an app initially designed for I phone using lawyers to facilitate their proceedings. Since 2017 it can be used by all android devices.

An eCourt has been operating since January 2018. This constitutes the first and (for the moment the only) ODR example in Turkey.[32]

These are excerpts from the website (which do not need comment).[33]

Our Goal

The aim of the eCourt Online Dispute Resolution Portal is to facilitate the solution of legal disputes online in the ordinary course of life, to make it economical, to accelerate the process of solution by shortening the process.

Nowadays, people are looking for the solution of legal disputes in courthouses because there is no another option. When the data of the Ministry of Justice is examined, the treatment of a file takes on average 266 days. Lawsuits are not economic at all. (…) When this data is evaluated, it is obvious that the courthouses and the classic dispute resolution methods are difficult. In this context, the eCourt aims to solve the legal problems of the Online Dispute Resolution Portal users in an economical, fast and reliable way.

What does the eCourt do?

The e-trial aims to provide users with the opportunity to negotiate and resolve their legal disputes online. Mediators are registered in the Ministry of Justice (…).

It is envisaged that eCourt users can apply online to experts in their disputes and calculate the potential risks in dispute. The conclusions of the users as a result of the e-trial process shall be obtained with the approval of the mediators registered to the mediation record and shall have the same legal guarantee as the court decision. The result of the appeal is to shorten the long period in the courthouses and to solve the problems economically, quickly and reliably.

Our Vision

The eCourt aims to be the address that can be applied to without any difficulties in (…) legal disputes (…). The e-mail users will be able to use the Online Dispute Resolution portal in confidence, wherever the internet and computer and mobile communication tools are located, without thinking about the time, space, formalities and impossibilities.

It aims to provide e-mail service to its members and applicants (…) and to reach a solution within 10 days (…). With eCourt Online Dispute Resolution, you can resolve your legal disputes economically, quickly and reliably.

eCourt – Technology is Changing All Our Habits in Every Area

Mankind has lived together (…) and built a civilization. Living together has contributed to the development of humanity, but has brought with it also problems. In order to solve these problems, humanity has found different ways with the development of modern law. Firstly, physical courts were established and people were seeking help in their problems in these courts. Afterwards, a search began for alternative dispute resolution ways because of the difficult transportation of these courts and the cost of the processes. Application of Alternative Dispute Resolution (ADR) has changed the

[32] It is a private initiative.

[33] '(…)' indicates that the text has been abbreviated by the author.

logic and habits of mankind's problem solving. As a result of this research, people started to use mediation as the most appropriate method.

> Mediation has provided people with privacy, flexible negotiation opportunities and solutions. In the early twenty-first century, the habits of human beings have changed remarkably with the development of methods of communication. The spread of the Internet all over the world resulted in the fact that people spend an average of 4 hours per day online. People can communicate with their distant relatives via the Internet, conduct their business meetings over the internet, and satisfy their food orders and clothing needs via the internet. So why should people not be able to solve their disputes online while meeting all their needs online? Here is the solution address (...).
>
> Thanks to the E-Court, users will be able to solve their problems while relaxing, working or on holiday. The result will have the same legal guarantee as the classic court decisions. The choice of other dispute resolution solutions are costly and long processes are not in accordance with today's habits (...).
>
> As a result eCourt as the Turkey's first Online Dispute Resolution offers its users the possibility to resolve their conflicts in accordance with the new habit'.[34]

As discussed earlier, mediation has become a case requirement in employment law. The Firm[35] refers also to this modification and provides an example in order to demonstrate that ODR remains the 'most effective' not only in terms of 'cost' and 'time', but also in terms of its capacity 'to replace' all these traditional stages with a 'new rational and practical way'. '(...) You will be able to resolve your dispute by continuing to deal with whatever you are doing'.[36]

It is added that:

> The eCourt Online Dispute Resolution Portal changes and develops every day according to the wishes of the community and mediators. It is now possible to negotiate mediation with mobile phones and tablets, making it very easy for our mediators, and 'privacy' is mentioned as 'the most essential and essential element of mediation'.[37]

As declared on the website of the Firm, the conflicts brought to the eCourt are mostly related to commercial and employment law. But, as also announced on the same site, services concerning family affairs (from divorce to child issues) will be proposed as soon as the rest of the juridical preparation is completed by the Ministry of Justice.[38] With respect to this, mediation is presented as the 'beginning of a new era' in the dispute resolutions related to family law:

> Even if people demand mostly from their legal systems the solution to their disputes stemming from their material rights and needs, in this developing world their spiritual problems and their need to ask for solutions to them are also increasing. The most important factor in the emergence of these spiritual concerns is related to the problems experienced in the family, in marriage and in divorce. The processes of

[34] www.emahkeme.com.tr/, accessed 18 February 2019.
[35] ibid.
[36] ibid.
[37] ibid.
[38] ibid.

solution for these problems are not theoretical and emotionless when we compare them to commercial relations. At the basis, we find privacy. Thanks to Family Mediation, in more than 100 countries around the world, the parties are overcoming this concern and the tension of the court, and efforts are being made to protect the unity of marriage.

According to TURKSTAT data, the number divorcing in 2016 is 126, 164. This number shows us:

- Around more than 1 million people get divorced in four years; this causes serious workload in the courts.
- Every four years, one million people carry all the details of their private life to the court.
- Only the first-instance court proceedings in divorces have a result in about one year.

Here is the 'friendly' way to facilitate the whole process for both parties and the judicial authorities. When the family mediation system starts to operate, it will present the following novelties:

- Persons who go to the judiciary for divorce, alimony, property sharing, compensation, custody, for establishing a personal relationship with the child will be oriented to the family mediator.
- In family mediation centres which will be created in accordance with the new legislation, there will not only be legal mediators, psychologists, and social workers but also experts from different fields will participate in resolution.
- The cases of divorce involving violence to the woman will remain exempted.
- The mediators will firstly try to reconcile the parties. The parties will be assisted in finding solutions to the interests of children. The compromise provided in the presence of the mediator will be approved by the family judge in all circumstances.

And the most important thing,

- Conflicts in mediation will remain confidential.

This institution will be clarified with the new legal arrangements planned in the next period. We hope that with the support of the judges, lawyers and parties, as in the developed world countries, it will contribute to our social life and our legal system.[39]

V. CONCLUSION

Finally, it seems hard to 'reach conclusions' during this very particular historical period that the country has been experiencing for nearly two decades. Everything is changing so fast; transformations are in transformation. We know that things are hidden and the role of the social scientist is to unveil what is hidden. But, when writing this chapter, I realised even more how successive changes in the laws (although I tried to summarise to give a general view here) in this authoritarian context create not only a very fragmented vision, but also make investigation itself difficult.

[39] ibid.

In other words, Turkey's situation, in which there is a two-way double movement of the judicialisation of politics and politicisation of the judiciary (Irtis, 2017) gives rise to more questions than answers. We see that Family Courts are a relatively recent institution. They have Family and Religious Guidance Offices next to them. Mediation too is a recent development. Digitisation is here now, but for how many people is it a reality?

Nevertheless, this coexistence of competing logics, norms and world visions demonstrates how the family is under pressure. As the Family and Religious Guidance Offices example shows us, the law operates on the family in various ways, by also implicitly expanding the field of 'classic family law'. The present state of family justice demonstrates how Turkey is squeezed between 'its own time' and the global one. The categories of 'private and public', 'formal and informal', and 'modern and traditional' (Kalem, 2010) all need to be reconsidered. To be able to understand these recent years and to provide a plausible analysis, the need for more time is obvious. At this stage, we can only say that, despite the increased politicisation of the family (and its law), private ordering, marketisation and fragmentation of legal services (Kaganas 2016: 326) are also gaining in importance in Turkey. Nevertheless, on consideration, we see that the Family Courts which seek to 'meet the long-term needs of the family as a whole, and in particular of the children' (Maclean et al. 2011: 339) remain the hub in the sense that they are the place of 'conclusion' for the conflicts.

In terms of professions, in spite of the existence of a sufficiently powerful professional organisation (and thus a relatively significant professional identity), the lawyers work under the dominant figure of the judge in general. But, in the Family Courts, I observed (Irtis, 2016) that even if the judges' power and domination is still clearly there, both judges and lawyers seem to be more comfortable and 'in their professions' compared to my other experiences with Juvenile and Juvenile High Criminal Courts.

We saw that in the case of mediation, the lawyers preserved their 'power'. But, if a new law comes into force by making possible the presence of social workers, pedagogues and psychologists in family mediation, this would affect their position. The involvement of lawyers via digital devices may weaken the judges' dominance. The lawyer who is not at the court can narrow 'the judge's scene'. Moreover, the expansion of the usage of digital technologies seems to create a new category among lawyers called 'new generation ones'.

Finally, it is important to underline that since the coup d'état attempt of July 2016[40] there have been several dismissals among judges and prosecutors as well as lawyers who have had severe problems (including incarceration and suicide) in the exercise of their professions. The conditions and procedures of education, training, selection and attribution are changing considerably, making the question of law and justice more eternal than ever.

[40] Coup d'Etat attempt.

REFERENCES

Adalet Bakanligi (2017) *Adli Istatistikler 2017* (Ankara, Adli Sicil ve Istatistik Genel Mudurlugu).

Ayata, G, Eryilmaz, S and Kalem, S (2011) *Ailenin Korunmasına Dair Kanun Kimi ve Neyi Koruyor? Hakim, Savcı ve Avukat Anlatıları* (Istanbul, Istanbul Bilgi Universitesi Yayinlari).

Bastard, B (2005) 'Mais à qui profite la médiation familiale?' *Dialogue* 4,170.

Bastard, B (2010) 'Family mediation in France: a new profession has been established, but where are the clients?', *Journal of Social Welfare & Family Law* 32(2).

Irtis, V (2016) 'Interacting within the Family Courts in Turkey', RCSL Working Group for Comparative Studies of Legal Professions Biennial Meeting, 6–9 July 2016, Acta Arthotel, Andorra La Vella.

Irtis, V (2017) 'Des "lois" à l'"identité": le travail du juge en Turquie', Seminar, Centre de recherches sociologiques sur le droit et les institutions pénales (CESDIP), 19 Septembre, Saint-Quentin-en Yvelines.

Kaganas, F (2016) 'Delivering Family Justice in the 21st Century', *Journal of Social Welfare and Family Law* 3, 38.

Kalem, S (2010) *Contested Meanings – Imagined Practices: Law at the Intersection of Mediation and Legal Profession. A Socio-legal Study of the Juridical Field in Turkey*, PhD dissertation, New School University.

Law No. 4787 on the Foundation of Family Courts, their Function and the Proceedings of the Judgment, 2003.

Law No. 6325 Mediation Law on Legal Disputes, 2012.

Law No. 633 on the Foundation of the Law on Establishment and Duties of the Presidency of Religious Affairs, 1965.

Maclean, M, Hunter, R, Wasoff, F, Ferguson, L, Bastard, B and Ryrstedt, R (2011) 'Family justice in hard times: can we learn from other jurisdictions?', *Journal of Social Welfare and Family Law* 4, 33.

Ozdemir, O (2013) *Aile Irsat ve Rehberlik Burolarinin Yetiskin Din Egitimine Katkisi (Adana Ili Ornegi)*, Master Diss, Cukurova Universitesi.

Sirman, N (2013) *Aile Irsat Merkezi Aslinda Ne Ise Yarar*, Evrensel Gazetesi: www.evrensel.net/haber/48611/aile-irsat-merkezi-aslinda-ne-ise-yarar, accessed 17 February 2019.

(2) The Professional Landscape

4

Legal Help by Student Lawyers: Harnessing the Thinking Behind Digital Expert Systems

LISA WEBLEY

I. INTRODUCTION

STATE FUNDED LEGAL assistance for most private law family law matters in England and Wales was radically reduced as a result of the Legal Aid, Sentencing and Punishment of Offenders Act 2012 (LASPO) reforms. There were already concerns that those of modest means were excluded from the then eligibility requirements for legal aid, and thus were finding it hard to seek professional legal help (See Cookson, 2011; 2013). This anxiety mounted when LASPO excluded many types of private family law matters from the legal aid scheme (Cobb, 2013; Bevan, 2013). Anecdotal evidence began to emerge from free legal and related advice providers indicating that clients with family law problems were beginning to seek help from those services when in the past they had not (McKeown and Morse, 2015; Camplin, 2017). Courts reported a sharp rise in the number of litigants in person, and the challenges they faced in the court system (See Webley, 2015a, for a detailed breakdown of the figures). The Ministry of Justice funded an in-depth study to examine this phenomenon (Trinder et al, 2014; Trinder and Hunter, 2015) and other studies also highlighted fears that people with family law problems were struggling to get the advice and information they need, let alone representation, to enable them to resolve their disputes or to have them adjudicated (Smith, Hitchings and Sefton, 2017; Barlow et al, 2017).

Proponents of the reforms have indicated that private family law issues are just that, private, and absent exceptional circumstances (such as domestic violence) taxpayers should not be required to fund legal advice and representation in contexts where clients had made choices that should be a matter of personal responsibility.[1] They also point to the availability of (limited) legal advice connected with family mediation services offered through the legal aid scheme.[2] Yet many people with family law issues have eschewed this route to potential redress (Barlow, 2017) and instead have sought to battle through either alone or with the help of piecemeal pro bono and/or less traditional forms of help (Wong and Cain, 2019; Maclean, 2014; 2015).

This chapter considers one of those responses to these reforms: legal help by university law students through university law clinics and/or court based assistance programmes supervised by law academics and legal practitioners. Rather than charting the development of these services, which has been done by others,[3] this chapter considers how the way in which students are taught family law could provide a means to support them to assist and/or signpost the otherwise unrepresented. This is in the context of ongoing access to family justice concerns in the absence of cost effective professional services that meet client needs. I am not advocating that student services be considered an appropriate replacement for fully qualified legal help (see Robins, 2012), and I am alive to criticisms that by providing assistance through pro bono mechanisms the state is better able to sidestep responsibility for providing funded legal help. My limited ambitions for this brief chapter are to examine whether clinical and legal education techniques may, in a family law context, provide insights into how digital information and triage systems could be harnessed better to help those who otherwise are without assistance. Such a system could, of course, be used by junior yet qualified lawyers[4] to provide legal help to family law clients through lower cost methods or to allow for partnership working between lawyers and their clients.

The chapter will first set the clinical legal education scene in general in England and Wales and then in family law terms. Next, it will consider how relatively modest amendments to relatively traditional approaches to teaching family law trialled on one module on the LLB (Hons) programme at the University of Westminster appeared to equip students better to engage with family law problems so as to help clients within clinic environments. Thirdly, it will suggest that these methods may be used as the basis for developing the kind of online triage tool that is already used in some branches of primary health care

[1] For a discussion of the ideological underpinnings see Kaganas (2017) Mant (2017); Webley (2015b) See too Maclean (ed) (2017) and Webley (2015a).

[2] For details of the interplay between legal aid, mediation and legally aided advice see: Maclean and Eekelaar (2016).

[3] See McKeown and Morse (2015) and Kemp, Munk and Gower (2016): http://hummedia.manchester.ac.uk/schools/law/main/news/Clinical-Legal-Education-Final-Report28.09.2016.pdf.

[4] England and Wales has professional divisions between different types of lawyers, with different routes to qualification and a distinct if overlapping set of reserved legal activities. Throughout this chapter I use the term 'qualified lawyer' to include those who are solicitors, barristers and chartered legal executives. This is to prevent the need to use each title or to suggest that one protected title represents all branches of the profession(s).

in England and Wales.[5] Such a tool could be used by junior qualified lawyers or, *in extremis*, law students, to provide signposting assistance and some basic information to would-be clients.[6] It will end with conclusions about students as law helpers in this context.

II. CLINICAL LEGAL EDUCATION IN ENGLAND AND WALES AND FORAYS INTO FAMILY LAW CLINICS

Clinical legal education became identifiable as a movement in England and Wales from the 1970s onwards,[7] but the relatively ready availability of low or free of cost legal help kept it contained to niche areas of law that were excluded from legal aid schemes (Bloch and Noone, 2010).[8] This is in contrast to its development in some other countries, such as the US (Kemp, Munk and Gower, 2016: ch 3). The turning point in England occurred when areas of law began to be cut from the system and by the late 2000s many university law schools were involved in some form of student clinical work.[9] The regulatory changes introduced by the Legal Services Act 2007 also opened the way for Law School clinics to offer fee-charging models of service as alternative business structures, although there has been little take up of for-cost models of clinical legal education and the vast majority of help is provided pro bono.[10] The Clinical Legal Education Organisation has sought to support clinical legal educators in their work[11] and a network of clinics and supervising lawyers developed more formally. Rhetoric from successive governments exhorting the legal profession(s) to undertake greater quantities of pro bono also accelerated these programmes (Baksi, 2016), as did a push from law students to gain more practical hands on experience of legal practice.[12] Clinical legal education became firmly

[5] Although it is noted that the evidence on the success of initiative such as the National Health Service 111 telephone triage service is mixed, see Pope et al (2017). There is also an online pilot that seeks to develop this service into an online chatbot app, the results of the pilot have not yet been released: Armstrong (2018).

[6] Clinical legal educators have already mooted this suggestion in the context of clinical legal education and law students: Jones, McFaul and Ryan (2017).

[7] See Kemp, Munk and Gower (2016) ch 4.

[8] The Open University has opened the first online law clinic in 2017, although does not offer family law advice currently: http://law-school.open.ac.uk/open-justice/get-legal-advice, accessed 7 April 2019.

[9] There were relatively few clinical legal programmes in the UK in the mid 2000s, in contrast to other jurisdictions: Marson, Wilson and van Hoorebeek (2005).

[10] See Kemp, Munk and Gower (2016, 26–27) setting out Nottingham Trent University's teaching law firm established as an alternative business structure authorised by the Solicitors Regulation Authority. The University of Law had also previously sought and been approved to provide some reserved activities as an alternative business structure: Connelly (2017).

[11] The Clinical Legal Education Organisation (CLEO) is a charitable organisation that seeks to foster, promote and develop clinical legal education in the UK: www.cleo-uk.org/, accessed 7 April 2019.

[12] For an example of student perceptions of the benefits of this kind of opportunity see Koroma and Antoniou (2017). Clinicians also note a range of benefits, see Marson, Wilson and van Hoorebeek (2005, 38–39). Guides have been written to support students in maximising their learning opportunities in clinical legal settings, see eg Kerrigan and Murray (2011).

established in law schools, even if often as extra curricula activity for a minority of students, rather than a mainstream and core component of the credit-bearing curriculum.

There are, however, challenges in providing effective clinical legal education opportunities that both address the educational needs of students and the legal needs of clients. The two are held in tension and law schools may, at times, have to prioritise the one of the other.[13] There are resourcing issues (students need supervision either by faculties with legal practice experience or by lawyers who are in private practice and participate as part of their commitment to pro bono), logistical issues (students and supervising lawyers have other commitments that may need to take priority at a time when clients need urgent help) and geographical ones (universities are not always well placed for clients, other town centre premises may need to be rented or otherwise sourced). Clinicians require some knowledge of learning theory and associated pedagogy, if they are to do clinical legal education well (Grimes, 1996). And there are regulatory and ethical considerations, including issues of client protection related to the quality of advice and assistance, what happens if things go wrong, and whether there is insurance in place too.[14]

Family lawyers and family law faculty did not often have to grapple with these concerns, as family law was such a mainstay of the legal aid scheme that clients rarely sought help with these kinds of cases. Many clinics expressly excluded these cases from their scope until the LASPO reforms. Yet, there are fewer hurdles in England and Wales to providing this kind of assistance than there are in many other jurisdictions, given the relatively narrow unauthorised legal practice rules in force.[15] It is possible to obtain appropriate indemnity insurance and there is a lot of guidance available from those with experience of clinics who generously share their good practice (see Thomas et al (eds), 2018). Increasingly sophisticated tools have been developed by clinical legal educators to help others to develop their programmes in other universities.

Since the reforms, a number of university law schools have introduced family law pro bono schemes including but not limited to: London South Bank, Northumbria and Birmingham (in court assistance as well as advice clinic schema); Huddersfield and Westminster (advice clinics) as well as other clinics that offer a broad spectrum of advice and assistance services that cover family law matters: Plymouth, Cardiff and Swansea universities. The Community Legal Outreach Collaboration, Keele scheme (CLOCK), started at Keele University and is now running in or planned to be running in conjunction with universities in court centres as follows: Keele, Stoke-on-Trent, Staffordshire; Brighton, Sussex; Canterbury, Kent; Salford, Greater Manchester and Essex, Birmingham

[13] See Camplin (2017) for the challenges of providing legal help outside term time.
[14] For a discussion of the regulatory issues, see Thomas (2017).
[15] See Webley (2015a) for details of activities reserved to fully admitted lawyers in the UK.

City, Birmingham and Liverpool John Moores, Liverpool.[16] These lists are not exhaustive, but illustrate that family law matters form part of a range of law school pro bono initiatives. They span help with form filling, to providing family law information, in some instances tailored legal advice, in others more in-depth assistance. Others include in-court help for self-represented litigants who seek support from students who talk them through the court process, up to MacKenzie Friend input[17] where law students provide help in court either on an informal basis or with judicial consent to assist the client to set out her case. Some of the law students involved will be law graduates who have already completed their law degrees and continued on to the next stage of vocational, practical legal education. Others will be relatively new to legal studies. All will have some form of supervisory support, although supervisory models vary considerably depending on whether the schemes are primarily clinical legal education, primarily pro bono initiatives or a combination of the two. Differences also emerge between initiatives controlled by law schools, by in practice legal professionals or are a partnership model.

During my time teaching family law in one of the institutions that was developing a family law clinic I began to realise that my then current teaching practice led students to be well versed in the law and legal problem solving for an idealised client, but not necessarily focused on using their legal knowledge and skill to provide practical solutions and focused advice to particular people. I wondered why that was the case given that students were set weekly simulated client cases to address that were designed to develop their abilities in client contexts. That made me consider whether, although the module was not designed as a feeder into the clinic, there were ways in which students could better be supported in their learning. Other legal educators have similarly explored this too. The next section outlines my approach.

III. FAMILY LAW'S PLACE IN THE LEGAL CURRICULUM: TEACHING FAMILY LAW FOR STUDENT PRO BONO CONTEXTS

Family law is not a compulsory part of the undergraduate or vocational stages of legal education in England and Wales and so is taught in a wide variety of interesting ways. These range from doctrinal modules that focus on the rules including the legislation and case law, to critical, contextualised modules that address theoretical and/or political and socio-legal debates associated with power and hierarchy within family structures and the law. Some modules combine the two. I have taught family law using a number of different lenses over my career, and have enjoyed taking different approaches depending on the institutional context

[16] For details see https://clock.uk.net/, accessed 7 April 2019.

[17] For more information on MacKenzie Friends see Smith, Hitchings and Sefton (2017).

and the student population. At the University of Westminster I had the privilege of teaching in a team, in the earlier years with a practitioner with a great deal of family law teaching experience as well as professional training experience, and later in a larger team with two academics who had also practised (a solicitor and a barrister) and who were involved in the law school student law clinic, and another academic who took a critical approach to family law and family justice. My observations in this section relate to my teaching in the larger team during a period when the work of the student law clinic was expanding and some of the family law students had taken the family law final year option to gain insights in that light. I was not involved in the clinic, other than as a bystander; I spent time talking to students on the module who were involved in the clinic and my two academic-practitioner colleagues were involved in both teaching on the family law module and overseeing and working in the clinic.

The module was a large one, both in student size (130 students) and in credit weighting: 30 then 40 credits (1/4 to 1/3 of the final year curriculum). This gave us great scope to develop our teaching practice and to combine both a first semester of 'the rules' and their application, followed by a second semester of critical family law content. We combined context, doctrinal law, socio-legal theory and law reform ambitions in a two-semester team-taught module. I taught most of the lectures, we all took weekly seminar groups, and the team remained stable for a number of years as did the content of the syllabus, but for regular updating as the law changed. This afforded us the opportunity to try new methods of teaching and learning with other elements of the module remaining relatively constant.

Much doctrinal law teaching is organised around topics, blocks of knowledge that make up the greater whole of the module. In the context of a private family law module this would often include, for example: coupling up (marriage, civil partnership, cohabitation); becoming a parent and parenting (who is a legal parent, a step-parent, responsibilities and rights etc); domestic violence; uncoupling (nullity, divorce, dissolution, cohabitation breakdown) and money, property and child related disputes that span these topics. Some modules will include gender identity, surrogacy and adoption. Students may be given some contextual and demographic information to assist them in understanding the range of family forms and the incidence of certain types of dispute. They may also cover different forms of dispute resolution including negotiation, mediation and adjudication.

Many modules taught in this kind of format address the legislative principles, their interpretation by the courts and then provide students with problem questions, vignettes that students are asked to use as the basis for providing legal advice. The problem questions aim to tease out the extent to which a student is able to apply the law in a nuanced way and spot questions that a legal professional would need to ask in order to gain a better understanding of the client's position. They may also be designed to test a student's ability to come up with workable proposed solutions that meet a client's needs. There are, of course, other ways to teach family law, including full problem-based learning.[18] Having said that, as an external examiner of a number of law programmes I have most often seen this form of syllabus in law schools that aim to teach family law as a doctrinal subject for the whole or part of the module.

And yet, even given this approach, developed in conjunction with legal practitioners, students still struggled to diagnose and treat the simulated family law issues in problem questions. Their queries in the context of clinic suggested that these difficulties were heightened in live situations. And it was only when I started to use the analogy of a doctor diagnosing then treating her patient (underscoring the need for the patient's full consent knowing the alternatives, their costs and their benefits) that I made a breakthrough with the students. I realised that I needed to switch to teaching through decision trees, as in some forms of medical education (see Podgorelec et al, 2002), rather than using a statutory and case-based method.

To begin with I developed my materials as diagrams setting out the key variables in each topic, for example: is the client: (a) married, (b) civil partnered, (c) cohabiting, or (d) not classed as any of the above, so that we could determine how a client would be classified by the legal system for the purposes of different types of legal issue. Sometimes relationship status makes no difference, but in other contexts it affects entitlements and responsibilities. My diagrams included a series of questions that a student may need to work through in order to investigate whether someone was legally married etc, predicated on the basis that this may not be immediately obvious from the information provided by the client. Over time, I developed the diagrams further into decision trees that operated, in effect, as a series of flow charts that had 'if yes then/if no then' branches running throughout them. The case law and statutory references were all contained within the boxes, but the charts were set out as questions with statutory and case law underpinnings. This was in contrast to my previous practice which was probably best characterised as being worked around the principles with explanations about why the principles mattered rather than putting the decision points to the fore.

It should not have been such a surprise that this transformed many of the students' abilities to engage with the subject matter and make much better use of their knowledge. But it was. It took me some time for me to work through the pedagogic reasons why it worked, backed up by some reading on decision trees and their use in other disciplines.[19] The diagrams became the means by which lectures were delivered, we made very few changes to the way in which the seminars operated, and the seminar problem questions remained similar to before as well.

[18] For fuller details on the pedagogy of problem-based learning see Boud and Feletti (eds) (2013). On simulation-based learning, see Apel (2011).

[19] See eg: Mushlin and Greene (2009) which is organised by topic similar to the way we often teach law; Lee et al (2009), which provides a means to understand how to structure the information to assist learners;. Magee (1964).

Yet learning increased and the atmosphere in the lectures was more interactive and positive. Some students also started to develop their own diagrams for other modules to help with the doctrinal components of those too. Some of the students who were engaged with clinical work indicated that they used the diagrams as effective triage tools with clients. I made some modifications to the diagrams in light of feedback, we moved the order of material around so that precursor information (relationship and parenting status) was addressed first before substantive dispute related content was considered. I continued to teach the module that way until I left to join another institution.

IV. ONLINE TRIAGE AND SIGNPOSTING SYSTEMS: SOME CONCLUSIONS ABOUT THE ROLE OF LAW STUDENTS AS LEGAL HELPERS

Once complex decisions have been reduced to a series of simple binaries, albeit set out as a multitude of questions, it becomes easier to identify the key issues that will affect the diagnosis of the client's problem. Further, it is possible to display the range of possible pathways to solutions in a similar way. This is how computer assisted diagnosis and treatment systems are developed in other fields and also how even the early attempts to develop online expert systems in law were conceived.[20] It is also the basis for more sophisticated predictive machine learning algorithms (although this requires high volumes of data to train the algorithm too), and is a mainstay of computer science decision-making. At the point when I moved to a new institution we were in the process of considering whether we could transform the decision trees into an online decision tool to structure client intake conversations; the next stage of the development discussion stopped when I left. It would not be that challenging to convert decision trees into a basic online system; there are law tech software systems to make this possible (Bridge, 2018). With additional work, and proper testing, it may be possible for a law tech developer to develop a sophisticated algorithm to guide decision-making through the life cycle of the legal problem but that would need data upon which the algorithm could be trained and its learning would only be as good as the data.[21] We are still some way away from this in a legal context in the UK; greater innovation has been possible in predictive technologies in the US given the greater volume of data that can be harvested from most levels of state and federal court legal judgments. Although this data only assists with predictions about cases that go to court, a phenomenon less likely to occur in the UK.

Such sophisticated tools are unlikely to be available in the near future in Britain and in any event will need to be used by lawyers who can interpret their

[20] See eg: Susskind (1987); Gardiner (1988); Capper and Susskind (1988); Walter (ed) (1985); Waterman, Paul and Peterson (1986); Greenleaf (1989); Zeleznikow (2002).

[21] For an explanation of how this works, see eg: Lee (2018).

outputs. A predictive algorithmic model tends to be operated as an expert system, rather than a client facing tool, and so is used by a trained professional who could consider the suggested approaches alongside the emotional and practical needs of the client and her family and work. The system may cut the costs of providing bespoke advice and allow the lawyer to spend more time, within resource constraints, empowering the client to give proper instructions. Such a system may also push up the threshold quality of advice and assistance. There is limited evidence for or against the quality of decision-making proposition in a medical context, as yet, although some studies suggest that the next generation of decision-support systems are more sophisticated and have greater utility than the models used to date (Cahan and Camino, 2017). As the quality and quantity of the data has improved, so have the algorithms.

In the context of university law clinics, the student's role is often limited to intake activities to establish 'the facts', the contentious issues and the unknowns, followed by a check-in with peers or a supervisor to consider next steps, follow up questions and possible routes that the client may wish to consider when thinking through actions to be taken. There are clinics that provide a fuller range of activities with students running cases under lawyer supervision, although these are labour intensive and fraught with concerns about the quality of the advice and assistance being given. Yet, if diagnosis can be systematised (noting that this is very challenging when dealing with vulnerable clients), supervisory resources may be concentrated on tasks linked to advice and next steps. This is the thinking behind the National Health Service 111 telephone triage and signposting service offered nationwide in Britain. Decision trees have been developed into an online system used by the nurses who operate the telephone mass triage service. They aim to make an initial diagnosis and take the next step for the patient: send those with potentially serious conditions to emergency specialist services, book an appointment for others with a doctor, and suggest that others head to a pharmacy for over the counter medication. Similar expert system decision-trees may have a role to play in family law too. It has already been suggested in other contexts, such as in teaching bankruptcy law (Tarvin, 2017).

As set out above, there are challenges associated with law students providing legal help to members of the public who would otherwise have little or no access to advice or assistance. Students may gain a useful insight into lawyering skills and the role of the lawyer; clients may gain help that they would otherwise miss out on. It could not be said, however, to be a like for like replacement for professional legal advice and assistance and it may embolden the state to cut the legal aid scheme yet further and privatise access to justice to the profession and nascent professionals. Intake, diagnosis and signposting under supervision, may be possible with support from a decision-tree system. But they cannot replace proper legal assistance and advocacy. Technology gains may give rise to cheaper professional legal help that some clients will then be able to afford. It may also provide a means to provide safer, more effective pro bono help by law students. There may be access to justice gains that we can make, even in this difficult funding environment. But they will not be resolved by students as legal helpers, or technology as a replacement for expert representation

REFERENCES

Apel, SB (2011) 'No More Casebooks: using simulation-based learning to educate future family law practitioners', *Family Court Review* 49(4), 700.

Armstrong, S (2018) 'The Apps Attempting to Transfer NHS 111 Online' *British Medical Journal* (London, 5 January): www.bmj.com/content/360/bmj.k156.full, accessed 7 April 2019.

Baksi, C (2016) 'The Politics of Pro Bono' *Legal Action* (March): www.lag.org.uk/article/202002/the-politics-of-pro-bono, accessed 7 April 2019.

Barlow, A (2017) 'Rising to the post-LASPO Challenge: How should mediation respond?', *Journal of Social Welfare and Family Law* 39(2), 203.

Barlow, A, Hunter, R, Smithson J and Ewing, J (2017) *Mapping Paths to Family Justice: resolving family justice in neoliberal times* (London, Palgrave Socio-Legal Studies, Palgrave Macmillan).

Bevan, C (2013) 'Self-represented Litigants: the overlooked and unintended consequence of legal aid reform', *Journal of Social Welfare and Family Law* 35(1), 43.

Bloch, FS and Noone, MA (2010) 'Legal Aid Origins of Clinical Legal Education' in FS Bloch (ed) *The Global Clinical Movement: Educating Lawyers for Social Justice* (Oxford, Oxford University Press) ch 10.

Boud, D and Feletti, G (eds) (2013) *The Challenge of Problem-based Learning* (Abingdon, Routledge).

Bridge, B (2018) 'Interview – Decision tree software in law studies' *Berkley Bridge Blog* (16 January): www.berkeleybridge.com/blog/decision-tree-software-in-law-studies/, accessed 7 April 2019.

Cahan, A and Cimino, JJ (2017) 'A Learning Health Care System Using Computer-Aided Diagnosis', *Journal of Medical Internet Research* 19(3): www.ncbi.nlm.nih.gov/pmc/articles/PMC5362695/, accessed 7 April 2019.

Camplin, H (2017) 'Changing Landscapes: the relationship between student law clinics, litigants in person and family law dispute resolution in England and Wales', *International Family Law, Policy and Practice* 5(1), 25.

Capper, P and Susskind, R (1988) *Latent Damage Law – The Expert System* (London, Butterworths).

Cobb, S (2013) 'Legal Aid Reform: its impact on family law', *Journal of Social Welfare and Family Law* 35, 3.

Connelly T (2017) 'Nottingham Trent's student-staffed 'teaching law firm' launches commercial advice arm' *Legal Cheek* (London, 25 May): www.legalcheek.com/2017/05/nottingham-trents-student-staffed-teaching-law-firm-launches-commercial-advice-arm/, accessed 7 April 2019.

Cookson, G (2011) *Unintended Consequences: the cost of the government's legal aid reforms* (London, King's College).

Cookson, G (2013) 'Analysing the Economic Justification for the Reforms to Social Welfare and Family Law Legal Aid', *Journal of Social Welfare and Family Law* 35, 21.

Gardiner, A von der Leith (1988) *An Artificial Intelligence Approach to Legal Reasoning* (Cambridge, Mass, MIT Press).

Greenleaf, G (1989) 'Legal Expert Systems – Robot Lawyers? An introduction to knowledge-based applications to law' *(Australian Legal Convention*, Sydney, August): www2.austlii.edu.au/cal/papers/robots89/, accessed 8 April 2019.

Grimes, R (1996) 'The Theory and Practice of Clinical Legal Education' in Julian Webb and Caroline Maugham (eds), *Teaching Lawyers' Skills* (London, Butterworths).

Kerrigan, K and Murray, V (eds), *A Student Guide to Clinical Legal Education and Pro Bono* (London, Palgrave Macmillan).

Jones, E, McFaul H and Ryan, F (2017) 'Clinical Legal Education in the United Kingdom: origins, growth and the technological innovations and challenges of its future', *German Journal of Legal Education* 4, 107.

Kaganas, F (2017) 'Justifying the LASPO Act: authenticity, necessity, suitability, responsibility and autonomy', *Journal of Social Welfare and Family Law* 39(2), 168.

Kemp, V, Munk T and Gower, S (2016) 'Clinical Legal Education and Experiential Learning: Looking to the future' (University of Manchester), ch 4: http://hummedia.manchester.ac.uk/schools/law/main/news/Clinical-Legal-Education-Final-Report28.09.2016.pdf.

Koroma, P and Antoniou, N (2017) *Law Students' Clinic Experience: is it all hype in relation to performance on black-letter law exams* (Practice Report): www.researchgate.net/publication/315531171_Law_students%27_clinic_experience_Is_it_all_hype_in_relation_to_performance_on_lack-letter_law_exams.

Lee, A, Joynt, GM, Ho, AMH, Keitz, S, McGinn, T and Wyer, PC (2009) 'Tips for Teachers of Evidence-based Medicine: Making Sense of Decision Analysis Using a Decision Tree', *Journal of General Internal Medicine* 24(5), 642.

Lee, J (2018) 'A Tour of The Top 10 Algorithms for Machine Learning Newbies' (Towardsdatascience.com, 20 January).

Maclean, M (2014) 'The Changing Professional Landscape', *Family Law* 42, 177.

Maclean, M (2015) 'New Ways to Seek Legal Information and Advice On Family Matters in England and Wales: From professional legal services to Google and private ordering' in M Maclean, J Eekelaar and B Bastard (eds) *Delivering Family Justice in the 21st Century* (Oxford, Hart Publishing, 2015).

Mavis Maclean (ed) (2017), *Delivering Family Justice in Late Modern Society in the Wake of Legal Aid Reform* (Abingdon, Routledge, 2017).

Maclean, M and Eekelaar, J (2016) *Lawyers and Mediators: the brave new world of services for separating families* (Oxford, Hart Publishing).

Magee, JF, (1964) 'Decision Trees for Decision Making' *Harvard Business Review* (July): https://hbr.org/1964/07/decision-trees-for-decision-making.

Mant, J (2017) 'Neoliberalism, Family Law and the Cost of Access to Justice', *Journal of Social Welfare and Family Law* 39(2), 246.

Marson, J, Wilson, A and van Hoorebeek, M (2005) 'The Necessity of Clinical Legal Education in University Law Schools: a UK perspective', *International Journal of Clinical Legal Education* 7, 29.

McKeown P and Morse, S (2015) 'Litigants in Person: is there a role for higher education?', *The Law Teacher* 45(1), 122.

Mushlin, SB and Greene, HL (2009) *Decision-making in Medicine: an algorithmic approach* (Elsevier Health Sciences).

Podgorelec, V, Kokol, P, Stiglic, B and Rozman, I (2002) 'Decision Trees: an overview and their use in medicine', *Journal of Medical Systems* 26(5), 445.

Pope, C, Turnbull, J, Jones, J, Prichard, J, Rowsell A and Halford, S (2017) 'Has the NHS 111 Urgent Care Telephone Service Been a Success? Case Study and Secondary Data Analysis in England' *British Medical Journal Open*: https://bmjopen.bmj.com/content/7/5/e014815.

Robins, J (2012) 'The idea of law students filling the legal aid gap makes my heart sink' *Guardian Law* online (London, 13 December): www.guardian.co.uk/law/2012/dec/13/law-students-legal-aid-gap, accessed 7 April 2019.

Smith, L, Hitchings E and Sefton, M (2017) *A Study of Fee-charging McKenzie Friends and their Work in Private Family Law Cases* (University of Cardiff and University of Bristol): http://orca.cf.ac.uk/101919/1/A%20study%20of%20fee-charging%20McKenzie%20Friends.pdf.

Susskind, R (1989) 'Pragmatism and purism in artificial intelligence and legal reasoning', *AI and Society* 3(1), 28: https://link.springer.com/article/10.1007/BF01892673, accessed 8 April 2019.

Susskind, R (1987) *Expert Systems in Law* (Oxford, Oxford University Press).

Tarvin, T (2017) 'Combating Professional Error in Bankruptcy Analysis Through the Design and Use of Decision Trees in Clinical Pedagogy', *St. John's Law Review* 91(2), 427: https://scholarship.law.stjohns.edu/lawreview/vol91/iss2/5, accessed 7 April 2019.

Thomas, L (2017) 'Law Clinics in England and Wales: a regulatory black hole', *The Law Teacher* 51(4), 469.

Thomas, L, Vaughan, S, Malkani, B and Lynch, T (eds) (2018) *Reimagining Clinical Legal Education* (Oxford, Hart Publishing).

Trinder, L and Hunter, R (2015) 'Access to Justice? litigants in person before and after LASPO', *Family Law* 45, 535–41.

Trinder, L, Hunter, R, Hitchings, E, Miles, J, Moorhead, R, Smith, L, Sefton, M, Hinchly, V, Bader, K and Pearce, J (2014) *Litigants in Person in Private Family Law Cases* (London, Ministry of Justice Analytical Services).

Walter, C (ed) (1985) *Computer Power and Legal Reasoning* (Eagan, Minn, West Publishing Co).

Waterman, DA, Paul, J and Peterson, M (1986) 'Expert Systems for Legal Decision-making' *Proceedings of the Second Australian Conference on Applications of Expert Systems* (Sydney, Institute of Technology).

Webley, L (2015a) 'When is a Family Lawyer, a Lawyer?' in M Maclean, J Eekelaar and B Bastard (eds) *Delivering Family Justice in the 21st Century* Hart (London, Bloomsbury) ch 17.

Webley, L (2015b), 'Legal Professional De(Re)Regulation, Equality, And Inclusion, And The Contested Space Of Professionalism Within The Legal Market In England And Wales', *Fordham Law Review* 83(5), 2349.

Wong, S and Cain, R (2019) 'The Impact of Cuts in Legal Aid Funding of Private Family Law Cases', *Journal of Social Welfare and Family Law* 41(1), 3.

Zeleznikow, J (2002) 'Risk, Negotiation and Argumentation- a decision support system based approach', *Law, Probability and Risk* 1, 37.

5

Mediation in Germany – The Possibilities for and Limits of Mediation

ADELHEID KÜHNE AND BARBARA WILLENBACHER

I. INTRODUCTION

THE AIM OF mediation, whether inside or outside the court, is conflict resolution. Sociology and social psychology have formulated theories of conflict development, but no theory of mediation or its application. When a conflict is based on the interaction of two or more persons, at least one of them has a great deal of negative experience, arising from incompatible thoughts, perceptions or motivation (Glasl, 2001). And in all conflicts there will be a normative nucleus. The development of conflict is marked by three stages: Naming: (conflict perception and definition); Blaming: (attribution of the noticeable harm); Claiming: (attribution of the injuries combined with a demand to rectify or compensate for the injustice) (Breidenbach, 1995).

II. MEDIATION METHODS

The main element in all mediation processes within or outside the court is to go back and examine the reality of the everyday content of the conflict. To be successful, mediation requires not only that the interests are balanced but also that the interaction between the parties and their expectations are discussed. The most widely practised approach is the so-called 'Harvard-Concept', grounded in economic thinking and an individualistic culture, but neglecting person-centred emotions and learned conflict behaviour. This is a western concept which depends on culture and language and is not transferable into another language or culture. In the educational context, it is necessary to discuss the concept and bring it into line with ideas about cultural change, and changing needs in the lives of pupils and students (Busch, 2009). Pedagogy can enlarge the Harvard concept with educational components to provide a sustainable working solution. The basic idea, however, is that it is not the people who are the problem but rather their different positions, interests and needs. Resolution of the conflict is the central focus, and the relationship between the opponents provides the background to this. Mediation should encourage change in the perspectives of the conflicted parties.

III. FORMS OF MEDIATION

There are a number of forms of mediation.

Peer mediation includes conflict solving with children where there are violent physical struggles between children and other young persons. Conflicts between students and teachers are rather rare. For this form of mediation to succeed, the reasons for the conflict have to be apparent, the culture of conflict has to change, and the conflicted parties have to accept responsibility and be aware of the underlying motivations. The ability to reflect and the level of self-esteem can then both develop and grow (Hartig, 2009). The solution depends on the ability of the opponents to develop empathy, to reflect on the position of the opponent and to learn about the emotional source of the conflict. The mediator – adult or student – works as an agent concerned with all the parties, accepting and respecting conflicted partners and being recognised by them as competent. The basic theory is borrowed from Humanistic Psychology with a fundamental philosophy of subjective reality, and a tendency towards actualisation and concept of self.

To clarify the conflict, the partners in the mediation process have to learn new forms of interaction; seeing the solving process as a win-win-situation. They have to identify the different levels of conflict, analyse the background, and differentiate their own position from the position of the other party. The opponents learn about conflict-free communication and interaction, and how to reflect on their own behaviour, and how to improve their concept of self and search for new perspectives. Clearing away the original normative expectations and providing training in the ability to reflect increases the chances of a solution and conflict prevention. A self-determining position about conflict solutions includes both an educational and a prevention of violence component.

Court mediation is voluntary, but peer mediation is often compulsory. The teacher and other attendants see aggressive actions, they then try to separate the opponents and send them to mediation. The conflict situation should be neutralised through a violence-free exchange. In the view of the school, mediation is a 'lesser evil' compared to a disciplinary intervention. Some schoolboys and girls see the process mediation as a form of violence, and come together to resist it.

They cannot accept that mediation helps; they see it only as a punishment. In those cases a real conflict begins, and attempts to improve the atmosphere of the school and prevent violence are likely to fail (Peschel, 2009).

Victim – offender – mediation (VOM) is a special form of mediation concerned with criminal offences. Since 2012 the European Parliament has required minimum standards for rights, support and protection for victims of crime (Europäische Kommission, 2016). VOM is in part mediation and in part restorative justice. If the offences are not too severe and aggressive, it involves an act of compensation by the offender to the victim, based on the idea of restorative justice. While mediation usually follows the Harvard Concept, described above, this is not suitable for VOM.

VOM is not voluntary but imposed as an alternative to the legal procedure, and does not follow the rationale of offender and victim, debt and punishment. An acknowledgement of guilt is not necessary as a precondition for VOM. International guidelines recommend taking responsibility for an offence and accepting that norms have been violated. Norms are not negotiable. VOM focuses on the everyday life experience of both conflicted partners. This includes both the offence of the offender and how the offender has behaved towards the victim subsequently (Pelikan, 2009). By involving the victim in the conciliation process, his or her emotional situation and the material damage done become apparent. Repairing the damage and confronting the offender with his or her offence and the victim should promote and support future social adjustment. The personal confrontation with the sorrow and anxiety of the victim should help the offender to understand the injustice caused and become aware of the consequences for the victim. Offender and victim interact to achieve compensation between the two parties without engaging the government.

The aims of victim-offender mediation are: critical recognition of the offence, resolution of the conflict and negotiation of compensation. Requirements for the conflicted parties are: voluntary participation, autonomy, confidence, decisions free of social and psychological pressure, seeking consent, following agreed rules, accepting the matter of concern, reducing the consequences of the conflict and subsequent conflicts, avoiding injustice.

We present below the results of the most recent Federal German Republic statistical inquiry into victim-offender mediation based on the numbers of victims and offenders who agreed to take part in the inquiry. The research was supported by the Federal Ministry of Justice and Consumer Protection (Hartmann et al, 2016). The survey shows an increasing number of victims (2015: 8,741; 2016: 9,376) and offenders (2015: 8,397; 2016: 8,946). Personal injuries are divided into physical, psychological and material harm. 72.2% of the victims suffered lasting harm, and this category is growing. In 40% of the cases damage suffered by the victims is physical, in 22% material and in 20% psychological.

The key findings are set out as follows.

Table 1 Victim-offender mediation

The most frequent types of conflict	
Neighbourhood conflicts:	20.3%
Domestic violence:	15.9%
The most frequent offences	
Personal injuries:	51.5%
Other injuries:	17.4%
False imprisonment:	14.9%
Damage to property:	12.1%
The mean age of the victims	
14–20 years:	21.6%
21–40 years:	39.5%
41–60 years:	27.4%
The mean age of the accused	
14–20 years:	28.1%
21–40 years:	41.5%
41–60 years:	6.6%
Other characteristics of the accused persons	
Male	60.3%
Female	39.4%
German citizens	71.9%
Other nationality	28.1%
Offender–victim relationship	
Well-known to eachother	41.9%
Were unknown	34.3%
Had met briefly	23.7%

The authority giving the contracts for the mediation is in most cases the public prosecutor's office (85.5%). The mediation is mainly provided by voluntary agencies and private mediation groups like the WAAGE (Balance) in Northern Germany, under juvenile and adult criminal law. Most cases occur in the western provinces of the old German federal republic such as North Rhine Westphalia (32.5%), Rhineland-Palatinate (13.2%), Lower Saxony (7.5%) and in the east Saxony-Anhalt (10%).

Most of the personal injury cases (70%) end with an apology, 30% by an agreement to change the aggressive behaviour, and in addition, 34% with compensation for injuries caused to the feelings of the victim. The apology is often combined with other forms of compensation. A strongly worded apology shows the offender's regret and the person harmed understands that he has suffered an injustice. Mediation takes place less with respect to robbery and blackmail but is increasing for physical injury (68%).

Sometimes an offender tries to avoid the sanction and supposes that violence can be negotiable, this is a recurrent risk of VOM. The accused have to recognise and learn that violence is not negotiable. If the victim is pushed towards VOM or the offender does not carry out the contract, the victim suffers so-called secondary victimisation. The mediator in victim-offender mediation accepts no excuses for refusal to give evidence; the victim may be forced to give evidence against the accused, for example in later proceedings.

IV. QUALITY ASSURANCE IN MEDIATION: PROBLEMS AND STANDARDS OF PRACTICE

In peer mediation, a frequently used and important area of practice in schools concerns bullying ('*Schikanieren*' in German). '*Schikane*' is originally a French word meaning to pervert the course of justice with malicious intent. School conflicts are in most cases aggressive arguments between students and disturb the everyday life of the school. The central conflict-producing emotions are indignation and blame. To handle the effect of such emotions they have to be controlled. That means it is necessary to encourage a change of perspective, and to provide training in empathy to learn more about the emotional aspect of the conflict. The position of the opponents has to be understood to enhance and protect the conflict solving.

Bullying is a subcategory of aggression and violence characterised by hostile intent, imbalance of power – real or perceived – between the bully and the victim, and repetition over a period of time. The victims suffer severe psychological, social or physical trauma. The bully is motivated by the perceived benefits of his aggressive behaviour. The underlying causes of school violence include gender and social norms and wider contextual and structural factors.

A. Standards of Practice for Peer Mediation

There is a need for scientific evaluation of peer mediation and research concerning the personality characteristics of mediators, and also the factors concerning the structure and process of mediation which may explain success. The working group on Mediation in Education (Fachgruppe Erziehung und Bildung, 2006) formulated standards to develop violence-free actions. The aims are encouragement of international attitudes, tolerance, and striving for justice, freedom and intercultural communication. Jeffreys-Duden (2000) has differentiated two approaches to mediation in school education and in the training of pupils and students to become mediators. The training is effective for the learning and practice of social competencies. Involving students with minor competence needs gives them an opportunity to receive encouragement which would not otherwise be possible. This programme can not only help to solve problems but also prevent further conflicts.

B. Family Mediation

Wardle (1994) interpreted the mediation movement as a reaction against the common law adversarial legal culture. The family justice system in Germany is a civil law system. But the family court process is adversarial in structure, with a petitioner making an application to which the other side responds before a judge in the following issues: financial matters, child support, spousal support, support for relatives, partnership support, entitlements after a birth, marital and partnership accrued gains, marriage and engagement, parent-child relationships and other partnership matters. The family court is authorised to obtain the disclosure of necessary information in regard to income and property from institutions and relevant informants (employer etc).

The family court process, however, is inquisitorial in childcare proceedings, parent and child cases, adoption applications, filial matters, domestic violence, splitting of pension assets and household affairs. The court is free to use all means of proof and to order all measures to improve the situation of the child. The judiciary takes an increasingly active role in managing these cases. The courts have a culture of negotiation and settlement. The predominance of conflict avoidance at the family court is the result of the dominant position of the court and the institutional framework, the influence of legal representation and legal aid. Publicly funded legal advice and representation is available to all litigants in all civil law cases according to means and merits tests at the family court. Legal aid is granted according to the economic situation of the litigants. There is an unequivocal relationship between the granting of legal aid and the rate of settlement in court, because, in contrast to settlements reached by the court, legal aid is not granted for drawing up a notarised agreement (which occurs out of court). And the rules of substantive and procedural law also support conciliation.

The German proponents of mediation in family law did not however take these differences into account and they systematically ignored socio-legal research on divorce by Rottleuthner-Lutter (1992). The pilot project of Bastine et al (1999) interviewed only a small number of mediators and separated parents from the upper middle class who evaluated self-determination and the absence of bureaucratic rules, whereas the pilot project of Proksch (2002) involved over 210 divorcing parents participating in publicly financed mediation. All the cases which had not already settled with an agreement on custody and access at the beginning of proceedings were categorised as contested. Only 41% of the parents accepted mediation and 31% of all the parents reached settlement by mediation. The author interpreted the results as evidence for the conflict reducing effects of mediation without even considering the outcomes of the respective court proceedings. He merely mentioned that 50% of parents had negative feelings vis-à-vis court proceedings.

The Child Law Reform Act 1998, with its new menu of orders, created more bargaining room and has encouraged resort to the court. The judiciary has moved towards a more educational approach, insofar as parental arrangements can be imposed as the lawyers and judges suggest. The only representative study concerning family mediation by Proksch (2001) collected data acquired by interviewing divorced German parents between 1999–2001. 7% of all parents with joint legal custody and 9% of all parents with sole custody had reached an agreement by mediation. But newly evolving conflicts were solved only in 1 or 2% of cases by mediation, while in child support controversies in 7%. Table 2 gives an example of the increase in the proportion of divorce-related cases where a judicial decision has been made in Germany as a whole, and in particular in Bavaria.

Table 2 Judicial decisions in divorce-related cases

Family Court statistics Germany 2016		
Number of custody cases pending with divorce	61,664	
Number of judicial decisions	1,661	2.7%
Family Court Statistics Germany 2000		
Number of Custody Cases pending divorce	268,959	
Number of judicial decisions	87,630	31%
Family Court Statistics Bavaria 2016		
Number of custody cases pending divorce	10,161	
Number of judicial decisions	318	3%
Family Court Statistics Bavaria 2000		
Number of custody cases pending with divorce	10,988	
Number of judicial decisions	7,732	70%

The FamFG 2009 (Procedure in Family Courts and free jurisdiction 2009) now forms the basis of family proceedings. The judiciary has moved away from an inquisitorial approach to a more educational approach in Germany. Negotiation is supported by oral proceedings in childcare cases thus expediting procedures. They aim to put the safeguarding of children at the forefront of the process by listing the first hearing within three–four weeks of issue. Different procedures concerning disputes in the same family will come to the same judge. There is a drive to move more towards decisions by mutual consent at the family court.

Mediation is one way of achieving this. The family court may order mediation. Legal aid will then be denied if parties refuse mediation. A new pilot project was initiated in Berlin in 2016 giving parties free access to mediation when legal aid is granted. But if they abandon mediation, legal aid will be adjudicated in court.

All child care proceedings follow the new expediting procedures. The oral hearing is to be held within a month of application in the presence of the dissenting parties, the reporting social worker, the representing lawyers and the guardian ad litem and/or an expert when appointed by the family court. This follows the Cochem model (described below). If parties refuse mediation, legal aid will be denied. The family court does not oversee arrangements for children following parental separation or divorce, when parents do not apply for custody. This encourages parents to reach agreements concerning joint uncontested legal custody.

The model of Cochem – a small town in Palatine – developed by a local Family Judge in 1993, includes mediation and proposes the cooperation of all professions involved in custody and contact proceedings. The family court informs the youth agency and sends disputing parents to be advised that parental discord and conflicts endanger the well-being of the child. The social worker is obliged to complete a consultation within 14 days, to take part at the next hearing of the family court and to give an oral report. If no agreement is reached, the disputing parents are sent to a counselling agency or to mediation. The counsellor or mediator will then take part in the next hearing of the family court. The aim is to impose joint custody even in highly disputed cases and to avoid judicial decisions. This intended goal is being reached and is appreciated by the Council of Europe which now favours shared parenting (Council of Europe, 2015). Many family courts have adapted this model. The effects may be seen in the low number of decisions in custody cases with the result that in only 3% of all cases is sole custody the outcome.

Greger (2010) found that only 1% of contested custody cases used mediation currently. Nevertheless he proposes the use of mediation. The majority of the 219 divorced parents investigated in his research contacted the local agency or other counselling service instead of using mediation. But 32% of the parents engaged in follow-up legal conflicts. 60% were represented by lawyers in custody matters, 95% in contact cases, and 70% received legal aid. Families using mediation agreed in only 30% of cases. They were content with the result but only 60% complied with the agreement reached. The personal appraisal of mothers and fathers differed: mothers valued mediation more often than fathers, who had to accept realistic solutions. Follow-up cases were not documented in this part of the study. Greger claimed that there was a long-term benign effect when agreement was reached by mediation, but without providing any supporting evidence.

The reason why mediation is still favoured by policymakers however is the supposed cost efficiency, insofar as the heavy case load of the judiciary and the costs of the court infrastructure could be reduced, as Staffke (2012) pointed out. The Cochem model of mediation contradicts the classical principles of mediation, which are voluntary participation, neutrality, self-determination and independence from judicial proceedings. Furthermore it cannot even be characterised as court connected according to the definition of Staffke who described court initiated mediation as taking place without any further involvement of the court, because the Cochem model does involve the further involvement of the court. The Cochem model of 'oppressive mediation' described above has never been evaluated and the treatment of domestic violence under this form of screening has not been discussed in the publications arising, as Kostka (2004) critically points out.

There has been a dramatic increase in litigation over contact and residence since 1998, even though the majority of parents come to an agreement as socio-legal research demonstrates. Changes in the legal framework did not succeed in reducing litigation concerning residence and access. Generally highly conflicted cases appeared to move away from the family courts but by 2016 35% emerged again in so called isolated hearings (that is in the procedures concerning mainly residence and visitation problems which take place after the main divorce matters have been settled by the court) compared to only 17% in 2000 (See Table 3).

Table 3 Custody cases in relation to pending divorce cases 2000 and 2016

Family Court Statistics Germany 2016		
Number of isolated custody cases in relation to cases pending with divorce	21,874	35%
Family Court Statistics Germany 2000		
Number of isolated custody cases in relation to cases pending with divorce	14,752	17%
Family Court Statistics Bavaria 2016		
Number of isolated custody cases in relation to cases with divorce	2,665	26%
Family Court Statistics Bavaria 2000 appeared to move away from the court		
Number of isolated custody cases in relation to cases with divorce	1,260	12%

International family law EU mediators try to work with complicated cases of cross border disputes. In the case of bi-national family law conflicts and child abduction with the consequence of parallel procedures in two EU countries who have failed to produce solutions, two mediators assigned from these countries will attempt to solve the conflict out of court, facilitated by the European Mediation Directive No. 2008/52/EC. Pati and Voet (2012) present the concepts of cross border mediation but give no information concerning the number of cases handled.

A new pilot project has been started in civil law developing the concept of conciliation judges. The family courts provide specialised judges shown on their websites who do not adjudicate. But family courts in general are characterised by a very small number of conciliations: only 1%, that is, 1,932 cases out of the total of 651,883 procedures at the family law court in 2016, were settled by conciliation judges, whereas of their cases 1,032 failed to settle. Their success rate amounts to 70% of all conciliation procedures and differs regionally (Bamberg 83%, Stuttgart 90%). In 44% of all mediation cases the agreement exceeds the original dispute and includes objects not mentioned at the beginning of the procedure.

In contrast to court based mediation and mediation independent from judicial proceedings the traditional settlement rate in family law courts exceeds the settlement rates with 12% of agreements settled by mediation. Legal aid is granted in 50% of the cases at the family court (33% to the petitioner and 20% to the respondent) and 65% of the parties are represented by lawyers (in 25% only the petitioner and in 40% both parties) (Statistisches Bundesamt, Rechtspflege Reihe 2.2. Familiengerichte 2016, 2000).

V. COURT BASED MEDIATION IN CIVIL CASES

Obligatory conciliation procedures preceding first instance civil law small claims have been abolished on account of their lack of success. Non-binding arbitration by conciliation offices (public or private) had been required as a prerequisite to litigation. The conciliation offices over the last decade had referred some cases to mediation. In a few provinces of Germany for a small range of cases obligatory conciliation procedures still exist. But the new pilot project with conciliation judges is taking over.

Many courts (civil law, family law, labour law, administrative law, tax law) point out that court based mediation is possible, and include the conciliation judges on their websites. The responsible judge decides which cases could be suitable for conciliation. The parties and the responsible conciliation judge then have to decide if they will accept the proposal. The conciliation judge uses mediation, but contrary to the traditional principles of mediation, the conciliation judge also gives legal advice to the parties.

However, in 2016 the number of trials handled by conciliation judges was still very low. Only 1% of civil law procedures at the local courts were accepted as a conciliation case. And in only 50% of these cases was an agreement achieved (Statistisches Bubdesamt, Rchtspflege Reihe 2.1. Zivilgerichte). In local courts, referral to mediation varied from province to province, from 0.2 to 2.4%. This held true for the settlement rate as well: Bavaria and Hamburg exceeded the other courts with an agreement rate of 70%, and 80% respectively. Regional courts characterised by cases with higher litigation values achieved higher rates of mediation: Schleswig-Holstein 9%, Mecklenburg Western Pomerania and Lower Saxony 8%, Berlin 7%. In half of the cases an agreement was reached, but there was considerable variation by area. Thuringia lead with 86%. Rates of Appeal in contrast were very low: only 0.6% of these cases were referred to conciliation judges. Typical objects of dispute at regional courts included inheritance, usage and work contracts, and at local courts neighbourhood and rent disputes, and at administration law courts: construction works. (Greger at www.reinhard-greger.de/datien).

The classic version of problem solving – settlement by the responsible judge, is still preferred to mediation by the conciliation judge, as in only 10% of the civil law cases is an agreement reached. The data below indicates the variation in success rates for conciliation judges in the different courts (see Table 4).

Table 4 Success rates for conciliation judges

Administrative Law Courts 2016	
Number of procedures:	239,376
Settlements by the responsible judge:	263
Settlements by the conciliation judge:	11
(Statistisches Bundesamt, Rechtspflege Reihe 2.4 2016)	
Social Law Courts 2016	
Number of procedures:	367,760
Settlements by the responsible judge:	31,794
Settlements by the conciliation judge:	179
(Statistisches Bundesamt, Rechtspflege Reihe 2.7 2016)	
Labour Law Courts 2016	
Number of procedures:	361,626
Settlements by the responsible judge:	223,416
Settlements by the conciliation judge:	171
(Statistisches Bundesamt Rechtspflege Reihe 2.8 2016)	

And the traditional settlements by judges have also increased to 10% since the civil procedures reform of 2002 in Germany. Willingness to reach agreement differs traditionally in distinct regions in Germany. The settlement rate is 25% in Bavaria. Economic reasons determine agreements in general. The courts characterised by higher conciliation rates are distinguished by higher traditional settlement rates as well: 41% agreements (company law 46%, inheritance 38%, family disputes 21%) and 30% disputed judgments. (Greger at www.reinhard-greger.de/datien.)

VI. ALTERNATIVE DISPUTE RESOLUTION

The legislation on alternative dispute resolution in consumer matters dates from 1 April 2016 and follows the ADR directive 2013/11 of the European Union. Accredited private associations offer non-binding arbitration with professional expertise, impartiality, independence and transparency, in which entrepreneurs have a duty to provide information in the case of disputes in consumer matters. The statistics for the consumer arbitration services 2016 demonstrate that 60,810 applications concerning contractual disputes between consumers and entrepreneurs were received: 26% were rejected, but when a conciliation proposal was proposed, 30% of the demands were accepted and in 2% of the cases a solution was found outside the procedure (Bundesamt für Justiz, 2016). Online Dispute Settlement of legal E-Commerce disputes in cross border disputes is offered by the Centre for Consumer Protection in Kehl, financed by different provincial ministries of consumer protection. In 2017 there were 11,000 cases with a 76% success rate (Jahresbericht des Zentrums für Europäischen Verbraucherschutz, 2017).

These preventive policies should reduce the number of civil procedures, because in the past this had been increasing year on year in Germany. The objects referred to, that is, insurance and capital investment; (with the exception of public transport) were those responsible for the increase in special legal actions at the civil law courts in the past. The situation may have been changed by the increasing recourse to debt collection companies in Germany when it was reported in 2017 that 22.3 million extrajudicial requests were handled, in the majority of cases (87%) out of court (Bundesverband deutscher Inkassounternehmer e.V. 2017). Special websites offer to claim what is owed in return for a share. In recent years the number of civil procedures decreased significantly by 23% between 2002 and 2012 at district courts, and by 19% at regional courts and also by 19% for appeals at regional courts. Only cases with a low litigation value (under 5,000 Euros) and a high litigation value (over 500,000 Euros) increased. Building cases declined by 40% between 2002 and 2012 in relation to the respective levels at district courts and by 26% at regional courts. However, the numbers of cases of disputed travel contracts increased by 50% between 2002 and 2012 at civil law courts, company law by 100%, insurance by 200% and capital investment by 350%. Educated guesses by social scientists suggest that the ambiguity of the legal situation, the specialisation of the courts, and the demographic development – an older and richer population – contributed to the decrease in the caseload at the courts (Graf-Schlieker, 2004). But the diminished number of civil procedures cannot be explained by an increase in mutual agreements. Lawyers specify that only 20% of their cases are solved by mutual agreements.

VII. EVALUATING MEDIATION

The first extensive research on peer mediation in schools including all federal counties took place in 2006 (Behn et al, 2006). This research aimed at describing all the important factors in order to identify which were preventing or restricting mediation. The research should give answers about the framework and the practice of mediation. The research was based on quantitative inquiries (pre- and post-tests), internal school statistics, qualitative single and group interviews, participant observation and inquiries of experts including control groups (schools with experience in mediation of less than 1.5 years).

The results show that peer mediation is not suitable for severe conflicts. But there are positive effects showing decreasing rates of disciplinary measures and cases delegated to the teachers. Wildfeuer (2009) gives a critical account of the results of peer mediation in Mecklenburg Vorpommern. Positive effects in his view include the improved ability of the mediators to communicate with regard to appropriate actions relating to conflicts, developing a mature personality and the ability to practice the skills learned. If mediation is part of the teacher's work, it improves the school atmosphere (34%) and the relationships between staff (15.7%).

Mediation is successful if conditions are good, the school context is cooperative and the participants accept the mediation and work in a transparent and integrative way. But there are no valid results concerning a change in violent cases. A longitudinal study in 2017 (Kaiser et al 2017) tried to identify factors affecting the structure and process and consequences of sustainable court mediation. These factors might also be necessary and important for school mediation. The results point to the importance of professional competence in conflict management, strategies to solve problems, ability to reflect on one's own actions, knowledge about interpersonal conflicts, self-consciousness and empathy. A stable emotional state, openness to new experiences and calmness support these effects. Personality traits develop from early childhood throughout a lifetime. They are compounded by psycho-social competence to deal with critical life events. Complexity of conflicts raises deficits in competence, and lack of competence if the person cannot call on psychological resources.

The consequences and preventive measures for practice and further education which are influencing the quality of structure include training, supervision and personal experience. To optimise the quality of the process it is necessary to look for significant criteria among the involved persons and systems to understand the relationships and conflicts. Empathic communication and high reciprocal regard, comprehensive clarification of all conflict related questions, and the neutrality and objectivity of the mediator, all of which are precise and checkable assumptions, optimise the results and their sustainability.

VIII. OPPORTUNITIES AND LIMITATIONS

Mediation is a good and successful way to solve conflicts between disputing parties especially if there is a good and confidential base for communication. Conflicts raise awareness of the possibility of solving existing problems. The necessary conditions are qualified mediators and the fundamental willingness of the conflicted parties to cooperate and to be open to new and creative thinking. Sometimes if the conflicted parties are willing, but not in an emotional and social position to communicate in a face to face situation, they can exchange proposals via the mediator. This may be an effective way, especially for parents unable to communicate without aggression and anger but interested in the best interests of the child. The experience with mediation in schools shows positive consequences with reference to moral, emotional and social development. Reducing reciprocal readiness to negotiate and the tendency to insist and justify one's own position increases the limitation of mediation and successful conflict solving.

Besides conflict settlement in institutions and between organisations – national or international – by arbitration or mediation – opinion polls demonstrate that 60% of Germans value problem solving by mediation, 44% consider mediation in case of conflicts, but only 10% engage in mediation. In legal conflicts which are concerned with personal rights, the number considering mediation is 76%, but falls to only 4% in the case of inheritance disputes (Roland RechtsReport, 2016). The government's own evaluation of the German mediation law demonstrated that mediation has not been adopted by the German population (Messer, 2017).

Mediators realise that legal problem solving is preferred to out of court mediation. The number of mediations has decreased in Germany according to surveys by the mediators association. There was about a 15% decrease in commercial matters, 36% in family and partnership and neighbourhood matters, and 49% within organisations (Schlieffen, 2016). They complain that the majority of mediators cannot make a living by mediation and campaign for public financing of mediation in general, some even request compulsory mediation (Bericht der Bundesregierung, 2017).

Regardless of the Mediation Directive 2008/52/EU, mediation in civil and commercial matters is used in less than 1% of cases in the EU (Europäische Kommission, 2016).

Conflicted parties in mediation rely on the supposed long-lasting pacifying effects of self determined agreements – independent of restriction by legal and bureaucratic structures. But their view of adversarial legal structures is not applicable to the majority of legal actions. Lawyers are not interested in highly disputed actions, their time management does not permit an engagement in time consuming adversarial actions, particularly as the financial benefits – especially in German family law – with the exception of cases characterised by high litigation values in civil law are not profitable. Civil law proceedings in first instance district courts are characterised in any case by fast tracking of claims. 50% of all law suits at the local civil courts are solved within three months and 25% more within sixth months (Zivilgerichte, 2016).

So why does the German Government and the EU support mediation? They hope for more cost-efficient and faster dispute resolution for the state, quicker and cheaper court proceedings insofar as they cherish the concept of a lean state and want to reduce the costs of the court infrastructures in continental European states, and set their hopes on the powers of the free market ignoring the unequal positions of the different legal parties. Or they try to use mediation at German family courts in the case of joint legal custody with the aim of encouraging parents to embrace the aims of the legislator, changing the law in a therapeutic setting, *and* making a connection between law and emotion.

REFERENCES

Bastine, R, Weinmann-Lutz, B und Wetzel, A (1999) *Unterstützung von Familien in Scheidung durch Familienmediation* (Stuttgart, Sozialministerium Baden-Württemberg).

Behn, S, Kugler, N, Lembeck, H-J, Pleiger, D, Shaffranke, D, Schroer, M, und Wink, S (2006) *Mediation an Schulen-eine bundesdeutsche Evaluation* (Berlin, Springer-Verlag fur Sozialwissenschaften).

Bericht der Bundesregierung über die Auswirkungen des Mediationsgesetzes in Deutschland und über die Situation der Aus- und Fortbildung der Mediatoren (2017): www.bmjv.de/service/evaluation.

Breidenbach, S (ed) (1995) *Mediation-Struktur, Chancen und Risiken von Vermittlung im Konflikt* (Koln, Dr Otto Schmidt).

Bundesamt für Justiz (2017) *Verbraucherschlichtungsjahresbericht 2016*: www.bundesjustizamt.de.

Bundesverband deutscher Inkassounternehmer e.V., *Pressemitteilungen: Neue Inkassomarktstudie 2017*: www.inkasso.de.

Bundesverband Mediation e.V., *Fachgruppe Bildung und Erziehung* (Berlin).

Busch, D (2009) 'Mediation als Kulturdilemma?', *Erwägen- Wissen-Ethik* 510–20.

Cooter, RD and Rubinfeld, DL (1995) 'Economic Analysis of Legal Disputes and Their Resolution' in S Breidenbach (ed) *Mediation – Struktur, Chancen und Risiken von Vermittlung im Konflikt* (Köln, Dr Otto Schmidt Köln).

Council of Europe (2015) *Rapport Doc 13870*, assembly.coe.int.

Europäische Kommission, Bericht der Kommission an den europäischen Wirtschaftsausschuss über die Anwendung der Richtlinie 2008/52/EG (Brüssel).

Fachgruppe Mediation in Erziehung und Bildung (2006) *Standards und Ausbildungsrichtliniem fur Schulmediation*, Diskussionspapier.

Glasl, F (2011) *Konfliktmanagement. Diagnose und Behandlung von Konflikten in Organisationen* (10th edn) (Bern, Huber).

Graf-Schlieker, ML (2004) 'Der Zivilprozess vor dem aus', *Anwaltsblatt* 573–77.

Greger, R (2010) *Pilotstudie zum Vergleich von Kosten und Folgekosten in Sorge-und Umgangsrechtskonflikten* (Berlin, Bundesministerium der Justiz, 2010).

Greger, R (2011) *Gerichtsinterne Mediation in der bayrischen Verwaltungsgerichtsbarkeit* (Műnchen, Bayrisches Staatsministerium des Inneren).

Greger, R and Unberath, H (2011) *Thüringer Projekt Güterichter* (Erfurt, Thüringer Justizministerium).

Gregor, R (nd) *Rechtstatsächliche Untersuchung zur Implementierung des Güterichterverfahrens*: www.reinhard-greger.de/dateien/Evaluationsbericht.1.pdf.

Guideline 2012/29/EU of the European Parliament (25 October 2012) *Official Journal of the European Communities* (EU from 11, 14 th 2012, L 315/57).

Hartig, C (2009) 'Das Standardmodell und seine Weiterentwicklung im pädagogischen Kontext', *Erwägen- Wissen-Ethik* 535–37.

Hartmann, A, Schmidt, M, Ede, K and Kerner, HJ (2016) *Täter-Opfer-Ausgleich in Deutschland – Auswertung der bundesweiten Täter-Opfer-Ausgleichs-Statistik für die Jahrgänge 2015 und 2016*. (Bericht für das Bundesministerium für Justiz und Verbraucherschutz): www.bmj.de.

Jahresbericht des Zentrums für europäischen Verbraucherschutz (2017): www.cec-zev.eu.

Jeffreys Duden, K (2000), *Konfliktlösung und Schlichtung* (Weinheim, Beltz).

Kaiser, P, Gabler, AM und Norden, I (2017) 'Wirkfaktoren für Qualität und Nachhaltigkeit von Mediation – Ergebnisse einer Längsschnittstudie zu gerichtlicher Mediation und allgemeine Implikationen' in K Kriegel-Schmidt (ed) *Mediation als Wissenschaftszweig. Im Spannungsfeld von Fachexpertise und Interdisziplinarität* (Berlin, Springer) 31–48.

Kostka, K (2004) *Im Interesse des Kindes?* (Frankfurt, Eigenverlag des deutschen Vereins für öffentliche und private Fürsorge).

Messer, K (2017) *Evaluierung des Mediationsgesetzes* (Speyer, Deutsches Institut für öffentliche Verwaltung).

Montada, L und Kals, E (2015) *Mediation – Lehrbuch für Psychologen und Juristen* (Weinheim, Beltz).

Montada, L (2009) 'Mediation – Pfade zum Frieden', *Erwägen- Wissen-Ethik* 501–11.

Pati, B and Voet, S (2012) *Family Mediation in International Family Conflicts: The European Context* (Research Report 20 April 2012): www.e-justice.europe.eu.

Pelikan, C (2009) 'Mediation, Peace-building and restorative justice', *Erwägen-Wissen-Ethik* 553–54.

Peschel, F (2009) 'Mediation in der Schule?', *Erwägen-Wissen-Ethik* 555–58.

Proksch, R (1998) *Praxiserprobung von Vermittlungen in streitigen Familiensachen* (Stuttgart, Kohlhammer).

Proksch, R (2002) Rechtstatsächliche Untersuchung zur Reform des Kindschaftsrechts (Köln, Bundesanzeiger-Verlag).

Roland Rechtsreport, (2016) Einstellung der Bevölkerung zum deutschen Rechtssystem und zur Mediation: www.roland-rechtsschutz.de.

Rottleuthner-Lutter, M (1992) *Gründe von Ehescheidungen in der Bundesrepublik Deutschland* (Köln, Bundesanzeiger-Verlag, 1992).

Schlieffen, K (2016) *Das neue Mediationsverständnis* (Jena, 8 Deutscher Mediationstag).

Staffke, F (2012) *Mediation in the European Union*: www.e-justice.europe.eu.

Statistisches Bundesamt, Rechtspflege *Reihe 2.1, Zivilgerichte 2016.*

Statistisches Bundesamt, Rechtspflege *Reihe 2.2, Familiengerichte 2016, 2000.*

Statistisches Bundesamt, *Rechtspflege Reihe 2.4 Verwaltungsgerichte 2016.*

Statistisches Bundesamt, *Rechtspflege Reihe 2.7 Sozialgerichte 2016.*

Statistisches Bundesamt, *Rechtspflege Reihe 2.8 Arbeitsgerichte 2016.*

Sukopp, T (2009) 'Mediation: Erweiterungen in interkultureller Perspektive', *Erwägen- Wissen-Ethik* 576–78.

Wardle, LD (1994) 'Liberty, Equality and the Quest of Family Justice in the United States' Paper presented at the Conference, Families and Justice, (Brussels).

Wildfeuer, W (2009) 'Mediation in der Schule – ein kritischer Blick', *Erwägen-Wissen-Ethik* 584–85.

6

Different Forms of Alternative Dispute Resolution: The Framework for Family Mediation in Spain

TERESA PICONTÓ NOVALES, ELENA LAUROBA, CRISTINA MERINO AND MARCOS LOREDO COLUNGA

I. THE FRAMEWORK FOR FAMILY MEDIATION IN SPAIN

FAMILY MEDIATION BEGAN in Spain at the beginning of the twenty-first century, following the example of countries including the USA, Canada and Argentina, and the experience of various associations in the Basque Country and Catalonia. The initiative for regulating family mediation came basically from the autonomous communities, starting with The Catalan Law of Family Mediation in 2001. As regards the interest of the Spanish State, the first reference to the possibility of family mediation appeared in Law 5/2005 concerning separation and divorce.

Given that there was no 'national' law until 2012 (The Law 5/2012) about civil and commercial mediation, the Autonomous Communities began regulating mediation using their own laws. This occurred in Catalonia, Valencia, Galicia, the Canary Islands, Castilla-La Mancha, Castilla-León, Asturias, Madrid, Andalusia, the Basque Country, the Balearic Islands, Murcia and Aragón.

> In Spain intra-judicial mediation was promoted by a pilot project initiated by the General Council of the Judiciary in 2006 in various courts (in Madrid, Barcelona, Málaga, Seville, Pamplona y Palma de Mallorca). In 2008 a protocol was drafted for implementing mediation in the courts in general. Specifically, in order to be able to incorporate mediation services, a court was required to have institutional support (from the Autonomous Communities, Local councils, Bar associations) and the necessary funding. The arrangements were developed by means of cooperation between the courts and mediation bodies (García-Herrera, 2016: 10).

Since the first regional laws concerning mediation and Directive 2008/52/ CEE and its incorporation into the Law 5/2012 on civil and commercial mediation, the implementation of mediation in Spain has continued to be a challenge (Lauroba, 2018: 10). Compared to other European countries, mediation in Spain is not widespread although its use is gradually increasing.

In Spain there is a distinction between 'Intra-Judicial' and 'Extra-Judicial' mediation. Intra-judicial mediation takes place when the judicial proceedings have already started and mediation has been encouraged by judges. In many Autonomous Communities, judges have taken the initiative in suggesting to parties involved in cases of divorce, separation or relationship breakdown that they consider following the mediation route (Lauroba, 2018: 11). The mediation process may also start before initiating any court action or after the court proceedings have finished. In both cases this is known as extra-judicial mediation (Merino, 2013: 75).

Intra-judicial mediation begins after the legal claim, the reply to the claim and the judicial process is suspended. If both parties reach an agreement, this must be ratified by the judge. In any case, the parties can go to mediation directly on their own initiative during the judicial process, or on the advice of the judge. Referrals to mediation may occur at any stage of the judicial process, even after the judicial decision.

Mediation in Spain is voluntary (Article 6.1, Law 5/2012). The law allows the parties to apply for mediation and consequently to suspend civil proceedings, but there must be mutual agreement to do so. In some autonomous communities, the judges can ask the parties to attend an information session or even the first mediation session. However, the parties are free to decide whether or not to proceed with mediation at any stage (Article 3, Directive 2008/52/CE). It is worth pointing out that Law 5/2012 obliges the courts to provide information to the parties about the possibilities of mediation. The mediation process may result in an agreement or not, and an agreement may be total or partial. In the latter case, the court proceedings have to be continued for those matters where consensus has not been reached.

There are certain matters that are excluded by law from any mediation process given their major importance. These include filiation, 'patria potestad' (parental responsibility), adoption, maintenance, child abuse, and domestic and gender violence (Decree 980/2013, 13 December, and Law 5/2012, 6 July, on mediation in family and commercial matters).

The issues which can be managed through mediation include:

- Arrangements for the care of children (eg, sole or shared custody).
- Child support payments.
- Use of the family home.
- Decisions relating to health and education of the child.

An issue regarding which there is intense debate in Spain among professionals and researchers is the advisability of mediation in some cases of gender violence (see Picontó Novales (2019: 251–62)). Legally, mediation is prohibited in cases of gender violence by Spanish Law (Article 44.5 of Organic Law 1/2004 for Integral Protection against Gender Violence). The prohibition refers to both criminal processes and civil processes (separation, divorce, custody, etc). Both processes come under the responsibility of the courts of gender violence against women when the victim is a woman partner or ex-partner.

More specifically, Organic Law 1/2004 for Integral Protection against Gender Violence establishes certain competences of the gender violence courts in civil matters (separation, divorce, custody and contact orders, issues relating to the family) when the victim of gender violence is a woman partner or ex-partner and any of the following offences have been committed: murder, injuries, offences against moral integrity, offences against sexual freedom, or any offence committed with violence or intimidation (Article 44). In all cases mediation is prohibited.

More recently, The State Pact against Gender Violence approved by the Spanish Parliament in September 2017 represents a significant commitment given that it was approved by all the political parties. Proposal 116 of this pact states the need to reinforce in the legislation and in procedures, which will be approved and revised, the absolute prohibition of mediation in cases of gender violence.

In the international field, this prohibition also appears in the Istanbul Convention (Council of Europe Convention on preventing and combating violence against women and domestic violence) which was ratified by Spain in 2014. Article 48 refers to 'Prohibition of mandatory alternative dispute resolution processes of sentencing' and states in section one that 'Parties shall take the necessary legislative or other measures to prohibit mandatory alternative dispute resolution processes, including mediation or conciliation, in relation to all forms of violence covered by the scope of this Convention'. What is prohibited in Spain is for alternative means of conflict resolution (such as Restorative Justice) to be considered as a substitute for the penal system.

In Spain, this form of legal prohibition against mediation has been generally accepted. However, in recent years there has been more criticism by some professionals and experts in gender violence who consider that the prohibition should not necessarily be applied in certain cases where there may be some advantages in mediation for victims and which could provide more effective prevention of such violence. Such criticism suggests that the legal prohibition of mediation in all cases of gender violence and in all fields may be wrong. In the first place, it assumes that all violence is the same, ignoring the varying degrees of seriousness and the diverse needs of women victims. Secondly, it fails to recognise that, at least in some cases, mediation could have benefits for the victim.

One of the most controversial issues in the possible use of the mediation process in cases of gender violence is precisely the question of equality between the parties. The victim must not be placed in a position of inequality in the dialogue with her aggressor. Therefore, mediation is not possible in cases of serious physical violence or repeated acts of violence where the woman is defenceless. In any case, it is essential that a professional psychologist should confirm that the victim has recovered her self-esteem to ensure the empowerment of the victim.

Catalonia and the Basque Country have been reference points for all the other Autonomous Communities in the initiative and development of mediation. The Catalan law of 2001 influenced other autonomous communities, which have also developed policies to encourage family mediation through their own family mediation laws.

In the Basque Country mediation is offered through in-court services as well as out-of-court services. In the courts this began in the area of criminal justice and was later extended to civil and family justice; specifically, in cases of divorce and separation where there were children involved (Merino and Moreno, 2018). Family mediation in the courts must be supported by the authorities (ie, by the Ministry of Justice). As Merino and Moreno said: 'it is essential to be supported by the authorities (the Justice Ministry) and coordinated and supervised by a public system which is complementary to the formal system and not opposed to it' (ibid).

In addition to mediation, there are other alternative dispute resolution processes in Spain although these tend to be very new and not widely used. One example is the figure of the parenting coordinator which has a strong presence in Catalonia but is only just emerging in other autonomous communities such as Andalusia and Aragon. Another example is collaborative law which is currently being assessed by various bar associations and encouraged by legal organisations such as the Basque Association of Collaborative Law, supported by the Basque Government, and the Catalan Association of Collaborative Law, supported by the Justice Department of the Catalan government.

In the following parts of this chapter, Elena Lauroba in Section II discusses the development of mediation in Catalonia and how the Catalan government is currently developing a plan to promote mediation and other forms of ADR (principally parental coordination and collaborative law). Cristina Merino in Section III describes the pre-court extrajudicial and pro-court mediation organised by the mediation service of the Basque Government. And finally, Marcos Loredo, in Section IV, provides an overview of some examples of collaborative law in Spain and perspectives for the future.

II. ADR IN CATALONIA: FROM MEDIATION TO COLLABORATIVE LAW

Catalonia was the first autonomous community in Spain to adopt a family mediation law, in 2001.[1] This law created the Family Mediation Centre of Catalonia (FMCC), which led to the development of family mediation and which controlled a panel of mediators who acted in public mediations – that is, mediations supervised by the FMCC.

[1] Act 1/2001 of 15 March, *de mediación familiar* (BOE, n 91 of 14 April 2001).

The Catalan law of 2001 was a reference point for other autonomous communities, which have also developed policies to encourage family mediation through their own family mediation laws. But the Catalan law of 2001 soon became insufficient to solve the wide plurality of family conflicts (this law was centred on conflicts relating to divorce or between couples with minors, and did not cover other family conflicts such as adoption, wills or family businesses) (See Lauroba, 2011: 21–31). Subsequently, the preparatory works in Europe which led to the Directive 2008/52/EC of the European Parliament and of the Council of 21 May 2008 on certain aspects of mediation in civil and commercial matters generated in the Catalan government the wish to have a more ambitious mediation law. This became a reality in 2009: the law of mediation in the field of private law.[2] The law aims to offer mediation in any area of conflict in family law, with an almost exhaustive enumeration of family disputes in Article 2.1 (which includes, eg, issues related to the inheritance of a family member and family conflicts between persons of different nationalities). In addition, the law also deals with conflicts (Article 2.2) characterised by the rupture of communication between the parties, and the will to rebuild relations in the future. This includes conflicts relating to condominium property, or associations and foundations.

To complete the legislative landscape, the Second Book of the *Catalonia Civil Code on persons and family*[3] which came into force on 1 January 2011, refers to mediation in several articles. This was especially important in its provisions regarding annulment of marriage, divorce and legal separation. Mediation was included as a constructive way of encouraging co-parenting after breakdown.[4] Article 233-6 includes specific references to *Family Mediation*. Two of its provisions are as follows:

> [233-6] 3. The judicial authority can refer the spouses to an information session on mediation if it considers, from the circumstances of the case, that an agreement can be reached.
>
> [233-6] 6. Agreements reached in mediation regarding the exercise of parental responsibility are deemed suitable for the minor's interest. The lack of approval by the judicial authority must be based on criteria of public policy and on the minor's interest.

There is currently a government initiative to reform the Article to make the information session mandatory, as in the Basque Country (Act 7/2015).

[2] Act 15/2009 of 22 July, *de mediación en el ámbito del derecho privado* (BOE n 198 of 17 August 2009). See I Viola et al (2018).

[3] www.parlament.cat/document/intrade/152428.

[4] The preamble of Law 25/2010 [III c) 15 affirms: 'The message of the second book is to encourage forms of co-parenting and the use of mediation as a tool to ensure the stability of relations after the breakdown between the parents, and the natural adaptation of the rules to changing circumstances …'

In parallel, in 2010 the *White Book on Mediation in Catalonia* (WBMC) was published, a research study involving more than 100 academics and experts from throughout Catalonia, which provided a complete profile of the implementation of mediation in areas such as business, schools, hospitals or consumer conflicts. It showed that there were more mediations than had been thought by analysts, but the lack of institutionalisation of mediation generated a feeling of insecurity among mediators. It also revealed that judges were not generally against mediation, but that they rarely advised parties to pursue it.[5] The WBMC ended with 15 recommendations. Number 13 reads as follows:

> We recommend encouraging mediation among citizens, underlining both the benefits for a better conflict management and the technical aspects. General strategies of communication have to be designed and scientific studies in all areas (of family and civil justice) have to be promoted. Professionals should be the focus of these strategies and studies, since they can use mediation and alternative conflict management and resolution techniques in these areas.

Many people remain unaware of mediation. Certainly, today there is a progressive increase in mediations in Catalonia, but this growth is far from making mediation a standard option for conflict resolution. When examining FMCC statistics we find that in 2017, 2,970 requests for mediation were processed, of which 2,324 were initiated directly by parties and 646 by the judiciary. A total of 784 were completed (461 directly and 323 by judicial referral), and 408 mediations were finalised with agreement (309 from the first group and 99 from the second).[6] It is an almost insignificant amount in terms of the total number of judicial conflicts. Moreover, the percentage of agreements is not very satisfactory, at about 52%.

In fact, Catalonia is a clear exponent of the so-called *European Mediation Paradox*. This refers to the paradoxical situation in which, despite the widespread conviction that mediation is a faster and cheaper procedure than the courts and that it provides a higher level of satisfaction for the parties in conflict, the adoption of mediation procedures continues to be almost minimal. Despite this, the fight for normalisation of ADRs continues. An example is the rapid implementation of parenting coordination. This form of ADR appeared in several sentences of the Provincial Court of Barcelona for the first time in 2013 and the High Court of Justice of Catalonia approved its employment in the Decision of 26 February 2015[7] – a leading case. Today parenting coordination has gone beyond the Catalan borders and the Ministry of Justice is studying its

[5] It showed too that when mediation was requested by the parties, the level of agreement exceeded 70%. In contrast, only 47.5% of mediations suggested by judges or in an open judicial proceeding reached an agreement (WBNC, ch 7).

[6] http://justicia.gencat.cat/ca/departament/Estadistiques/mediacio/.

[7] For an exhaustive list of judgments about the parenting coordinator in Catalonia, see García-Herrera (2016).

implementation throughout the state through pilot programmes. However, to guarantee success a clear single concept for this new ADR is needed, which is not always the case. For some enthusiasts, the parenting coordinator has therapeutic connotations while others – significantly lawyers – do not share this view.[8] And even before its implementation some experts worry about the high costs involved.

Given the willingness to develop actions that contribute to consolidate ADR, the Justice Department of the Generalitat de Catalunya in 2016 commissioned a report in order to identify measures in this regard.[9] After analysing its proposals, members of the Justice Department have explained in numerous conferences the new steps to be taken. Perhaps the most important conclusion is the necessity of a major investment in ADR, not only financial but also in terms of publicity, and the possibility of opening the field to new ADR beyond mediation.[10]

That said, what is the situation nowadays following the coming into force of the two Acts?

To begin with, we must assume that a significant sector of the legal profession still does not have full confidence in mediation or is not sufficiently familiar with the procedure. This situation is linked, among other reasons, to the fact that lawyers have often been excluded from mediation procedures – especially family mediations. It is true that their exclusion is partial as they are essential for drafting the agreements. But many lawyers do not understand – and sometimes they are absolutely right – why they are excluded from mediation sessions.

On the other hand, many lawyers were trained after the introduction of the first mediation law (2001) to became mediators too. They were convinced that mediation would be a new and possibly lucrative field of work. But this was wishful thinking, not a reality. As the WBMC reminds us: 'The expectations created by the above mentioned act were reflected in the increase of the activity of mediators in 2002 and 2003. However, there was a remarkable decrease in 2004 as regards the activity of mediators and the interest in training courses. Trends are created by expectations' (WBMC: 1164). The situation has not substantially changed more than 14 years later, not even with the Mediation Act of 2009. Today, with palpable disenchantment, these lawyers have found that mediations are rare and that trained lawyers in mediation coexist with mediators from other professions, mainly psychologists or social workers.

However, given the weight of the legal profession, lawyers are irreplaceable in their role as advisers to the parties that attend mediation processes. In this area,

[8] An example of this lack of a clear definition is the STSJC 12.1.2017, which designates a parental coordinator to address a conflict between a parent and a minor, not between parents.

[9] The main driver for the initiative has been Xavier Bernadí i Gil, the General Director of Law and Juridical Entities at the Justice Department of Catalonia. The hitherto unpublished work was elaborated by Montserrat Tur Racero (lawyer, mediator and divorce coach) and Elena Lauroba.

[10] The best introduction to these ADR as a pedagogical tool for Catalan jurists is Ortuño (2018).

no other profession can compete with them. Thus, specific training has recently been proposed for lawyers, linked to their status as counsellors of parties in mediation. This training aims to familiarise them with the structure of the procedure and with the best tools to succeed in it. If lawyers feel comfortable, they will be more favourable to advise mediation. In 2018, the Bar Association of Barcelona offered two training courses for lawyers who wish to achieve the status of 'mediation friendly lawyers', that is, the condition of qualified lawyers to accompany parties in mediation. Now, a priority objective is to organise this training in other Bar Associations in Catalonia. More than mediator-lawyers, what are really needed in order to consolidate this ADR are *mediation-friendly* lawyers.

The Catalan Justice Department has promoted mediation in administrative courts for the last two years. From their point of view, the Generalitat would not have the legitimacy to affirm that it is serious about encouraging mediation if it excludes this procedure in conflicts where the public administration is one of the parties.

Currently, there is a conviction that mediation is not the right tool for all kinds of conflicts. For this reason, other forms of dispute resolution have been initiated, for example, the promotion of parenting coordinators. Moreover, collaborative law[11] is emerging as a modality of ADR. It is considered as an ideal instrument for lawyers (Lauroba, 2018). In addition, the commitment to collaborative law on the part of the government of the Basque Country represented an initiative to be imitated in Catalonia. In September 2017, the Justice Department promoted a conference to bring collaborative law to the attention of juridical operators. The conference was the occasion to present the *Associació Catalana de Dret Col·laboratiu* (ACDC).[12] In October 2018, the ACDC began its first training programme that will allow participants to be considered collaborative lawyers, in accordance with the standards of the *International Academy of Collaborative Professionals*. We hope to have the first group of accredited collaborative lawyers in spring 2019. The inclusion of new ADRs will probably lead to a change in the name of the official Centre of Mediation. In 2001, it was called the Family Mediation Centre; in 2009, it became the Private Mediation Centre. In 2019, it will probably be renamed for a second time. The decision is yet to be made, but the government is thinking of naming it the Mediation Centre (without the qualification of private) or the Mediation and other ADR Centre.

Catalonia is now considering Online Dispute Resolution (ODR), the little brother of ADR that is growing at meteoric speed. This approach is also linked with the management of consumer complaints.

[11] See Section IV of this chapter.
[12] www.dretcolaboratiu.cat. The ACDC has currently about 30 members.

III. OUT OF COURT FAMILY MEDIATION IN THE BASQUE COUNTRY: FAMILY MEDIATION SERVICE OF THE BASQUE GOVERNMENT SOCIAL POLICIES (1996–2018)

The Basque Government started the first Family Mediation Service as a pilot project in Bilbao in October 1996 and more than two decades later it is offered in every capital of the three provinces of the Basque Country (Bilbao, San Sebastian and Vitoria).

In the 1990s the statistical data in the Basque Country community reflected a progressive increase in petitions for separation and divorce. In every separation or divorce process, together with and prior to the legal proceedings in court, there is an emotional breakdown of the marriage or couple which involves a set of personal reactions to the relationship which is being dissolved. This emotional component as a whole affects any full understanding of the new reality, hindering dissolution of the original economic unit and adaptation to the new relationship.

One of the main goals of the out of court Family Mediation Service is to help couples in overcoming these situations and limiting the trauma. Mediation is a method designed to pave the way to mutual consent, and avoid legal confrontations. It could be used before or after going to court, thus it is pre-judicial or post-judicial (once the judicial procedure has already finished).

Mediation is a face-to-face process. The mediator maintains direct contact with the parties in order to promote communication and dialogue to help the parties to reach an agreement which will involve less emotional damage to the children as well as for future family relations. The mediator does not himself or herself decide, but assists the parties in reaching joint decisions. With the agreements reached, the couple must then resort to a lawyer who will process their separation or divorce through the courts. In cases where the parties are already divorced and take part in the mediation process to improve the judicial decision, they will go back to the court to request a change in the terms of the original decision.

Mediators have at their disposal interdisciplinary teams which include lawyers, psychologists, social workers and educational workers with knowledge and experience in conflict-solving processes, mediation, negotiation skills, emotional and interpersonal relationships, and with knowledge of the existing legal framework. Every team also has an administrative assistant with knowledge of mediation.

The main characteristics of the Family Mediation Services can be summarised as follows (Merino, 2010):

> The-out-of-court Family Mediation Services are publicly financed and therefore are controlled by the Department of Social Policies of the Basque Government. However, in court mediation services are controlled by the Department of Justice.
>
> - The Mediation Service is coordinated with all kinds of social and community services.
> - It is free for the users.

- It is voluntary, which means that it is possible to attend information sessions individually, but to start the process the mediation must be accepted by both parties.
- The team members who are directly involved during the mediation processes remain totally on the margins of the judicial proceedings.
- The cases are always handed over directly to the *Bar Associations*, and never to individual lawyer's offices.

The basic lines of family mediation imply that any family suffering an interpersonal conflict or a couple who wish to separate or divorce, can ask for an information session in the Mediation Service. When the conflict is related to separation, in order to gain access to amicable legal proceedings the couple will have to reach a series of agreements concerning what is the best way to regulate their life in the future, as well as that of their children.

To work as a mediator in the Basque Government *out of court* family mediation programmes, it is compulsory to be registered officially. This registration requires a University degree and a 200-hour training course on conflict resolution skills, family law, the legal framework, evolutionary psychology and family mediation processes. The training required is focused on dealing with family conflicts in order to minimise the impact on the children and to prevent a judicialisation of family problems.

The target groups for the programme are the following:

- Any person who is suffering a conflict with their family and is looking for a place to talk with their relatives.
- Couples who wish to regulate their relationship without resorting to a legal process of separation in the early stages.
- Couples who have decided to separate but have not initiated separation proceedings.
- Couples who have legally resolved their separation or divorce, but continue to experience a situation of crisis.
- Couples who are involved at any stage of legal separation proceedings and wish to resort to a new mediation process can apply to the Mediation Services.

There are several stages in the mediation process:

Stage 1: Approaching the service

The application can be made by either member of the couple, or by both of them at the same time. When there is a family conflict one of the family members can ask for an informative session individually or with any other members of the family. In this first meeting applicants are informed about the objectives of the Family Mediation Service. At the same time, they will be reminded that if they want to initiate legal proceedings they must do so accompanied by their respective lawyers.

Stage 2: Organisation of the petition

Being an out of court service, applicants do not usually have a lawyer. However, if they have contacted lawyers, we inform the lawyers about the basic lines of the mediation process. They will be informed that this is a collaboration service aimed at achieving agreements, and that they will continue to represent their clients, being responsible for the formalisation of the agreements reached.

Stage 3: Initiating the process

The attempt is made, through individual or joint interviews, to find a space for reflection, in order to discover those issues which might hinder the negotiations. At this point it is important that both partners or spouses accept the reality of their situation and seek to replace the concept of blame by responsibility, thinking less in terms of asserting their claims and more about looking for solutions. At this point the remaining stages of the mediation process are explained to them.

Stage 4: Signing the mediation document

Once the decision to go ahead has been made, the terms of the private mediation document are discussed and agreed. Then it is signed by the two parties in a partnership conflict and by the mediator, or by all of the members of the family in a family conflict and by the mediators. Therefore, the signing of this document is the beginning of the mediation process properly speaking.

Stage 5: Setting the agenda and negotiation

Setting the agenda is one of the keys to the process. At this stage efforts are made to reach agreement on the immediate issue they want to deal with in the mediation process. The agenda will allow the negotiation process to begin in a more relaxed way for the parties in conflict. In negotiation, the points of agreement and dispute between the parties are identified in order to reach a definitive consensus in relation to the final drawing up of the agreement, which they must sign.

Stage 6: Final agreement

The regulatory contract is drawn up. The couple or family members have time to read it calmly and reflect on the agreement written down in a draft. If they agree on every detail, then they will sign it. When the conflict is related to separation or divorce, then this will have to be legally formalised in the corresponding separation process, through the intervention of the lawyers.

Stage 7: Follow up and continuous support

Follow up will be carried out after one year from the date of the signature. The aim of the follow up is to know the effect of the mediation process, in order to check if the agreement is correctly observed, renegotiate any possible changes and seek the opinion of the users with regard to the Family Mediation Service once a certain amount of time has passed after the conclusion of the process. The mediation team will always be available for future negotiation of any aspects on which an agreement has already been reached, but where subsequent circumstances make fulfillment difficult.

The Family Mediation Service has been very well welcome by the public, as it is shown by the extensive demand for its services during its 22 years of operation. Mention should also be made of the interest shown by a variety of public institutions since it was created, particularly by the Social Welfare Services of city councils, the Ombudsman's office, Family Associations, the Bar Association's Legal Guidance Service, all professionals related to family issues such as therapists, social workers and education professionals.

From the beginning, given the non-existence of any provision in this respect in our legal system, the Family Mediation Service has been operated on an absolutely voluntary basis. After 22 years, not only institutions but also 'previous users' recommend couples or families in crisis to resort to this service

The data corresponding to the out of court service in 2017 are the following:

Figure 1 Mediation data

<table>
<tr><td colspan="2">Out of court Mediation data 2017[13]
2,064 cases
Pre-mediation (first stages of mediation) 634
Complete mediation processes 854
Follow-up processes 576</td></tr>
<tr><td rowspan="2">Mediation process finished
854 cases</td><td>Agreements
658 (77%)</td></tr>
<tr><td>No agreement
196 (23%)</td></tr>
</table>

Source: Annual Report (VV.AA., 2018).

The follow-up stage takes place a year after the agreement was reached. In 2017, the follow-up data showed that almost all the parties to mediation had complied with the signed agreement in 2016. In detail, for 93.6% of the total of agreements reached the commitments made were met. Only 6.4% of parties failed to comply with the agreements.

We consider ADR offers a range of processes. The alternative processes in family contexts are mediation, family group conferences, restorative practices, even individual assessment focused on conflict management. This variety of processes implies that the response to family conflict can be specifically adapted to every family, context and conflict. So flexibility and adaptation are two of

[13] For further information visit the Basque Government website: www.euskadi.eus/web01-a2famil/es/contenidos/informacion/.

the main advantages of this approach (Merino, 2013). As mentioned earlier, the teams working *in court* and *out of court* mediation programmes are interdisciplinary. For this reason the teams can adopt a global approach to conflicts.

The principle of confidentiality leads the mediators to have more information than is available in a judicial process. People feel more comfortable in a mediation process than in court to talk about their feelings and family issues with a professional. The interdisciplinary approach is considered one of the keys of mediation best practices. The chance of working in a team, even to intervene as a professional couple (called co-mediation) allow for the design of an accurate process for every conflict and every family.

At the same time, there are some risks that concern us. For instance, the time scales of the judicial procedure differ from those of the mediation process. In this sense, the development of standard mediation procedures in our country has a great impact on the flexibility of the mediation. In the field of family conflict, this intervention requires more individual sessions and longer mediation processes than in criminal cases. One of the goals of the mediation is to achieve confidence and respect to build a dialogue in order to generate trust between the parties. This takes time and requires adaptation to the rhythm of the emotional process. Consequently it is really important to be efficient and respectful during the interaction with the parties in order to get back to the judicial process within a reasonable time period.

In conclusion we can say that, one of the strengths of mediation in the Basque Country lies in the training of the mediators. They are not lay advisers. Most of the mediators are well-qualified in fields including family law, psychology and social and restorative intervention practices. It is also considered as a strength that each process can be developed with flexibility and an open-minded attitude (Alzate and Merino, 2011). Participation in these processes is always voluntary, both to begin and to leave, which makes them more attractive even if they are conducted within a judicial process.

In summary, the mediation process takes place in face to face meetings, and this direct dialogue allows mediators to deal with conflict and take into account the personality traits of the parties in the conflict.

IV. COLLABORATIVE PRACTICE IN SPAIN: THE CURRENT SITUATION AND FUTURE PROSPECTS

Family law is facing a great challenge at this point in time: how best to offer effective tools for the appropriate approach, management and resolution of conflicts in family relationships. In line with this statement, this part of the chapter offers an overview of collaborative practice, a methodology to manage marriage crisis with two main objectives: to facilitate the dissolution of the communal life of a couple in an orderly and peaceful manner; and satisfy the interests and needs of all those affected by the breakup. So, collaborative practice is an ADR method based on negotiation, that has been in existence for almost 30 years and has a great deal of potential, but it is little known in Spain, and requires explanation in this chapter.

An appropriate introduction to collaborative practice requires that we take into account some previous reflections. Each family falls apart in a unique way, which discourages a standardised and uniform treatment of all breakups. On the contrary, the peculiarities of each family unit translate into different needs and interests in the face of a crisis. An appropriate legal response should involve offering various alternatives, so that the most appropriate can be chosen according to the circumstances of the case. Traditionally, two different approaches have been followed (Tesler and Thompson, 2006):

- Delegate the decision-making power to the judge (usual formula: confrontation or battle for the parties to obtain the best for him or herself and to harm the other as much as possible):
    - Confrontation in terms of win-lose.
    - Resolution often unsatisfactory and unfeasible from a practical perspective.
    - Irreversible deterioration of the relationship.
- Or maintain control of the process (through direct negotiation, mediation and other formulas):
    - Approach from a win-win perspective.
    - Agreement that satisfies each party's interests and needs.
    - Continuation of the relationship and better communication.

Given this panorama, it is obvious that mediation offers better results, but it can also be limited in some situations such as asymmetric relationships, emotional disturbance, inability to negotiate autonomously, or some specific needs (psychological or therapeutic help, tax advice or educational support). To fill this gap, a specific option has been developed, negotiation within a collaborative environment, a methodology alluded to in various ways: collaborative method, collaborative practice, collaborative process, collaborative law or even, collaborative divorce. That said, when talking about collaborative practice, the following conditions must be met:[14]

- A private negotiation aimed at obtaining the highest degree of satisfaction for all those involved.
- Personal intervention by the parties, who are assisted by their respective lawyers and other neutral professionals if they are required (psychologist, therapist, coach, financial adviser, mediator, etc).

[14] International Academy of Collaborative Professionals: www.collaborativepractice.com/what-collaborative-practice, accessed 15 May 2018.

- A disqualification clause: if the negotiation fails, both lawyers and any other professionals that may be involved, will be disqualified from intervening in any possible contentious judicial process that may arise between the parties.
- Confidentiality: unless otherwise agreed, both the information and the documentation handled during the negotiation will be confidential and cannot be used in litigation.

Two of these conditions are specific to this approach, and make it unique: the possibility of taking a multidisciplinary approach to the problem, and the mandatory exclusion of the professionals involved in any future judicial proceedings. And in accordance with these premises, the key to its success lies in the obvious waste of time, money and effort if the negotiation fails (since it would force the whole process to start over again), and as such the incentives for reaching an agreement are greater. In line with those premises, certain issues can be highlighted (Loredo, 2011):

- Collaborative practice is an ADR method based on negotiation. As such, fundamental aspects are shared with mediation: voluntariness, flexibility, confidentiality and control of the procedure, for instance.
- Collaborative practice impacts the judicial process in different ways:
  - It is necessary to suspend any previous judicial process in order to start a collaborative negotiation.
  - A lawsuit ends the negotiation.
  - The breakdown of the negotiation leaves the judicial channel open.
  - The final agreement can be incorporated into the judicial process for approval.
- Collaborative practice is the only method that offers comprehensive and multidisciplinary professional assistance: communication, managing emotions, managing finances or parenting skills.
- In collaborative practice only the intervention of lawyers is mandatory, that of other professionals is contingent. These professionals help to carry out the negotiation and advise the parties on anything necessary for them to take appropriate decisions. The professionals act as experts in their corresponding field, forming a collaborative team, for which specific training is required.

Collaborative practice has had only a short life, given that it was developed only 30 years ago. There is no need to dwell on these issues, but it is helpful to highlight the key milestones and recognise the merits of those who first promoted this approach.[15]

The starting point was at the end of the 1980s in Minneapolis, and the protagonist was Stuart Webb, a family lawyer with more than 20 years of experience.

[15] International Academy of Collaborative Professionals (history): www.collaborativepractice.com/resources, accessed 15 May 2018.

He was disenchanted with the traditional methods of litigation in family law, and came up with ADR, developing the collaborative technique: assisted negotiation with the intervention of lawyers, who are replaced if there is no agreement and the matter moves to court. His commitment to this formula was such that, in 1990, he declared himself a 'collaborative lawyer', informing his colleagues and potential clients of his willingness to not participate in contentious litigation. He took the risk of standing alone in his endeavour, but he managed to convince couples and colleagues of its value, and thus collaborative practice was born (Webb, 2008).

By this time (at the beginning of the 1990s), Peggy Thomson and Rodney Nurse, two psychologists from California, incorporated the multidisciplinary perspective into their work with couples in crisis. And in 1993, at a professional conference, they heard about collaborative practice, and decide to combine the two elements.

From then on, groups of collaborative professionals were organised in various states. These groups communicated and collaborated with each other, and in 1999, they took three decisive steps:[16]

- Created the first network, the *American Institute of Collaborative Professionals.*
- Held their first annual forum.[17]
- Began to publish *The Collaborative Review*.[18]

Shortly after, in 2001, after expanding into Canada, the organisation became the International Academy of Collaborative Professionals (IACP), an organisation committed to professional excellence in conflict resolution through negotiation in a collaborative environment, and which has the following objectives:[19]

- Training and dissemination.
- Establishment of training and practice standards.[20]
- Determination of deontological rules.[21]
- Legislative harmonisation.

[16] International Academy of Collaborative Professionals: www.collaborativepractice.com/collaborative-practice-faqs, accessed 15 May 2018.
[17] Next one in Seattle: www.cpcal.com/events/19th-annual-networking-educational-forum/, accessed 15 May 2018.
[18] International Academy of Collaborative Professionals: www.collaborativepractice.com/collaborative-review, accessed 15 May 2018.
[19] International Academy of Collaborative Professionals: www.collaborativepractice.com/about-iacp, accessed 15 May 2018.
[20] International Academy of Collaborative Professionals (standards and ethics): www.collaborativepractice.com/resources. accessed 15 May 2018.
[21] ibid.

Over the years they have trained more than 20,000 professionals and have over 5,000 members from more than 24 countries: the USA, Bermuda and Canada on the American continent, Austria, the Czech Republic, France, Germany, Italy, the Netherlands, Spain, Switzerland and the United Kingdom in Europe; Israel in the Near East; India in Asia; South Africa and Uganda in Africa; and Australia and New Zealand in Oceania.

In addition, thanks to their work they have obtained the approval of specific legislation in some North American States (such as California, Florida, North Carolina, Texas and Utah).

What about Spain? There is a national organisation,[22] several local associations and some collaborative professionals at least in Asturias,[23] the Basque Country,[24] Cantabria,[25] Castilla-La Mancha,[26] Cataluña, Galicia,[27] Madrid,[28] Navarra,[29] and Valencia, but no general and practical implementation. Some institutions offer specific training[30] and there are several dissemination campaigns, but the future is quite uncertain despite the obvious potential of this methodology.

In sum we can say:

1. Collaborative practice has not yet revolutionised the world of ADR or family law, but it does open up new horizons within the framework of negotiation and agreement, and has great potential, since it broadens the options available and offers original and creative solutions.
2. Collaborative practice shares the advantages of mediation over the judicial process and, in addition, it offers greater protection to the parties and personalised assistance, and allows a multidisciplinary approach to the problem and the adoption of creative and integrated solutions.
3. In a different vein, from the lawyer's perspective, it also has some advantages: it offers an original product with which they can attract new clients; a more satisfying and creative professional exercise; achieve more satisfactory results for clients; and more positive relationships with other professionals (Soleto Muñoz, 2017).

[22] La Asociación de Abogados Colaborativos de Familia: www.abogadoscolaborativosdefamilia.com/, accessed 15 May 2018.

[23] Asociación de Derecho Colaborativo del Principado de Asturias: www.derechocolaborativoasturias.com/, accessed 15 May 2018.

[24] Asociación de Derecho Colaborativo de Euskadi: www.derechocolaborativo.es/, accessed 15 May 2018.

[25] Asociación de Derecho Colaborativo de Cantabria: http://derechocolaborativo.eu/, accessed 15 May 2018.

[26] Asociación de Derecho Colaborativo de Castilla-La Mancha: www.facebook.com/adcclm/?ref=page_internal, accessed 15 May 2018.

[27] Asociación Gallega de Derecho Colaborativo: https://es-es.facebook.com/AGADECO/, accessed 15 May 2018.

[28] Asociación de Derecho Colaborativo de Madrid: http://adcmadrid.es/, accessed 15 May 2018.

[29] Fundación Navarra para la Resolución Alternativa de Conflictos: /www.fundacionnarac.org/index.php, accessed 15 May 2018.

[30] eg the Asociación de Derecho Colaborativo de Euskadi or the Universidad Carlos III de Madrid.

4. However, there are criticisms, mainly of the difficulty in selecting the cases; and the questionable disqualification clause of the professionals.
5. In any case, despite the fact that there are no official data, the IACP claims that agreement is reached in almost 90% of cases, based on the information provided by professional members, which seems to indicate its effectiveness.[31]
6. Agreements are not always reached. Occasionally, the process fails in a resounding way and personal relationships are inexorably destroyed. Or sometimes, the negotiations drag on for months, or stagnate, raising doubts about the viability of the method. Often there are difficult moments, disagreements, protestations, anger or tensions, and very difficult decisions, which involve renouncing potential rights in favour of another, always have to be taken. That said, it is worth trying, because another type of divorce is possible.

And finally, collaborative practice has recently arrived in Spain, where there is a national organisation, several local associations and some collaborative professionals, but not a general and practical implementation. Some institutions offer specific training and there are several dissemination campaigns, but the future is still uncertain despite the potential of this methodology.

V. CONCLUSIONS

We have described how family mediation began in Spain at the beginning of the twenty-first century following initiatives in the Basque Country and Catalonia. The first regional laws concerning mediation and the European Directive 2008/52/ CEE with incorporation into the 'national' Law 5/2012 on civil and commercial mediation, set out a clear legal framework for alternative dispute resolution in Spain. But the implementation of mediation has continued to be a challenge. Compared to other European countries, mediation in Spain is not widespread although its use is gradually increasing.

Mediation in Spain remains voluntary (Article 6.1 of Law 5/2012). The law allows the parties to apply for mediation and consequently to suspend civil proceedings, but there must be mutual agreement to do so. In some autonomous communities, the judges can ask the parties to attend an information session or even the first mediation session. However, the parties remain free to decide whether or not to proceed with mediation at any stage. Law 5/2012 obliges the courts to provide information to the parties about the possibilities of mediation.

The mediation process may or may not result in an agreement, which may be total or partial. If only partial agreement is reached, the court proceedings have to be continued to deal with those matters where agreement has been reached.

[31] International Academy of Collaborative Professionals (effectiveness): www.collaborativepractice.com/resources, accessed 15 May 2018.

Where there is an agreement which both parties have signed, in the majority of cases the agreements are complied with. In cases where the agreements are breached, the parties have to return to and continue with the court process and the judge takes into account the terms of the agreement when reaching a decision.

The issues which can be managed through mediation include: arrangements for the care of children (eg, sole or shared custody), child support payments, use of the family home and decisions relating to the health and education of the child. Other matters are excluded by law from any mediation process given their major importance. These include filiation, 'patria potestad' (parental responsibility), adoption, maintenance, child abuse and domestic and gender violence, though there is ongoing discussion about whether domestic violence should automatically preclude using mediation.

Every mediation service consists of an interdisciplinary team in which the mediators are lawyers, psychologists, social workers and educational workers. It is important to stress that family mediation is publicly financed by the regional governments in the majority of the autonomous regions and users of the service do not have to pay. There are also private family mediators but these are used considerably less than the public services. Obviously, users have to pay the total costs of private family mediation.

One of the strengths of mediation in the Basque Country is the training of the mediators. They are not lay advisers. Most of the mediators are already well qualified in fields including family law, psychology and social and restorative intervention practices.

As regards the relationship between mediators and lawyers,[32] it must be said that in Spain all legal advice remains the responsibility of the lawyer. The mediator is not allowed to offer such advice. Therefore, it is necessary to use a lawyer in the legal process of divorce and separation, fundamentally when there are court proceedings. In Spain, many mediators are also lawyers (especially in the Basque Country). Some teams of mediators include lawyers.

Many people remain unaware of the institution of mediation. Certainly, today there is a progressive increase in mediations in Catalonia and in the Basque Country, but this growth is far from making mediation a standard option for conflict resolution.

On 11 January 2019 the Spanish Council of Ministers (the equivalent of the British cabinet) approved an 'Anteproyecto de Ley' (Draft Bill) to promote mediation in Spain,[33] which should be debated in Parliament at some point in the future.

[32] As regards the roles of mediators and lawyers in the case of the UK: '(…) the two main grounds upon which the mediator's activities are said to be different from those of the lawyers are that mediators provide information (which suggests a neutral act), not advice, and that mediators primarily deal with resolving current conflicts, whereas lawyers are not restricted to this but can offer advice and support in planning for the future (…)': Maclean and Eekelaar (2016) 125–26.

[33] The Draft Bill can be seen at: www.mjusticia.gob.es/cs/Satellite/Portal/1292429062854.

In addition to mediation, there are other ADR processes in Spain although these tend to be very new and not widely used. Specifically, there is a conviction that mediation is not the right tool for all kinds of conflicts. For this reason, other forms of dispute resolution have been initiated, for example, the promotion of parenting coordinators. Moreover, collaborative law is emerging as a modality of ADR.

The figure of the parenting coordinator has a strong presence in Catalonia but is only just emerging in other communities such as Andalusia and Aragon. Collaborative law is currently being assessed by various bar associations and encouraged by legal organisations throughout Spain, but it is rarely used in practice.

However, the development of digital techniques for processing cases coming to court, or seeking resolution of conflict online or even mediation on line has not yet occurred in Spain, although the introduction of ODR is currently being considered in Catalonia. It is highly likely that other regions will follow this initiative in the future.

REFERENCES

Álzate, R and Merino, C (2010) 'Principios éticos y Código de conducta para personas y entidades mediadoras', *Doxa. Cuadernos de Filosofía del Derecho* 33, 659–70.

García-Herrera, A (2016) 'Reestructuración de la familia tras la separación parental: mediación intrajudicial, mediación en el punto de encuentro familiar y coordinación de parentalidad', *InDret* 2.

Lauroba, E (2011) 'L'aposta del legislador català: de la mediació familiar a la mediació en l'àmbit del dret privat' in E Lauroba, I Barral and I Viola, *Materials jurídics del Llibre Blan de la Mediació a Catalunya, Generalitat de Catalunya* (Centre d'Estudis Jurídics i Formació Especialitzada) 21–31.

Lauroba, E (2018) 'Instrumentos para una gestión constructiva de los conflictos familiares: mediación, derecho colaborativo, arbitraje ¿y…?', *InDret* 4: www.indret.com/pdf/1417.pdf.

Loredo, CM (2011) 'El método colaborativo: nuevos horizontes en el marco de la autocomposición' in R Castillejo Manzanares, *Violencia de género, Justicia restaurativa y mediación* (Madrid: La Ley) 529–65.

Maclean, M and Eekelaar, J (2016) *Lawyers and Mediators. The Brave New World of Services for Separating Families* (Oxford, Hart Publishing).

Merino, C (2010) 'Gestión de conflictos familiares desde un Servicio Público de Mediación Familiar 1996–2009' en *Mediación, Arbitraje y resolución extrajudicial de Conflictos en el siglo XXI* (Madrid: Ed. Reus).

Merino, C (2013) *La mediación en situaciones asimétricas: procesos de gestión de conflictos con episodios de violencia, drogodependencias, enfermedad mental y desequilibrio de poder* (Colección de Mediación y Resolución de Conflictos, Editorial Reus).

Merino, C and Moreno, R (2018) 'Family Mediation in the Basque Country: Strengths and Risks' in *Oñati Socio-Legal Series* 8(7): http://opo.iisj.net/index.php/osls/issue/view/79.

Ortuño, Pascual (2018), *Justicia sin jueces. Métodos alternativos a la justicia tradicional* (Barcelona, Ariel).

Picontó Novales, T (2019) 'Violencia de género y mediación' in JL Argudo (dir), MA Júlvez, and FA González Campo (coords), *Mediación y tutela judicial efectiva. La justicia del siglo XXI* (Madrid, Editorial Reus) 251–62.

Soleto Muñoz, H (2017) *El abogado colaborativo* (Madrid, Tecnos).

Tesler, PH and Thompson, P (2006) *Collaborative divorce* (New York, Harper Collins Publishers).

Viola, I (dir), Barral, I, Lauroba, E (coords) (2018) *Comentarios a la Ley catalana 15/2009, de 22 de julio, de mediación en el ámbito del Derecho privado y concordantes* (Madrid, Marcial Pons).

VVAA (2018). Family Mediation Service, Department of Social Policies, Basque Governement: www.euskadi.eus/web01-a2famil/es/contenidos/informacion/.

WBMC (2011) Casanovas, Pompeu; Jaume Magre y Mª Elena Lauroba (Dtrs), *Libro Blanco de la Mediación en Cataluña (White Book on Mediation in Catalonian,* WBMC) (Barcelona: Generalitat de Catalunya/Departament de Justícia).

Webb, S (2008) 'Collaborative Law: A Practitioner's Perspective on Its History and Current Practice', *Journal of the American Academy of Matrimonial Lawyers* 21, 155–70.

Part B

The Development of Digital Family Justice

7

Family Justice in France: Two Dimensions of Digitisation

BENOIT BASTARD

I. INTRODUCTION

TALKING ABOUT THE 'digitisation of justice' can give the impression of a uniform phenomenon, a wave that would carry everything in its path like a tsunami. However, digital change is not homogeneous, but protean and chaotic. The modalities it uses are multiple and their effects are to be sought in different directions. Moreover, the development of digital technology, even if it appears to be entirely new, is not independent of other transformations in society. It cannot therefore be studied in isolation as if it had effects of its own. On the contrary, it should be linked to other ongoing developments and the links with them should be sought: what is the purpose of digital technology? Who does it serve? What is it used for?

Considering the effects of digitisation in the field of family justice alone, and more specifically with regard to the treatment of family breakdown, two main dimensions can be identified that make it possible to understand the changes underway in France: digitisation as a new field of application for the management of court resources management (*managérialisation*) and as a resource in the transformation of case allocation (the development of private ordering or *privatisation* in French). Each of these two dimensions will be presented and discussed, using material collected during exploratory surveys of what has been called 'dematerialisation' (the disappearance of hard paper copy) in courts and in the work of lawyers

II. DIGITISATION AND THE MANAGEMENT OF FAMILY COURTS

A. Civil Justice Under Pressure

The first dimension of the development of digital technology touches the very heart of the judicial institution, the treatment of cases – in civil as well as criminal matters (Ackermann and Bastard, 1993, 1996; Vauchez and Willemez, 2007; Vigour, 2018).

This development originated several decades ago, when family cases represented more than half of all civil cases and family judges were confronted with a tidal wave, while they have only limited resources – overworked exhausted staff with no possibility of increasing their numbers. Family matters, particularly cases of marital breakdown (divorce, separation of unmarried parents, post-divorce matters), represented nearly 300,000 cases per year. The term 'mass litigation' has rightly been used to describe a situation that continued until recently (1 January 2017) due to the change that will be described below, with the introduction of a divorce without the judge.

In this situation, family judges were in charge of handling these cases and could see no other way than to receive and deal with them all. Unlike the criminal sector, in which there is the possibility of taking 'no further action', civil courts are not in control of their agenda. The idea of encouraging any form of diversion from the courts seemed an insult to their role and capacity. The plan to deal with part of the litigation without judges was thought to be scandalous (see Bastard, 2000).

Like prosecutors and criminal judges, who were looking for answers to deal with the increase in their caseload, the magistrates in civil courts did not stop thinking, innovating, and developing new procedural or practical means to answer what they considered to be a challenge. It has been constantly difficult for them, since the mid-1970s, not to let themselves be overwhelmed, to keep services 'afloat', and not to let delays build up, particularly in order to give hearing dates to new cases regarding couples with children in difficulty or in acute conflict (Bastard et al, 2015).

These solutions included legal provisions: encouraging divorce by mutual consent; reducing the number of hearings required for divorce by mutual consent; reducing the length of the time required before divorce following a long-term separation, etc. All these provisions were included in the previous reform, which came into force in January 2005. This reform also contained practical measures which had been designed to control the parties and their lawyers using various terms: '*la mise en état des affaires*' is based on agendas, 'procedural contracts' which the magistrates seek to reinforce but which can hardly achieve their goal – when confronted with the imponderables of the trajectories of couples, the violence of conflicts or the avatars of the professional practice of lawyers. Technical solutions have also been sought: the development of information technology, use of electronic files, and the development of pre-written decision templates for a whole range of situations.

Finally, the family judges have taken a great deal upon themselves – without necessarily being encouraged to do so by the justice system, but rather due to a sense of duty. They became speed champions (at the hearings, in the way they treat lawyers, in the drafting of judgments, etc). They increased their work load to decide on 80 cases per month, which is much more than what is expected of a judge in civil matters. And they also mobilised many of the people who worked with them, including the clerks, who also helped to cope with the mass of cases, by putting in place, with the magistrates, effective solutions.

This way of operating family justice services is usually described as the '*managérialisation*' of justice, a trend that emerged long before the advent of digital justice and has become more pronounced in recent decades.

B. The Transition to Digital, a New Stage

When new digital developments have become more widely known, magistrates have taken them up and have seen how they could be used in civil justice. Without it being necessary to tell the whole story, it can be said that the digital initiative came firstly from the courts (Fabri, 2001; Velicogna, 2012; Velicogna, Errera and Derlange, 2011). They developed the first applications and sought to involve the bar associations. As a matter of fact, as far as France is concerned, the courts have imposed online working on the lawyers. In 2005, decisions were taken to create and link two VPN,[1] one for courts RPVJ (*Réseau privé virtuel des juridictions*) and one for the bar associations, RPVA (*Réseau privé virtuel des avocats*). The Ministry of Justice and the CNB (*Conseil national des barreaux*) were associated and desired very much to succeed in this enterprise (Ghera and Calvet, 2011). This was also the effect of certain European directives. The implementation encountered huge difficulties, but digital applications gradually covered the whole of civil justice. In practice, the bar associations moved forward at different speeds. Until recently, major difficulties resulted from the divisions between Paris and all other bar associations, with several digital systems coexisting among lawyers: different providers, different competing access systems. Recently, however, digital connection between bar associations and courts has become not only optional but mandatory. For instance, action in any appeal court requires exclusively electronic access at a first stage. This change has coincided with the removal of the *avoués (solicitors)* from the appellate courts, in January 2012.

Gradually, all exchanges of documents before civil courts (*tribunal de grande instance*) are made through both VPNs. In the same courts, many of the hearings in adversarial proceedings (*audiences de mise en état*) are also digitised. However, the completion of the digitisation of civil proceedings remains uncertain. In particular, the ultimate application in the jurisdictions, PORTALIS, which will include all of the functionalities currently performed by previous programmes, has not yet been implemented. This has been constantly delayed for reasons mainly of cost. The Ministry of Justice has announced their intention very recently to relaunch this project. (*Ministère de la Justice*, 2018).

[1] Virtual Private Network.

C. New Features, Old Questions

The entry into digital justice constitutes an extension and a new stage of managerialisation. The resulting 'progress' and the questions raised by this new evolution are in line with the previous stages of the evolution towards this 'new' justice ('21st century justice' to use the title of a recent Act[2]).

Some questions relate to the very functioning of these digital devices. All kinds of difficulties have affected their implementation – and they are not yet solved. The costs are considerable – making updates difficult for an institution as poor as justice and delaying new developments. There are also data protection issues, failure issues, and so on. At the Paris Court of Appeal, for example, all services are blocked and hundreds of employees find themselves without activity when an IT breakdown occurs. Also, it is still unclear how to ensure the cooperation of lawyers: there is resistance, and there are questions of professional jurisdictions, transfer costs, and so on.

Even if one thinks that this is only a 'price to pay' for an inevitable and promising change, there are still other questions arising which more generally address the effects of managerialisation. Digitisation can be seen as a facilitator of communication between the bar and the courts. It is supposed to simplify and speed up the proceedings. However, little or nothing is known about its less visible effects. What impact does switching to digital have on the duration of a case, on the procedure, on the deadlines, or on the way to implement them? Is it possible to achieve better compliance with deadlines when they are set 'automatically'? Who does it benefit? Does digital technology lead to trial times becoming less flexible? What effect does digitisation have on the informal dimension of court activities? Lawyers now seldom go to court – only for major hearings. It greatly reduces the opportunity for informal contacts with judges and clerks. Digitisation is like a further step in the evolution marked by the reduction of judicial debate – a development that can be observed in both civil and criminal cases.

III. DIGITISATION AND PRIVATE ORDERING

A. An Old Trend

The second dimension to consider in understanding the effects of digitisation in the field of family justice is already long established. It dates back to the 1970s, when the increase in the number of divorces led to a rethinking of access to justice in order to satisfy couples who wished to divorce in a non-adversarial way. In 1975, the introduction of mutual consent in family law marked a first

[2] Loi de modernisation de la justice du XXIème siècle, n° 2016-1547 du 18 novembre 2016.

legal step in this evolution, which was already underway in the courts. Indeed, family judges have gradually been converted to the idea that the best divorce is the one where the terms are determined by the parties themselves. They showed it in their hearings, congratulating couples who were able to agree on how to take care of their children and share their property, while encouraging those who asked them to resolve their conflict to progress on their own (Bastard, 2002; Le Collectif Onze, 2013).

The legislator has gradually confirmed the priority given to the search for amicable solutions. The reforms of parental authority bear witness to this: the 'invention' of joint parental authority, first as an option for parents who wanted it, then as the default solution in all divorces; alternating residence and finally, co-parenting. The 'duty to agree' has become the key expression in family law, as well as the idea that it is the parties themselves who are responsible for finding solutions to the problems posed by family breakdown and reorganisation. In this way of dealing with marital breakdown, judges keep as far back as possible. They endorse decisions made by the spouses and intervene only in cases of persistent disagreement – a 'system' that has worked for several decades and can be said to represent a first version of the privatisation of divorce – in the precise sense that the judge, in the background, refers the decisions to be made to the parties themselves (Cardia-Vonèche and Bastard, 1986).

Another particularly striking sign of the strength of the trend towards *privatisation* is the development of family mediation. As an alternative to the judicial process, mediation is another vehicle for finding solutions that belong to the spouses themselves. In France, mediation was introduced at the end of the 1980s, coming from Québec. It was gradually recognised and institutionalised. French mediators have consistently presented themselves as powerless innovators, serving the empowerment of couples. Behind this screen, however, they advocated for the adoption of a single formula, co-parenting, hoping to become in turn newly accredited stakeholders and permanently lobbying public authorities to obtain it. Secretly, they may have dreamed of one day taking the judges' place. Their perseverance was rewarded, since family mediation was given special recognition under their pressure. Not only was it introduced into the law, so that it became one of the tools available to the judge,[3] but it was also the subject of provisions that led to the creation of a profession, endowed with all the necessary attributes – a diploma, certification and protection.

Everything seemed to be converging, at the very beginning of the twenty-first century: the withdrawal of judges, reform of the law in favour of co-parenting, the development of mediation. However, at this stage, the idea of a real transfer of responsibility for private decisions to the couples themselves faced resistance which appeared on different occasions when attempts were made to simplify the divorce process. These attempts, led by Ministers of Justice who liked the

[3] French Civil code, Art 373-2-10, Loi n° 2002-305 du 4 Mars 2002 relative à l'autorité parentale.

idea of being able to reduce the burden of the courts and the associated costs, have met with a favourable response from the public, ready to acknowledge that couples who agree on the terms of their divorce can do so without recourse to a judge. But they also encountered apparently irreducible opposition, particularly from lawyers and magistrates. The former feared that a door would be opened that could lead to the end of their monopoly of representation in civil matters. The latter liked to think that, even in the case of consensual divorce, they exercised some control over the situations submitted to them, making it possible to prevent abuses and the adoption of decisions that could be harmful to women and children.

Despite this opposition, the trend towards privatisation continued and prevailed. Paradoxically, this progress did not benefit the mediators but rather the lawyers, who had absolutely rejected the idea of a divorce without a judge in the previous period – and perhaps also, benefitted from the digitisation of family justice.

B. A Step Forward: Divorce Without a Judge

The law that came into force in 2017 introduced divorce without a judge. The government carried out this major reform in quite a brutal way, through an amendment which was adopted without any debate.[4] This change was not prepared for by any consultation with legal professionals. Discussions took place only after the event, on the modalities of its implementation (the professionals arguing that the lack of preparation for the reform had left whole parts of its application in a complete blur). The law transformed the conditions of access to a divorce agreement, with the explicit aim of alleviating the burden of the courts, while giving divorcees responsibility for their separation. Once the spouses agree, the divorce is settled without any intervention by the judge or the court. Each party should be assisted by a lawyer. This provision served as a guarantee to the profession so that it would not oppose this reform that it had previously constantly fought against. It means that the procedure, instead of being simplified, is made more complex and more expensive (the previous divorce by mutual consent could be presented to the judge by a single lawyer on behalf of both spouses). The measures agreed by the parties must include all the effects of divorce and the settlement of the matrimonial property. Children should be informed of the project of their parents; they have to sign a document in order to confirm it and can ask for some assistance – if they do, a judge will review the decisions taken. The couple and both lawyers sign the agreement. It is then presented to a notary who, without having the function of checking its validity, registers it.

[4] Loi 2016-1547 de modernisation de la justice du XXIe siècle du18 novembre 2016 (Arts 44 à 47 et 50). Décret 2016-1507 du 28 décembre 2016 relatif au divorce.

The implementation of this reform has been underway for two years and the predicted disaster has not occurred. The survey that we carried out amongst lawyers suggests that no major problems have disrupted the implementation of this new form of divorce treatment. The overall number of separations has remained unchanged – with an increase in divorces by mutual consent, according to family lawyers. Litigants are satisfied with their access to this procedure. This result does not seem surprising, since it is true that couples, before the reform, considered such a step desirable. Their satisfaction, according to the lawyers, comes precisely from the absence of the judge, which removes formality from the decision-making process. Also, divorcing couples are especially concerned that things should move as quickly as possible, which can, at least in part, be ensured by the new process – for instance they do not have to wait months for a hearing date.

As for lawyers, they are obviously satisfied with the fact that this reform, which was decided without them, is in fact made for them – it gives them a predominant place, which they may not have expected, in the treatment of marital breakdown. Beyond the mechanical increase in the number of clients, they see the attribution of this new role to them as a form of recognition of their competence and responsibility. 'It's legitimate, it's good that we do it,' said one of the lawyers interviewed during the survey.

Specialised lawyers say they continue to work in exactly the same way as before the reform, especially when it comes to finalising the agreements between the parties. For them, exercising their responsibility in this new framework does not change the responsibility they already assumed in the past. When asked, they say they do not feel the change, as if they do not miss the judge. However, we can observe certain signs of change that has occurred with regard to this question of professional responsibility: on the one hand some lawyers explain that the judge is no longer there to serve as a 'scarecrow' with clients who have unreasonable demands (Sarat and Felstiner, 1975); see also research. On the other hand, all indicate that the work required by each divorce agreement has increased considerably for lawyers as a result of the reform. Agreements between divorcing parties did not need much justification before the reform as they were presented to and validated by the courts. Today, lawyers have become accustomed to detailing the conditions under which divorce is granted and its terms. It is up to them to ensure the validity of consent in a face-to-face meeting with both parties; and they are careful to trace the reasons given by the parties to justify the decisions they wish to make, especially when they deviate from what might seem a normal solution. This is how they maintain their credibility and protect themselves from any possible attack on their professional liability.

Regardless of the additional work and responsibility, lawyers more generally minimise the change that has occurred in the way consensual breakdowns are now treated. They seem not to be affected or worried by the idea that they are thus participating in a more general movement that places the decision outside the public orbit of the court and given an exclusively private dimension.

We will mention here the place of notaries as a reminder. After a period of familiarisation with the reform, they have become accustomed to it and raise no difficulties with lawyers who seek their assistance. However, they do not appreciate the new way their services are used: their role is limited to checking the presence of documents; moreover they consider the fixed rate for their registration ridiculously low, at 50 euros. They prefer to deal with situations in which divorcees are their regular clients: it is then possible for them not only to register the divorce, but also to liquidate the matrimonial property regime, a formality which is mandatory before an agreement can be concluded in this new type of divorce,

Before coming to the effects of digital technology in relation to this new form of divorce, it is necessary to give some further details on the implementation of the law. With regard to children, the rule that seemed to allow a child wishing to appear before the judge to somehow intervene in the choice of divorce procedure by his or her parents seems to have been hardly ever used, so fears in this respect were unfounded.

However, there are situations in which the parties, even though they agree on all aspects of their separation, organise themselves to escape divorce without a judge. Without going into detail, these are cases in which couples want to avoid settling their matrimonial property regime in order to avoid a special tax, representing an amount of 2.5% of the total amount of shared property. Using a contested divorce, even if it is a fiction, would make it possible to postpone this settlement and to defer, possibly indefinitely, the payment of this tax.

Finally, there are real difficulties associated with divorce without a judge, probably due to the lack of preparation of the reform, and in particular the fact that it is not open to couples in which at least one of the spouses is not of French nationality, even if they agree on all aspects of the divorce. Such couples are required to go through a contested divorce, sanctioned by a judge.

C. Step 1: Online Divorce

Private ordering is easily combined with digital devices. Since separations are private matters, and are managed between the parties, stakeholders may be tempted to prepare and organise decisions using digital tools.

Even though divorce and the handling of family matters remained anchored in the family courts, lawyers began to develop their online activity towards divorce candidates in a more intensive way: digital platforms were created on the Internet, offering low-cost divorce formulas (for less than 1,000 euros for a divorce by mutual consent). People had to provide the necessary elements for the constitution of their divorce file themselves; the legal document including their agreement was addressed to them in return and could be brought on their behalf by a lawyer before the competent court.

This new offer reflected the more general transformation in the way lawyers now approach their clients. It developed, thanks to the Internet, even when lawyers were forbidden to advertise. Since then, this has been allowed under certain conditions. Firms have created websites and offer videos, interviews of partners and tutorials, in order to attract clients. This has developed very strongly in certain specific sectors. In the field of family justice, we have witnessed the development of real 'brands' with some lawyers promising a quick and inexpensive divorce.

The development of these new forms of work did have an effect on the very organisation of the legal profession. Without going back too far, until recently the bar was a profession of 'solo practitioners' attached to a local jurisdiction – associations of lawyers have only existed since the 1950s. Each lawyer was attached to only one of the 160 bar associations in France, and to one specified judicial area. Pleading before another court, even in the area of the same appeal court, required asking for the services of a colleague registered with that particular bar (this is called '*postulation*' and the local lawyer is called '*un avocat postulant*'). However, the platforms that have developed in recent years to provide 'low-cost' procedures, specifically for consensual divorce, respect but circumvent the rules relating to postulation. Under the same 'brand' that bears the name of a founding lawyer – the most well know is Maître Omer – it is now possible to find a network of lawyers that covers the entire territory. In step 1, before 2017, the couple provided the data, the firm formatted it and suggested a local lawyer who would meet the couple, check their identity and agreement, then take their application to the appropriate court and attend the hearing (in this case, only one hearing was required). The fees were shared. If a more individualised service was required, the firm could not act and directed the clients to a traditional service. (The local lawyer had a chance to play a role in this kind of case.)

It is difficult to know how extensively these forms of work are used. There are no studies on the subject. We know that they have been submitted to ethical committees in local bars and not rejected. Also, by 'testing' several of these platforms, we saw that they took advantage of digital functionalities. Once the data has been filled in, the customer who does not follow up will be repeatedly asked for the necessary information.

These low-cost formulas are in line with the European and 'Macronian' trend towards the liberalisation of legal services. It is reflected in the change of the rules on advertising or *postulation*.[5] At a time when the digitisation of procedures is spreading and when the lawyer, from home, can initiate proceedings before any jurisdiction, it seems difficult to maintain rules that confine and limit their practice.

This type of development, already under way before the reform that came into force in 2017, can be developed today.

[5] In France, there are 36 courts of appeal, each of them having a very diverse set of jurisdictions. Since 2015, lawyers can plead before all jurisdictions in the court of appeal where they are registered without having to use the services of a local lawyer, which was not previously the case. They still need a *postulant*, when they act in the territory of another court of appeal.

D. Step 2: Towards the Uberisation of Family Justice?

As soon as the divorce no longer involves bringing a petition before a court, lawyers are 'free ranging'; they are no longer required to intervene in the space of a given bar association or court of appeal. In effect, they can work with clients living throughout France to gather their wishes and develop their agreements in interaction with a colleague, who may or may not also be located near these clients. The only remaining requirement, as far as can be ascertained, is to organise an appointment involving all the stakeholders, both lawyers and the couple.

The Omer firm, which was already organised to carry out this type of operation before the reform, sought to respond to the new configuration that emerged. The solution proposed, in order to remain in touch with the various areas, consisted, for the Parisian lawyer, in proposing to his local 'correspondents', with whom he had associated in the previous period, to continue to deal with divorces with him according to a new protocol. Once a couple has contacted the firm's website and completed the necessary elements for drafting an agreement, the Parisian lawyer offers to assist one of the couple's members and offers to the other assistance from the local correspondent close to his or her home. The meeting to sign this agreement takes place at the correspondent's office: the couple is present with the local lawyer, while the Parisian lawyer intervenes by videoconference. Omer has offered to equip their correspondents' office with the necessary material, arguing that they could then operate as corresponding lawyers for a great number of divorces, across large areas. It is difficult to know whether this way of working has actually been implemented and whether it has been validated from the point of view of lawyers' professional ethics.

In any case, we can see that new forms of legal work are developing, based on communication technologies, but this is a great cause for concern among bar associations and lawyers who have continued to work in traditional ways. In the family justice area these developments are still limited, and have not been contested to any degree even if they are regarded with suspicion by the majority of lawyers. In other fields of legal practice, national bar associations tried and fought against some of the new platforms offering legal services, but without much success.

Can we speak of an uberisation of legal services? Is the service offered efficient? Is it the same as that usually expected by divorce applicants? What happens as soon as we no longer deal with the simplest divorce? What effect does the development of this type of service have for litigants, for the image they have of justice and the legal professions? May we assume that they have no fear in this regard and that they are satisfied if it is cheaper and if it leads to quick decisions?

IV. CONCLUSION

In this chapter, two important dimensions of social change have been discussed that extend into the functioning of the justice system, and in particular into the functioning of family justice.

On the one hand, the idea of the efficiency of the public service, more generally linked to the dissemination of management requirements, is being extended in order to speed up the functioning of civil courts and to respond in the most cost-effective way to the needs of litigants. The result is a constant process of renewal of procedures that uses digital tools as soon as they become accessible and demonstrates their efficiency. For France, all communications between lawyers and courts are thus in the process of being digitised. While this undoubtedly facilitates the exchange of documents, it remains extremely difficult to know to what extent this change has an impact on court proceedings and even whether they will continue at all. Can the change in the medium not have consequences either on the timing of the trials or even on the content of the decisions, with the drastic reduction in the oral part of the procedure?

The second trend, the spread of private ordering in the family field, is of even greater importance, since it has led to the courts being deprived of a whole section of the cases they were dealing with and which the judges claimed to control. This shift is of great benefit to lawyers, whose role is confirmed. Paradoxically, this has happened at the expense of mediators, whose profession, although recognised as the main promoter of private ordering, is not given a clear role in the new divorce configuration. While there is little dispute about the implementation of the reform, analysis remains as yet incomplete from the point of view of the resulting consequences for the balance of family justice. France is not the first country in which divorce happens without judicial intervention – and it is not a bad thing that this is so. But this is a particularly important breach in what until now seemed to be social control over family functioning. The fact that some lawyers take the opportunity to develop online forms of divorce raises all kinds of questions about how family breakdown processes will now be managed.

In addition, these changes are accompanied by transformations that deeply affect the legal profession, moving it away from the courts, giving it a new autonomy in the management of private affairs and allowing some of its members to develop low-cost applications. This could ultimately affect it profoundly as a profession.

REFERENCES

Ackermann, W and Bastard, B (1993) *Innovation et gestion dans l'institution judiciaire* (Paris, Libraire générale de droit et de jurisprudence, Coll. Droit et société).

Ackermann, W and Bastard, B (1996) 'La modernisation de l'institution judiciaire: la surprenante diffusion des tableaux de bord' in C Grémion and R Fraisse (eds) *Le service public en recherche. Quelle modernisation?* (Paris, La Documentation française) 187–201.

Bastard, B (2000) 'Administrative Divorce in France: A Controversy over a Reform that Never Reached the Statute Book' in J Eekelaar and M Maclean (eds) *Making Law for Families* (Oxford, Hart Publishing) 51–71.

Bastard, B (2002) *Les démarieurs. Enquête sur les nouvelles pratiques du divorce* (Paris, La Découverte).

Bastard, B and Mouhanna, C (2007) *Une justice dans l'urgence. Le traitement en temps réel des affaires pénales* (Paris, PUF).

Bastard, B, Delvaux, D, Mouhanna, C and Schoenaers, F (2015) 'Controlling Time? Speeding Up Divorce Proceedings in France and Belgium' in M Maclean, J Eekelaar and B Bastard (eds) *Delivering Family Justice in the 21st Century* (Oxford, Hart Publishing/Bloomsbury) 281–303.

Bastard, B, avec la collaboration de Boigeol, A, Benech-Le Roux, P, Jamet, L and Printz, P (2016) *Ethique et TIC. A quoi sert l'Ordre des avocats?* (Cachan, ISP).

Cardia-Vonèche, L and Bastard, B (1986) 'Les silences du juge ou la privatisation du divorce. Une analyse empirique des décisions judiciaires de première instance', *Droit et Société* 4, 497–506.

Collectif Onze, Le (2013) *Au tribunal des couples: enquêtes sur des affaires familiales* (Paris, Odile Jacob).

Fabri, M (2001) 'State of the art, critical issues, and trends of ICT in European Judicial Systems' in M Fabri and F Contini (eds), *Justice and Technology in Europe: How ICT is Changing the Judicial Business?* (The Hague, Kluwer Law International) 1–18.

Ghera, T, and Calvet, F (2011) *Dématérialisation des procédures judiciaires en France et en Europe: l'équilibre des professions à l'épreuve de l'évolution culturelle.* IEPJ: www.congreso.es/docu/docum/ddocum/dosieres/sleg/legislatura_10/spl_81/pdfs/36.pdf.

Ministère de la justice (2018) *Transformation numérique* (Référents: Jean-François Beynet, Didier Casas) publié le 5 janvier 2018: www.justice.gouv.fr/publication/chantiers_justice/Chantiers_justice_Livret_01.pdf.

Sarat, A and Felstiner, WLF (1975) *Divorce Lawyers and their Clients. Power and Meaning in the Legal Process* (Oxford, Oxford University Press).

Vauchez, A and Willemez, L (2007) *La justice face à ses réformateurs* (Paris, PUF).

Velicogna, M (2011) 'Electronic Access to Justice: From Theory to Practice and Back' *Droit et cultures* [En ligne] 61 | 2011-1, mis en ligne le 18 octobre 2011, consulté le 16 décembre 2012: http://droitcultures.revues.org/2447.

Velicogna, M, Errera, A et Derlange, S (2011) 'E-justice in France: the e-Barreau experience', *Utrecht Law review* 7(1) (January): www.utrechtlawreview.org.

Vigour, C (2018) *Réformes de la justice en Europe. Entre politique et gestion* (Louvain-La-Neuve, De Boeck).

8

From ADR to ODR in Scots Family Justice: No Clear Direction of Travel

JANE MAIR

I. INTRODUCTION

'FROM ADR TO ODR' is a phrase that suggests progress, a strong sense of building momentum and a clear direction of forward travel. This use within the phrase of acronyms signals a level of settled familiarity with the underlying concepts of both alternative and online dispute resolution. In its conciseness, there is a definite sense of speed. When the title for the workshop, which gave rise to this book, was first discussed, the phrase seemed apt. In our workshop papers, the metaphor most often used was that of a train, already speeding at a fair pace down a pre-laid track. Now in retrospect, in Scotland at least, there is little evidence of a fixed direction of travel or of significant distance covered. In Scots family law and family justice, the movement towards Alternative Dispute Resolution has itself been somewhat halting and to date there is no clear line of progression from Alternative to Online.

What is becoming increasingly clear in Scotland is a new public narrative of civil justice, including family justice, in which both ADR and ODR, or more broadly 'digitisation', are situated. Emerging from reviews and reports by, for example, the Scottish Legal Aid Board (Scottish Government, 2014a), the Scottish Civil Justice Council (2014), the Scottish Courts and Tribunals Service (SCTS), the Justice Committee of the Scottish Parliament (Justice Committee, 2018) and the Scottish Government (2017), the language is of modernisation and transformation. There is a drive towards progress, and the delivery of a modern system of justice, which will require both the alternative and the digital. In the specific context of family justice, detail is as yet limited but, of growing concern in the vision of where we are going, is a lack of engagement with where we are now. What is it about the current system of family dispute resolution that requires modernisation and transformation, and in the drive for progressive change do we risk overlooking what works?

Of particular note is the extent to which the emerging strategy for modern civil justice in Scotland posits litigation as the default position. ADR is presented as a necessary diversion from court, and digitisation to date has been concentrated predominantly on modernisation of judicial processes and court systems. What is missing from this narrative is the current Scottish reality of resolution of family issues, which for many is already well established as being neither court-based nor in many instances a matter of dispute. Access to the courts is of course an essential element of access to justice but it is only part of the story.[1] This chapter will trace the construction of ADR and ODR within an emerging Scottish story of civil justice, highlight the extent to which a litigation-focused narrative ignores already well established out-of-court and non-dispute based practice[2] and, in so doing, promotes a misplaced and misleading, vision of the range of needs and possibilities for Scottish families. While the government's aspiration to create an inclusive system, open to all, is undoubtedly welcome, a fixed focus on litigation and a persistently dichotomous framing of debate about the mainstream and the alternative, risks Scotland becoming stuck in somewhat circular and cyclical motion rather than improving what already works reasonably well and making measurable progress[3] towards a vision of modern justice.

II. THE SCOTTISH LANDSCAPE

Scotland has its own system of substantive family law, quite distinct in many ways from that of its nearest neighbour, England and Wales, and it also has a markedly different civil justice landscape. Until recently, there have been few concentrated efforts to shape the practical delivery of family justice, other than through the development of substantive family law reform. In particular there has been no sustained policy agenda in Scotland to compare with that which has recently dominated in England and Wales where, 'from 2001 onwards, it has been explicit government policy to reduce the proportion of disputes resolved by resort to the civil courts.' (Genn, 2010: 197–8).[4] Part of the explanation may be that over-reliance on the courts in family matters has not been identified as a pressing concern in Scotland. The latest available civil court statistics show that 73,640 civil cases were initiated in the Scottish courts in 2016–17, a 5% reduction on the previous year and continuing

[1] A point hinted at by one of the witnesses to the Justice Committee of the Scottish Parliament in their recent review of ADR but sadly left unexplored: Liam Kerr, 'Is there a danger that we talk about access to justice when what we really mean is access to the courts.' Justice Committee Meeting 2018, Session 5, Official Report 2 February 2018, col 29.

[2] Drawing on two empirical studies of financial provision on divorce in Scotland, the first concentrating on negotiated agreements and the second on litigated outcomes: Mair, Wasoff and Mackay (2013) and Mair, Mordaunt and Wasoff (2016).

[3] To date there has been nothing comparable in Scotland to the excellent recommendations for evaluation of reform published by The Legal Education Foundation: see Byrom (2019).

[4] For an overview of the sustained policy attempts to increase the use of mediation in England and Wales see Hunter (2017).

the clear downward trend of a 44% fall since 2008 (Scottish Government, 2018a: 5). Of all civil cases, 13,250 (18%) were family actions. While family cases saw a small increase of 3% from the previous year, there is an overall downward trend there too, with an 11% reduction since 2008 (ibid).

The decision to reduce the cost of legal aid has been a key driver of change in family justice in England and Wales.[5] The contemporary context in Scotland, however, is different to the 'brave new world' south of the border,[6] in that civil legal aid remains available for divorce and related matters. In a recent independent review of legal aid (Evans, 2018) and in the Scottish Government's response to that review (Scottish Government, 2018b), there is continuing commitment to legal aid as 'an important public service' (Scottish Government, 2012: 32). Legal aid for civil matters is currently available in two forms: Advice and Assistance, covering for example initial advice, letter writing and negotiation, and Civil Legal Aid, for court-based work. It is estimated that approximately '70% of the Scottish population is eligible on the basis of their income for civil legal aid to fund at least part of their legal actions' (Evans, 2018: 19) and this availability of some level of legal advice and assistance to many families is likely to be another reason behind the lower sense of urgency about change in family justice in Scotland than in England and Wales. Lawyers in Scotland remain reasonably accessible and therefore the driver of necessity away from them is relatively weak.[7]

III. CIVIL JUSTICE IN SCOTLAND

A. Vision and Strategy

Against that background, family dispute resolution in Scotland has been left to develop largely in the hands of family law practitioners. Any movement towards alternative, digital or other particular forms of dispute resolution has been bottom-up[8] and, until quite recently, the idea of shaping the delivery of

[5] Resulting in the reforms introduced by Part 2 of the Legal Aid, Sentencing and Punishment of Offenders Act 2012 (LASPO). These cuts in legal aid and their consequences for families and family law have been analysed extensively in academic literature: see, eg Wong and Cain (2019).

[6] Which is described and analysed in detail in Maclean and Eekelaar (2016).

[7] This is by no means intended to underplay the difficulties around legal aid funding or the fact that many law firms do not undertake legal aid work. In recent research with family law solicitors, many of those interviewed explained that they did not undertake legal aid work or that they did so only exceptionally: Mair, Mordaunt and Wasoff, 'A note on legal aid' (2016) 42.

[8] For example, through associations such as CALM, Comprehensive Accredited Lawyer Mediators: www.calmscotland.co.uk; the Family Law Arbitration Group Scotland (FLAGS): www.flagsarb.com; Consensus Collaboration Scotland: www.consensus-scotland.com. Many solicitors not only advertise their dispute resolution services online but are also increasingly providing some guidance and resources on their websites and there are examples of predominantly online services such as Scottish Divorce Online: www.scottishdivorceonline.co.uk.

'family justice', as distinct from reforming family law, has received relatively little top-down attention.[9] The Scottish Law Commission was highly active in family law reform during the 1980s and 1990s with significant new Scottish legislation being enacted in the UK Parliament.[10] Key aims of those reforms included the creation of laws which were clear, certain and, where possible, codified, in order to maximise fairness and access to justice and to promote private ordering and party autonomy. With devolution and the establishment of the Scottish Parliament at Holyrood in 1998, family law became a devolved matter and, although there was limited family reform in the early years, the pace has since quickened.[11] The initial focus of the Scottish Government remained primarily on the substance of family law, with much less obvious interest in broader justice policy or family law in practice. That relatively laissez-faire approach may now be changing, with the emergence of a more explicit and directive public justice agenda.

Tracing in detail the precise origins of the current policy on civil justice in Scotland is beyond the scope of this chapter but a useful starting point is the Scottish Executive's 2007 Report on Civil Justice in Scotland, *Modern Laws for a Modern Scotland* (Scottish Executive, 2007). In her foreword to the Report, the then Minister for Justice, Cathy Jamieson MSP, noted that the Scottish Government had to date focused on law reform, and that, while substantive reform would continue, they now believed 'the time is right to concentrate on reviewing and modernising the delivery of civil justice in Scotland' (ibid: 1). The Scottish vision of civil justice was to be broad and inclusive; always seeing the 'big picture' (ibid: 3). Two priorities were highlighted: the first 'to increase access to good quality legal information, advice and representation in civil matters' and the second to undertake a major review of the civil courts under the leadership of the then Lord Justice Clerk, Lord Gill (ibid: 20[12]). Family law was reasonably prominent in the 2007 Report, perhaps reflecting the recent and significant reforms of divorce, parental responsibilities and rights and cohabitation which had been introduced by the Family Law (Scotland) Act 2006. Commitments to keep those reforms under review and

[9] The absence of any civil justice review was noted with regret by the Scottish Consumer Council in its 2001 Report, *Consensus Without Court*, 6: https://webarchive.nationalarchives.gov.uk/20090724141013/http://scotcons.demonweb.co.uk/publications/reports/reports01/rp09cons.pdf.

[10] Most notably reform of matrimonial property and financial provision on divorce in the Family Law (Scotland) Act 1995 and a major new framework for parental responsibilities and rights and child welfare in the Children (Scotland) Act 1995.

[11] For an overview of key reforms see Scottish Executive (2007) 8. For further analysis, see Sutherland (2011) ch 4.

[12] Court reform has subsequently been the principal focus for civil justice reform in Scotland. Following from a major review by Lord Gill, significant restructuring of the civil courts has been implemented and the process of court reform continues. Details of Lord Gill's review, its outcomes and the ongoing process of implementation, are available on the website of the Scottish Courts and Tribunals Service at www.scotcourts.gov.uk/about-the-scottish-court-service/the-scottish-civil-courts-reform.

to develop a new 'information initiative to support family law reform' were highlighted (ibid: 24).[13]

In 2012, the Scottish Government published its first *Strategy for Justice in Scotland* (Scottish Government, 2012). Its vision was of:

> a justice system that contributes positively to a flourishing Scotland, helping to create an inclusive and respectful society, in which all people and communities live in safety and security, individual and collective rights are supported, and disputes are resolved fairly and swiftly (ibid: 2).

Although it was reiterated, as in 2007, that 'justice' was to be defined broadly, 'encompassing criminal, civil and administrative justice' (ibid: 2) in fact the focus of the strategy was trained narrowly on crime and security and, in contrast to the 2007 Report, family law and family justice were barely mentioned. Of 11 priorities identified in the Strategy, only one was specifically focused on civil matters: Priority 9, Transforming civil and administrative justice (ibid: 55) which related to implementation of significant court restructuring following from the earlier proposals by Lord Gill (ibid: at n 26).

Building on the 2012 *Strategy*, a further document, entitled *Justice in Scotland: Vision and Priorities* (Scottish Government, 2017) was published by the Scottish Government in 2017 and here again, despite the same broad and inclusive definition of justice, the focus and substance was dominated by crime. The importance of research into how family law was working in practice and the continued commitment to the provision of high quality legal advice for families, both of which had been stressed in the 2007 Report, were missing. In the 2017 *Vision*, there was, however, specific reference to *Family Justice Modernisation* (ibid: 21).[14] This promising modernisation plan had been heralded in the *2015–16 Programme for Government*, where a commitment was made to 'work with the courts, legal and social work professions, parents and children to improve the experience of children and families involved in family justice matters' (Scottish Government, 2015: 52). Further details for the *Family Justice Modernisation* Strategy emerged in a subsequent Open Paper from the Scottish Government, which, perhaps surprisingly considering the broad and inclusive sounding title, began to make it clear that in fact the focus would be narrow:

> The Strategy is about improving procedures. It is not about changes to the substantive law. The Strategy would just cover cases involving children and would not cover other family cases (eg divorce cases where children are not involved).[15]

[13] It might be noted that in fact it was 2016 before a very brief, and by necessity limited, review of the 2006 Act reforms was initiated by the Justice Committee of the Scottish Parliament: www.parliament.scot/parliamentarybusiness/CurrentCommittees/96301.aspx. Significant problems were highlighted with the legislation, some of which are now being explored by the Scottish Government (review of child law) and the Scottish Law Commission (review of cohabitants' rights).

[14] The Family Justice Modernisation strategy has not yet been published: www2.gov.scot/Topics/Justice/law/17867/fjms.

[15] Scottish Government, Family Justice Modernisation Strategy: www2.gov.scot/Topics/Justice/law/17867/fjms/FJMS-summit-responses.

This construction of family justice as being concentrated on children, and in particular children at the centre of disputed cases, has been confirmed by the recent Scottish Government consultation on review of the Children (Scotland) Act 1995.[16] It signalled a separation between substance and process, quite different from the Scottish Law Commission reform approach of earlier decades which saw the substance and form of the legislation as intrinsically linked to practice and process. In the end, the consultation process combined a mix of questions on substance and practice; big conceptual issues unhelpfully interspersed with detailed matters of implementation. Precisely how the review of substantive child law and the family justice modernisation strategy will develop remains unknown as, while the consultation has now closed, there is as yet no indication of its outcome.

What has become increasingly clear through these various policy documents is that the Scottish Government has an active and growing interest in family justice. While initially defined broadly and inclusively, the strategy is in fact being shaped by very specific concerns, which apply to the minority. The commitments of the 2007 Report, *Modern Laws for a Modern Scotland* (Scottish Executive, 2007) to 'good quality legal information, advice and representation' and to ongoing information and review to support and inform family law have been overtaken by the priority of managing and minimising court-based disputes concerning children, in particular child contact. For the moment it seems that the modernisation agenda is firmly fixed on the use of litigation and court process. Missing from the debate is any sense of the long established and widely used practices of family dispute resolution which happen well away from court and consequently there is a risk that whatever strategies and delivery plans may emerge from this Family Justice Modernisation agenda will fail to reflect the experience and address the needs of the majority of Scottish families. A court-centric vision of family dispute resolution in Scotland is not only misleading but it has significant implications for debates concerning ADR and ODR and for the plans as to how these techniques might be used in the delivery of civil justice.

B. ADR: Alternative to What?

In Scotland, the most common form of ADR for families and relationships is mediation,[17] while arbitration[18] and collaborative law[19] are also available.

[16] For details of the consultation see www2.gov.scot/Topics/Justice/law/17867/review-of-children-scotland-act-1995.

[17] Mediation was first offered in 1984 by the Scottish Family Conciliation Service and is now provided by Relationship Scotland. There is also a significant group of family solicitors who are also trained mediators: Comprehensive Accredited Lawyer Mediators (CALM). For further discussion see Griffiths, Fotheringham and McCarthy (2015) paras 15-33–15-41.

[18] The availability of family arbitration in Scotland has experienced a rise in profile since the Arbitration (Scotland) Act 2010 and the establishment of the Family Law Arbitration Group, Scotland (FLAGS). See further Griffiths, Fotheringham and McCarthy (2015) paras 15-46–15-49.

[19] For discussion of collaborative law in Scotland see Griffiths, Fotheringham and McCarthy (2015) paras 15-42–15-45.

Parties may choose to refer their family dispute to ADR on their own initiative, they may be directed towards it by their lawyer or they may be referred by the court but, regardless of the pathway, there is no compulsion. The cost of mediation can in suitable cases be covered by civil legal aid and there is some centralised funding but there is also a high proportion of *pro bono* provision. Family mediation has been on offer in Scotland since the 1980s but, through a series of reviews and reports from then until the present time, the debates, the issues and the limitations seem strikingly consistent. While there is considerable enthusiasm for and individual satisfaction with ADR techniques, knowledge of the services and access to them tend to be uneven. There is a continuing perception that ADR is underused.[20] Linked to this perception, and preventing it becoming clear fact, is a recurring theme concerning the lack of reliable publicly available data, which further hampers meaningful debate and the development of effective policy (Scottish Government, 2014a: 29).

In 2014, the Scottish Legal Aid Board conducted an extensive review entitled *Making Justice Work: Overview Report of Alternative Dispute Resolution in Scotland*, November 2014 (Scottish Government, 2014a) and more recently, in 2018, the Justice Committee of the Scottish Parliament, following two evidence sessions on the issue, published their report, *I won't see you in court: alternative dispute resolution in Scotland* (Justice Committee, 2018). The Justice Committee was convinced that there is potential for ADR 'to encourage the earlier and more effective resolution of disputes' and regretted therefore that it 'remains underused' (ibid: 1). While the Committee concluded that compulsory ADR should not be introduced, it recognised that previous attempts to encourage ADR had had limited effect and it recommended that 'more fundamental changes which could facilitate a step-change in the uptake of ADR in Scotland should now be explored' (ibid: 23). These more fundamental changes might include the introduction of something similar to the MIAMS used in England and Wales or perhaps a statutory framework similar to that recently introduced in Ireland by the Mediation Act 2017.

While the Justice Committee report has been generally welcomed, it gives rise to some frustrations. There are definite signs of growing momentum on the part of Scottish policy makers in respect of ADR, but whether this is simply the latest round in the cyclical debate or the beginning of a seismic shift remains to be seen. Even if there is a shift, it seems likely that it will only be a shift from one side of a divide to the other. What does not seem to change is our inability to move beyond preconceived divisions and fixed framings, to move towards integration[21] rather than choice or competition. The phrase Alternative Dispute

[20] See eg Lewis (1999). The Scottish Office: 'the legal system currently provides somewhat uneven Access to mediation' and cf the very recent comments of the Justice Committee (2018) in respect of referrals to mediation being 'patchy', at 11.

[21] As suggested by Maclean and Eekelaar, 'Towards an Integrated Service?' (2016) ch 7.

Resolution has become such an accepted part of our language that it can be difficult to question it, but what is meant by that word 'alternative'? The Scottish Civil Justice Council (2014: 1) in their literature review of ADR listed the following six examples: 'negotiation, mediation, arbitration, conciliation, collaborative law and early neutral evaluation' whereas the Justice Committee in its recent report listed five slightly different examples: mediation, conciliation, arbitration, adjudication and ombudsmen, with the latter list notably omitting negotiation. And what of the underlying assumption that the default in family dispute resolution is litigation; that 'alternative' dispute resolution is the exception to a court-based norm or that court-based processes are, by definition, disputed?

Can a form of dispute resolution be alternative when it is alternative to litigation and the courts or, to qualify as ADR, must it also be alternative to law and to lawyers? In the practical resolution of family matters in Scotland these are key questions because if ADR includes dispute resolution through negotiated settlement, which is alternative to the courts but primarily solicitor-led, then it is an already very well, and long, established method. It is disappointing to see these questions repeatedly raised but routinely left to one side. One of the key issues for the 2007 review was whether 'as a matter of public policy, the court should be regarded as the last resort … or whether it is simply one of a "menu" of dispute resolution options from which parties may choose'.[22] In the recent Justice Committee Report, a very similar suggestion was again made that litigation be thought of simply as one of a range – 'a spectrum' – of methods (Justice Committee, 2018: 3). A number of expert witnesses to the Committee made calls for the Committee to think not only about how to encourage Alternative Dispute Resolution but about how to answer the question of 'alternative to what?'. While in its conclusions the Justice Committee acknowledged these points and accepted that 'there may be merit in moving away from this terminology' in favour of an inclusive phrase such as 'appropriate dispute resolution' or simply 'dispute resolution', ultimately it chose not to do so, concluding that, as 'the terms "alternative dispute resolution" and "ADR" are still in common usage in Scotland' they would continue to use them in the Report (ibid: 4). To shift the framing could revitalise the debate, broaden the options for policy development and foster real modernisation of family justice but so far, despite the inclusive Scottish vision of justice for the twenty-first century, it has not happened.

C. Digital Technology and Transformation

While debates and strategies in terms of digital technology are new and there is much less revisiting of old themes, in developments so far there are similar concerns over the limitations of a narrow focus. The Scottish Government in

[22] *Scottish Civil Courts Review: A Consultation Paper*, 2007, 3: www.scotcourts.gov.uk/docs/default-source/civil-courts-reform/scccompleter-(2)7CDD54ABAE89.pdf?sfvrsn=2.

its 2017 *Justice in Scotland: Vision and Priorities* (Scottish Government, 2017), made specific reference to technology: 'To deliver justice fit for the 21st century, our justice systems need to embrace digital technology' (ibid: 31). In this they reflected closely the opening commitment of their 2014 *Digital Strategy for Justice in Scotland* (Scottish Government, 2014b): 'we need to look beyond traditional methods and transform how we think; how we engage and how we deliver services to citizens and users'. In line with a broad philosophy of justice as a public service, the primary objective was presented as widening access and improving quality with cost and savings as an added bonus:

> We want to use digital technology wherever possible to broaden access to justice, improve quality of service and safeguard the rights of citizens and users. By digitising our justice systems and operating efficient processes, we can at the same time lower our costs. (ibid: 1).

The Digital Strategy identified three objectives. The first was to 'allow people to access the right information at the right time,' the second to provide fully digitised systems and the third to 'make data work for us' (ibid: 3–8). Under the first objective, to enable access to the right information at the right time, the Scottish Government committed to developing a 'justice public information portal' in the form of mygov.scot. In the confusing digital world of information overload, a single, reliable source of focused, trustworthy and accurate advice, information and resources would significantly enhance individual access to justice and could assist in the early resolution or at least preparation for resolution of family disputes. To date, however, the information provided on the justice portal is generic and lacking in structure or system, with the default message often being to 'contact a solicitor'. While some disputes will always benefit from expert advice, much clearer and more specific information about the law and legal rights could quite easily be made available through this justice portal and would reflect the commitment of the Scottish Government, in their 2007 Report (Scottish Executive, 2007), to 'increase access to good quality legal information'.

The second objective is to provide fully digitised systems. This is of course a major task, and pragmatic prioritisation is to be expected but once again the focus has been, first on criminal justice and secondly on the courts and, although there are important developments in terms of an online system for small civil claims, as yet, there is little sign of digital thinking for family law and a wider, more inclusive model of family justice. In the family legislative reforms of the 1980s and 1990s, there was an ambition to make family law as accessible as possible through well drafted, clearly structured statutes. Digital technology offers exciting opportunities for law reformers and law makers to combine that twentieth century, access to justice thinking with twenty-first century know-how. We need 'modern laws for a modern Scotland' which include transforming not simply the substance but the creation and dissemination of our laws: 'a fully reengineered process reaching from drafting through legislation to the citizen' (Sibbald, 2003: 92). If digital system strategy focuses solely on 'good result efficiency' it risks missing the potential to make more radical transformations (Allbon, 2018).

The third objective of the Digital Strategy is to make data work for us. In the Digital Strategy Document, this third objective is discussed principally in the context of crime, with multiple examples of how data can be used to predict outcomes and therefore to minimise future risks. At present, there is little sign of any thinking about how this objective might be pursued in the context of family law and family justice. One obvious area for development could be financial provision on divorce. The Family Law (Scotland) Act 1985 was designed to maximise clarity, certainty and consistency. Based around five statutory principles, it is a clearly drafted, but at the same time sophisticated system, which might lend itself well to the possibilities offered by AI. Years before the Scottish Government's Digital Strategy was developed, an academic project set out to design and develop an online tool to support advice-giving in respect of financial provision on divorce (Duguid, Edwards and Kingston, 2001). While that particular project did not proceed, the opportunities are clear and a decade later, it is a striking example of an idea whose time has come.

As with the general Justice Strategy and Vision, highlighted above, the Digital Strategy makes clear that it is intended to cover all aspects of Administrative, Criminal and Civil justice but, so far, new initiatives have focused on criminal law and small civil claims. Family justice to date has been little affected or improved by digitisation; in fact the endless expansion of online information, much of which can be misleading or even inaccurate, may be a backward step. The recent establishment of a Justice Digital and Strategy team within the Justice Directorate of the Scottish Government is perhaps a positive sign of progress.[23] In their mission to 'drive, support and enable transformation' it is hoped that they will look beyond the courts and the single priority of case management and engage not only with the future but also with the past of Scots family law which offers considerable inspiration for development.

IV. DIVORCE IN SCOTLAND

Current justice strategy focuses principally on what is 'not working'; in the context of family justice that is specifically child contact disputes. What if we look instead at areas of family law which seem to work reasonably well? Instead of concentrating on the disputes which most trouble the courts, what if start from family disputes which very rarely trouble the courts? What might we learn from experience in practice of what works? How might alternative and digital methods be developed to support those disputes? One such area of

[23] https://blogs.gov.scot/justice-safety/2018/08/09/introducing-justice-digital-strategy.

Scots family law is divorce and financial provision. While all divorces must be granted by a court, the vast majority are undefended and around two thirds are obtained by the very simple, almost administrative, simplified procedure. This is a court-based resolution process, which to a large extent requires only virtual engagement and where there is little sign of 'dispute'. In terms of financial provision on divorce, a significant proportion of couples in Scotland reach agreement without any need for court involvement. By so doing they are using an alternative method of dispute resolution albeit there is relatively little evidence of 'ADR' as commonly or strictly defined.

A. Not Quite Online

Divorce in Scotland may be sought by means of the Ordinary or the Simplified Procedure. The latter is commonly referred to as 'do-it–yourself' divorce and it has been central to the apparently smooth functioning of divorce law in Scotland in contrast to the current position in England and Wales where divorce reform is high on the agenda.[24] Simplified Procedure is currently available only where divorce is sought on one of the two non-cohabitation grounds,[25] where there are no disputes as to property or financial provision and where there are no children under the age of 16.[26] Where these conditions are met, the parties complete and submit a form, which is then sent to the court for consideration and granting of the decree. Generally no further evidence is required beyond what is stated on the form but the parties do have to swear, before a Notary Public or Justice of the Peace, that the information they have provided is accurate. This is a simple, quick and relatively cheap process, albeit it remains a court-based process and in order to be used there must be some level of agreement between the parties.

In 2015–16, 8875 divorces were granted in the sheriff court and, of those, 96% were undefended and 62% used the Simplified Procedure.[27] Simplified divorce in Scotland was loosely referred to as being 'online' long before the recent explosion of interest in legal tech, digitisation and AI. It was in many ways already hailed as quite 'modern' before the recent modernisation agenda developed and yet it is increasingly obvious how far the process is falling behind.[28] The application forms are available to download from the website of the Scottish Courts

[24] There are currently no plans for reform of divorce law in Scotland: Sarah Harvie-Clark, 'It's the end of the line but no one's to blame' (SPICe, 2018): https://spice-spotlight.scot/2018/09/12/its-the-end-of-the-line-but-no-ones-to-blame-no-fault-divorce-in-the-uk/.

[25] One year's non-cohabitation with the consent of the defender or two years' non-cohabitation, regardless of consent: Divorce (Scotland) Act 1976, s 1(2)(d) or (e).

[26] The simplified procedure was introduced in 1982 and is governed in the Court of Session by RCS, r 49.72 and in the sheriff court by OCR, r 33.73.

[27] *Civil Justice Statistics in Scotland 2015–2016*, ch 6: www.gov.scot/publications/civil-justice-statistics-scotland-2015-16/pages/7/.

[28] cf the online system for divorce now provided in England and Wales: www.gov.uk/divorce/file-for-divorce.

and Tribunals Service but they cannot be completed and submitted electronically. Although a solicitor is not otherwise required to assist with the divorce application, and relatively clear guidance is provided online, the forms require to be signed by a Notary Public or a Justice of the Peace: a striking juxtaposition of the old and the new and far from the streamlined digital process of the Digital and Justice Strategies. Where official sites are falling behind, enterprising firms are stepping up and an online search will produce various hits promising online divorce at discount rates albeit the small print reveals the same requirements for real as opposed to electronic signatures, not to mention some concerns at the unregulated nature of these services (Gallagher, 2018).

B. Already 'Alternative'

It is extraordinary that, in a jurisdiction where there is so little adjudication, the debate has become framed in terms of ADR versus court-imposed rulings. This false dichotomy ignores the main mode of dispute management in family (and other civil matters), which is lawyer-led negotiation, usually concluded in a settlement culture without a court appearance except to check and record a consent order for the purposes of fairness and enforceability (Maclean, 2010: 106).

This dichotomisation is even less appropriate in Scotland where neither court appearance nor judicial consent is needed, to give effect to a negotiated financial settlement. In Scotland there is, and has long been, a very strong and settled pattern of separation agreements, usually, although not necessarily, drafted with the aid of solicitors and enforceable without the need for any judicial involvement.[29] Where there are children, the court must be satisfied of the arrangements for their post-divorce care but once again there is a strong preference for private negotiation and agreement, with the court directed to make an order in respect of residence and contact only where to do so would be better than making no order at all.[30] There is clear evidence that this system of private agreement is widespread and works very well in practice. Two studies of separation agreements, the first in the mid-1990s (Wasoff, McGuckin and Edwards, 1997) and the second in 2013 (Mair, Wasoff and Mackay, 2013), explored the use, nature and extent of such agreements. There is long-standing practice of registering separation agreements, often called minutes of agreement, in the Books of Council and Session, a public register. While registration is not required in order to make an agreement legally binding,[31] it does make the process of enforcement very simple. Registration gives the agreement the same legal force as a court decree and it becomes directly enforceable without the need for any court involvement.

[29] For further discussion of the operation of this system, see Mair, Wasoff and Mackay (2015).
[30] Children (Scotland) Act 1995, s 11(7).
[31] It is binding between the parties simply as a matter of contract.

In 2013, a random sample of 600 agreements, registered in 2010, was analysed and interviews were conducted with parties to agreements and with solicitors. There is no index or record of the subject matter of registered agreements and therefore no way of knowing precisely how many separation agreements are registered. The 2013 study estimated, however, that 5,000 agreements were registered in Scotland in 2010, compared with around 10,000 divorces granted in the same year. This represented a substantial increase since the early 1990s when a similar exercise had estimated 3,000 agreements; one agreement in every four divorces at that time (Wasoff, McGuckin and Edwards, 1997). Not all such agreements will be registered and therefore the level of settlement of financial and property disputes arising from divorce or dissolution of civil partnership, and indeed from the breakdown of cohabitation, is likely to be much higher.

Within the context of negotiated settlement facilitated by solicitors, what evidence is there of specific use of ADR methods? Of the sample of 13 solicitors interviewed as part of the project, three were accredited collaborative lawyers, one accredited to do CALM[32] and three were accredited to do both. Solicitors explained the impact of training in ADR on their practice. In respect of CALM:

> I felt from the moment that I'd started the [CALM] training course it just made you look at the whole thing in a different way. And it made you much more careful about what you wrote in letters and how you dealt with the case generally because often in mediation there can be quite a lot of time spent discussing what solicitors have put in letters and the way things have been said because it's an adversarial system [but] you look at it in a completely different way as a mediator. [Solicitor 9]

and in respect of collaborative law:

> I think it's made me even more passionate to work out solutions that are suitable for them, because collaborative law allows them to hear it from both sides, it's handy in the event that if one of the parties is being really stupid, they will have two solicitors against them. But, also, you can make suggestions in a collaborative situation, like if they're arguing about the pension share and the house, for instance, you can say, well how about this? Would that be a way forward? You can make suggestions to both of them that you wouldn't normally make in just an adversarial system. [Solicitor 1]

One solicitor who had been in practice since 1979 had noticed the impact of ADR upon family law practice over that time:

> When I first started it was very much a kind of aggressive kind of horrible letters going back and forth and much more confrontational and adversarial. Whereas I think with these … mediation and collaboration there is a lot more sophistication going on and the realisation that in family law an adversarial approach is not really going to serve your clients the best … okay we might have all sorts of difficult issues to consider over the next short while, but at the end of the day these children will always be yours. And there will be certain life events that you'll want to see and mum

[32] See n 8 above.

> will be there as well, or dad will be there as well, and really do you want to be able to dance at your daughter's wedding? [Solicitor 9]

While another solicitor also clearly acknowledged the benefits of this kind of approach for nurturing an ongoing business relationship:

> I want that client to come back to our firm to get their will done or if they set up a business I want to take them to the commercial department ... It's very difficult I think for people to come away from these experiences with anything positive out of it and I think that if we can do that and people can behave with a bit of dignity when they are separating, then the whole family is better for it. [Solicitor 5]

Some solicitors who were not themselves trained in collaborative practice were nonetheless not hostile towards it and one described taking part in an 'alternative' form of negotiation:

> We went to the offices of the other solicitor, and they found a room for my client and myself, and they found a room for their client and their solicitor, and then periodically the solicitors met and one of them went back and tried to persuade their client. We did get something sorted out. I suppose what we did was reduce four or eight weeks of letters into one afternoon, so ... but that was really a negotiation, rather than conciliation. I'm told that the lady didn't want to meet my client again, but I wouldn't have been very comfortable being in the room with both of them. I'd be willing to repeat it. [Solicitor 12]

Practitioners were, however, also aware that not all those undertaking family law work had been influenced by the move towards conciliatory family law practice:

> I think perhaps the problem arises when people go in to see solicitors that maybe have a criminal practice where they have got a very definite kind of attitude towards courts and everything else ... they think that being aggressive and the old Rottweiler analogy is the one that is going to serve their client well. But for the vast majority of cases, they can't deliver, or they just aren't able to achieve what they're setting out to achieve ... and they say, oh well if don't like it, just go somewhere else, so ... The poor people are then having to sort of pick up the pieces. [Solicitor 9]

As with the evidence of access to specific forms of ADR, coming into contact with a solicitor who offers mediation or is influenced by more 'alternative' forms of practice is often left to chance.

If ADR is, as the Justice Committee (2018: 3) recently said, a collective term to describe 'methods designed to enable people to resolve disputes outside the court system' then negotiated and registered agreements are, surely, a form of ADR. If this form of dispute resolution is classified as ADR then ADR immediately shifts from alternative to mainstream. Negotiated agreements are nothing new in Scots family law which has long respected personal autonomy in marriage and made space in the legal framework for private ordering.[33] For centuries,

[33] It is clear, for example, that a couple may agree to oust the jurisdiction of the courts in respect of financial provision on divorce and there is only limited scope to vary or set aside the terms of any agreement: *Milne v Milne* 1987 SLT 45 at 47 per Lord Kincraig.

couples in Scotland have been making and enforcing private agreements to regulate aspects of their marriage, separation and consequences of divorce. This is a form of non-judicial dispute resolution which has a long and continuous history in Scotland, albeit it fits well with current thinking and practice around family law and dispute resolution and if the Scottish Government is committed to increasing the use of ADR, there is much it might learn from this example of 'what works'.

Greater clarity is needed in Scotland and in the emerging Government justice strategy as to what it wants from ADR. Is it about diverting disputes away from the court system, or is it about moving away from the legal system? Is it about encouraging all those who may assist in resolving family disputes to employ a range of techniques or is it about diverting parties away from lawyers and towards other practitioners of ADR? At present, the debate is stuck in a model which still seems to assume that most disputes are headed for court whereas the evidence of what happens in practice is that court is very much a last resort. Rather than focus on how to divert family disputes away from law, more productive energy might be invested in how to make a range of effective dispute resolution options available to all. The vast majority of the sample of separation agreements analysed, appeared to have been drafted by legal practitioners. Of a sample of 600, only one or two had the appearance of being entirely do-it-yourself. Within those which had been written and registered by solicitors, there was, however, a wide range, from the highly technical and clearly bespoke to those which, while set out in legal format and printed on lawyers' paper, included lay words and terms which sounded much more personal than legalistic. In principle, there is no reason why couples cannot reach their own agreement and then ask a lawyer – or to use an old fashioned term, a writer – to put their agreement into words. There is nothing to stop them from completing the whole process themselves. A key reason behind the widespread use of separation agreements in Scotland and the relative ease of their negotiation, particularly in simple cases, is the clarity and certainty of the statutory framework for financial provision on divorce.[34] It is not difficult to imagine the provision of very high quality, trusted and accurate information to parties through an online resource – the Scottish Government's mygov.scot for instance – which could assist them in reaching their own settlement. Although the Books of Council and Session where many of these agreements are registered is an ancient repository, the Registers of Scotland where it is housed is an increasingly high-tech and open access resource[35] and, again, with some thought it is not difficult to imagine an easily accessible, online service for registration. In this centuries old Scottish system

[34] Particularly the five statutory principles set out in the Family Law (Scotland) Act 1985, s 9.

[35] A point clearly made in the RoS timeline at www.ros.gov.uk/about/what-we-do/our-history.

of negotiation and registration of agreements, there is huge potential for both alternative and digital modernisation.

V. FAMILY JUSTICE

Family issues, which engage law and civil justice, take many forms and by no means all conform to the model of highly contested, lengthy, court-centred litigation. Strategies and delivery plans, perhaps by necessity, focus on narrowly drawn priorities and highlight areas of practice most in need of transformation but by so doing they may skew perceptions of the wider system. Initially, the development of a justice strategy in Scotland concentrated on criminal law, when it turned to civil law it focused on the courts and court system and, more recently, when it has begun to look at family justice, it has remained court-centric. The starting point for modernising and transforming family justice in Scotland is the model of a court-based dispute. Child contact disputes, leading to protracted and highly contested litigation, are increasingly to the fore in Scotland as they are in many other jurisdictions and it is therefore unsurprising that the courts and the government see this form of family dispute as a priority. Such disputes are not, however, representative of the experience of the vast majority of families seeking to resolve family issues and to move through points and periods of transition in family relationships. From the emerging public narrative of civil justice and family dispute resolution in Scotland, much of the family dispute landscape is so far missing. Any strategy for the future development of family justice, constructed on such a narrow and incomplete understanding, is unlikely to reflect or meet the needs of all. To reprise the words of the Minister for Justice in her foreword to the 2007 Report *Modern Laws for a Modern Scotland*, we need to look at the 'big picture' because '[f]ocussing on the detail of one part can mean that we los[e] sight of the overall effect.' (Scottish Executive, 2007: 3).

REFERENCES

Allbon, E (2018) 'Beyond text: exploiting the visual in law', *Australian Law Librarian* 26(2), 54.

Byrom, N (2019) 'Developing the detail: Evaluating the Impact of Court Reform in England and Wales on Access to Justice' (2019).

Duguid, S, Edwards L and Kingston, J (2001) 'A Web-based Decision Support System for Divorce Lawyers', *International Review of Law, Computers & Technology* 15(3), 265.

Evans, M (2018) *Rethinking Legal Aid: an independent strategic review*, February 2018.

Gallagher, J (2018), 'Online and out of line', *Journal of the Law Society of Scotland* 15 October.

Genn, H (2010) 'Civil mediation: a measured approach?', *Journal of Social Welfare and Family Law* 32(2), 195.

Griffiths, A, Fotheringham J and McCarthy, F (2015) *Family Law* (4th edn), (Edinburgh, W Green).

Hunter, R (2017) 'Inducing demand for family mediation – before and after LASPO', *Journal of Social Welfare and Family Law* 39(2), 189.

Justice Committee (2018) *I won't see you in court: alternative dispute resolution in Scotland*, SP Paper 381 9th Report, 2018 (Session 5), 3: https://digitalpublications.parliament.scot/Committees/Report/J/2018/10/1/I-won-t-see-you-in-court--alternative-dispute-resolution-in-Scotland.

Lewis, J (1999) *The Role of Mediation in Family Disputes in Scotland*, Legal Studies Research Findings No 23.

Maclean, M (2010) 'Family mediation: alternative or additional dispute resolution?', *Journal of Social Welfare and Family Law* 32(2), 105.

Maclean, M and Eekelaar, J (2016) *Lawyers and Mediators: the brave new world of services for separating families* (Oxford, Hart Publishing).

Mair, J, Wasoff, F and Mackay, K (2013) *All Settled? A study of legally binding separation agreements and private ordering in Scotland*: www.crfr.ac.uk/assets/MinutesofAgreement20131.pdf.

Mair, J, Wasoff F and Mackay, K (2015) 'Family Justice Without Courts: Property Settlement on Separation Using Contracts in Scotland' in M Maclean, J Eekelaar and B Bastard (eds) *Delivering Family Justice in the 21st Century* (Oxford: Bloomsbury) ch 10.

Mair, J, Mordaunt E and Wasoff, F (2016) *Built to Last: The Family Law (Scotland) Act 1985 – 30 years of financial provision on divorce*: www.nuffieldfoundation.org/financial-provision-divorce-under-family-law-scotland-act-1985.

Scottish Civil Courts Review: A Consultation Paper (2007) 3: www.scotcourts.gov.uk/docs/default-source/civil-courts-reform/scccompleter-(2)7CDD54ABAE89.pdf?sfvrsn=2.

Scottish Civil Justice Council (2014) *Access to Justice Literature Review: ADR methods*, December 2014: www.scottishciviljusticecouncil.gov.uk/publications/scjc-and-other-organisations'-publications.

Scottish Executive (2007) *Modern Laws for a Modern Scotland: A Report on Civil Justice in Scotland* (Edinburgh): www2.gov.scot/Publications/2007/02/09110006/8.

Scottish Government (2012) *The Strategy for Justice in Scotland: Evidence*: www2.gov.scot/Publications/2012/09/5924/0.

Scottish Government (2014a) *Making Justice Work: Overview Report of Alternative Dispute Resolution in Scotland*, November 2014: www.slab.org.uk/about-us/what-we-do/policyanddevelopmentoverview/AlternativeDisputeResolution/.

Scottish Government (2014b) *Digital Strategy for Justice in Scotland*: www.gov.scot/Resource/0045/00458026.pdf.

Scottish Government (2015) *A Stronger Scotland: The Government's Programme for Scotland 2015–16*: www.gov.scot/publications/programme-government-2015-16/.

Scottish Government (2017) *Justice in Scotland: vision and priorities*, 2017: www.gov.scot/publications/justice-scotland-vision-priorities/.

Scottish Government (2018a), Civil Justice Statistics in Scotland 2016–2017: www.gov.scot/publications/civil-justice-statistics-scotland-2016-17.

Scottish Government (2018b) *Independent Review of legal aid: our response*: www.gov.scot/publications/scottish-government-response-independent-review-legal-aid-scotland/.

SCTS (nd) *Digital Strategy 2018–2023*: www.scotcourts.gov.uk/docs/default-source/aboutscs/reports-and-data/reports-data/scts-digital-strategy---final.pdf.

Sibbald, J (2003) 'A Scots Law Portal: Putting Scots Law on the Digital Map', *Legal Information Management* 3(2), 90.

Sutherland, EE (2011) 'Child and Family Law: Progress and Pusillanimity' in EE Sutherland, KE Goodall, GFM Little and FP Davidson (eds), *Law Making and the Scottish Parliament: the Early Years* (Edinburgh, Edinburgh University Press).

Wasoff, F, McGuckin, A and Edwards, L (1997) *Mutual Consent: Written Agreements in Family Law* (Edinburgh, The Scottish Office).

Wong, S and Cain, R (2019) 'The impact of cuts in legal aid funding of private family law cases', *Journal of Social Welfare and Family Law* 41(1) 3–14.

9

Representations of Family Justice in Online Communities

LEANNE SMITH

I. INTRODUCTION

As THE CHAPTERS of this volume demonstrate, there has in recent years been much talk of the potential of digital materials to streamline family justice processes and aid or impede access to family justice. A great deal of discussion and activity has similarly explored the pros, cons and viability of online dispute resolution processes as a substitute for other types of family dispute resolution.[1] My concern in this chapter is to illustrate that the potential transformations to family justice heralded by the digital age could be wider – and rather wilder – than carefully planned introduction of digital materials and dispute resolution processes. The World Wide Web is more than an information repository, a scaffold for transactions and service delivery and a set of apparatus for structuring communications. It is also a new social space inhabited by communities in which experiences, ideas and relationships are shared and constructed. It is the relevance of online communities to the changing landscape of family justice and family dispute resolution that this chapter considers.

My focus is on online communities characterised by spontaneous interactions between users, which both generate social connections and facilitate information exchange. The typical example of an online community is a discussion forum, which might be hosted through any one of a variety of different platforms. Online communities can also be formed within social networking sites, such as Facebook.[2] Recently, I spent some time exploring how such communities are used by those experiencing justiciable family disputes.[3] Even the briefest

1

[2] In relation to Facebook, which is probably the most widely used online community, open or closed 'groups' can operate in a very similar way to online discussion forums.

[3] My approach was to explore the content of posts on open access, dormant threads, with a view to assessing whether online communities might be a worthwhile field of study for a research project. There is a growing body of literature on the ethics of online research. This includes debates as to

of online searches reveals that they are used frequently. On the most widely used forums it is possible to find tens of separate threads started daily that are related to a dispute over arrangements for children. Some threads rapidly garner tens of responses. It is not possible to ascertain the number who later read the threads without actively contributing to them but, given that threads remain visible through searches entered on standard search engines, it could run into the multiple hundreds. It is striking that the most widely used forums appear to be those hosted on platforms that speak to particular family identity groups, such as mums, dads or grandparents.[4] My impression is that discussion forums on issue-focused platforms, such as those hosted by organisations that aim to help single parents or people experiencing divorce, are used considerably less often and less widely.[5] What this might mean for the distribution of partisan or polarised views is a matter of some concern.

A quick scan of online forums reveals that some use them to air views and seek support on how to resolve family conflicts privately, others to share or seek advice on experiences of family court processes; they function as a dynamic space in which people share and develop views on both formal and informal family dispute resolution. Participants therefore assume roles as co-producers of information and also act as their own information 'gatekeepers', meaning that they must judge for themselves what is worthy of attention and trust.[6] As social psychologists David Westerman et al have observed, in traditional media such functions have been fulfilled by professionals, authors or journalists, who have selected and published information based on its quality (Westerman, Spence and Van der Heide, 2014: 173). How adeptly individuals are able to fulfil these roles for themselves is a question of some importance to which the answer is unknown. It raises further concerns about the quality of the information shared in online communities.

Somewhat surprisingly, the use of online communities by individuals experiencing a family dispute has been subject to almost no research so we know little

whether visible forums should be treated as public documents that are fair game for researchers, or literary works with copyrights attached to them. These dilemmas were not relevant at this exploratory stage of my research but would not to be considered in a project that involved collecting data. For a good summary of the issues see Paechter (2012a).

[4] This assessment is based on early impressions rather than any systematic collection of data. In the UK Mumsnet and Netmums appear to be particularly widely used. There are plenty of sites focused on fathers, but my experience is that they are more likely to be closed forums that cannot be perused by the casual observer.

[5] Gingerbread and Wikivorce are examples of such organisations in the UK. Gingerbread is a charity that provides support for single parents. Wikivorce is a social enterprise that does have a high membership (the site reports 150,000 members and up to 5,000 visitors a day). Both offer visitors to their websites opportunities to participate in discussion forums.

[6] Many platforms that host online communities will employ moderators with some power to remove information. However, those moderators often work within very limited parameters focused on, for example, spotting offensive or commercially sensitive material.

about the role it might play in dispute resolution, either in positive or negative terms.[7] This situation is in marked contrast to other fields. In healthcare, for example, the utility and impact of online discussion forums have been widely researched over the last 10 years or so (eg, Cole, Watkins and Kleine, 2016; Fox, 2011; Hu and Sundar, 2009; Sillence, Hardy, Briggs and Harris, 2013). Similarly, in education, pedagogy has been informed by research that has sought to understand the conditions in which online discussion with others might enhance or impede learning (eg, Kent, Laslo and Rafaeli, 2016; Rovai, 2007; Thomas, 2002).

Below, I make the case for researchers and policymakers with an interest in family justice to engage in their own explorations of online communities because neglecting to consider them will result in a constricted understanding of how the digital world can impact on family dispute resolution. I begin by showing that online communities provide useful insights into attitudes to family justice and approaches to dispute resolution that are usually hidden. However, I then draw on insights from social and cognitive psychology (insights that have been put to use in the healthcare and education research) to suggest that online communities have the potential to be uniquely powerful. I advance two reasons in support of this argument. First, online communities have the capacity to amplify the effects of social networks and particular social groups on attitudes and approaches to family justice. Secondly, their character as social spaces makes them particularly influential as sources of information; the very act of contributing to discussions of family disputes in an online community is likely to increase an individual's propensity to value the information shared in that community. I conclude by reflecting on whether online communities might present positive opportunities for supporting family dispute resolution.

II. THE ROLE OF SOCIAL INTERACTION IN FAMILY DISPUTE RESOLUTION

There is nothing revelatory in the realisation that individuals who are experiencing family disputes have informal discussions about those disputes with other people who form part of their social network. Writing about shifts in the nature and provision of professional advice for family disputes in the 1980s, Gwynn Davis dedicated a whole chapter to the recognised importance of what he termed 'informal mediation', or simply advice, provided by networks of friends, family members and others (Davis, 1988: ch 4). For example, Davis reported that 50% of those involved in his studies of divorce discussed their family dispute with their parents. He went on to argue that the parental input could manifest itself through direct interventions in the problem (a sort of informal mediation) or

[7] Paechter (2012b) did carry out a study of the use of Wikivorce as a community of practice providing divorce support in 2007.

indirectly through the operation of their advice on the subsequent actions of the advice seeker (ibid: 35).

More recently we have learned that, although people are very likely to use a formal dispute resolution process – or at least legal or professional advice – to help solve a family dispute, they are even more likely to seek the advice of family and friends on the dispute. In England and Wales, a recent *Legal Problem and Resolutions Survey* found that, 'Over two-thirds of adults with relationship breakdown problems (68%) reported getting information, advice or help from their friends and family' (Franklyn, Budd, Verrill and Willoughby, 2017: 80). This was much higher than the proportion of people who used such informal social relationships to help solve other types of legal problem, with the number doing so ranging between 32% and 47% depending on the particular problem. Moreover, a quarter of people relied entirely on this type of self-help strategy (ibid: 38 and 61). The figure also means that informal social relationships were the most common type of self-help resource used in relation to family disputes.

So we know that informal communications with social contacts about justiciable family disputes have always been common. The content of these social communications could well be a signifier of what people perceive the law and justice (in its lay sense) to be in this context. Such communications should therefore be of considerable interest to researchers, lawyers and policymakers who seek to understand how family law and family justice are perceived, as well as how those perceptions are applied by those who resolve their disputes privately. These issues are of increasing importance in an environment in which private settlement has been normatively valorised and structurally enforced through family justice policies.[8]

In some preeminent analyses of the operation of family justice, certain things have been widely assumed in relation to private bargaining and settlement. Mnookin and Kornhauser (1979), for example, famously surmised that legal norms would impact on the behaviours, strategies and bargaining strength of individuals trying to resolve a family dispute, leading to a form of 'bargaining in the shadow of the law'.[9] Later, John Dewar (1998: 474) made a similar assertion, arguing that lawyers and others deploy 'stabilising practices of interpretation' of legal norms in such a way as to 'set the tone for private ordering, or alternative dispute resolution'. In truth, however, we know very little about the

[8] Most notably, this has happened through the promotion of mediation as superior to court processes and as a better option than negotiations supported by lawyers. This approach has characterised family justice policy in England and Wales for a long time. It is reflected in the report of the Family Justice Review Panel (2011) and was intensified through the Legal Aid, Sentencing and Punishment of Offenders act 2012. Along with other, roughly contemporaneous, new legislation (eg, The Children and Families Act 2014) this Act served to compel many people to consider mediation and deter them from using lawyers and the courts. See Diduck (2013) for discussion of the ramifications of the push towards private negotiation and settlement.

[9] It has become a widespread assumption that the 'shadow of the law' referred to by Mnookin and Kornhauser was to be cast by advice from lawyers operating as a backdrop to private negotiations between individuals. In fact, it is not clear from their article that they did believe this.

extent to which legal norms really are reflected in the processes and outcomes of family dispute resolutions that do not go through the courts – still less about situations where a lawyer is not even consulted. A few studies have sought to explore the general public's understandings of family law norms, in contexts such as assessing child support payments (Bryson et al, 2015) and distinguishing the legal consequences of marriage and cohabitation (Barlow, Duncan, James and Park, 2005). In fact, the case for saying that law is likely to influence family dispute resolution decisions is diluted by such research, which tends to reveal a substantial gap between what the law is and what the public perceive it to be.

Unfortunately, evidence revealing how the majority who do not use the legal process actually approach the resolution of a real family dispute has remained stubbornly elusive. Indeed, part of the problem has been the difficulty of analysing influences that are hidden from view precisely because they have only been considered or expressed in private. The existence of online communities, however, transfers many informal social communications about family disputes into public space, enabling us to examine previously invisible but ever-present informal approaches to family dispute resolution. My own exploration of online discussion forums suggests that they are rich sources of information on: perceptions and experiences of the family justice system and relevant professionals; understandings and misunderstandings of family law and procedure; approaches to negotiation and settlement; and different conflict resolution strategies. As such they have the potential to provide wholly new insights into perceptions of family law and family justice, as well as the factors shaping private dispute resolution.

Researchers and policymakers might also find that exploring how people interact with online discussion forums shines a light on another important issue. A considerable amount of research tells us that it is not just those a person communicates with that is important, but also the groups in society that they identify with. It has been several decades since social psychologists Tajfel and Turner (1979) presented their influential social identity theory to explain how membership of a social group can shape the norms according to which individuals behave and make sense of their behaviour (see also Turner, 1991). Tom Tyler has found that social identity theory has ramifications in the specific context of attitudes to justice (Blader and Tyler, 2003; Lind and Tyler, 1988; Smith et al, 1998; Tyler, 2009). His extensive research shows that the groups with which a person identifies may qualitatively alter the manner in which the person 'relates' to the rules and procedures of a justice system, provided they are groups that affect a person's identity in a relevant way. Perceptions of the 'quality of treatment' delivered by a justice system will be coloured by the fit between the treatment and the group's interests or concerns (Blader and Tyler, 2003: 748).[10]

[10] Moorhead and Sefton (2000) 75 have also found that, when it comes to being satisfied with an encounter with the justice system, 'issues such as age, health, education, ethnicity, gender and social and economic group all show some influence'.

Tyler's research helps to explain the findings of Smart et al (2005). Their qualitative research into the outcomes and experiences of litigants in residence and contact dispute cases found that both mothers and fathers are respectively likely to report a perception that the family justice system is biased against mothers or fathers as a group (ibid: 29–31). Members of the two groups give different reasons for the perceived bias[11] and it seems likely that the tendency to express these conflicting perspectives is not just mediated by gender, but also by the more specific and distinguishable experiences as mothers and fathers.[12] Motherhood and fatherhood become highly salient aspects of a person's identity in the context of many family disputes and it is hardly surprising that individuals might frame their positions with reference to what they perceive to be the experiences of mothers and fathers in general.

Unfortunately, we know very little about the factors that might make individuals experiencing family disputes more or less susceptible to identifying with different social groups. However, as I indicated earlier, many popular online communities related to family dispute resolution are organised around the salient identities of motherhood and fatherhood. Such communities might increase the exposure of individuals to social groups that they identify with and indeed create channels through which relevant social groups can communicate. This makes them fascinating and there is good reason for seeking to understand their functions in this regard.

Recently, concerns have been expressed about how communications with particular groups might be orienting those experiencing family disputes towards particular perspectives.[13] Melville (2017: 150) has written about this in the context of observations of McKenzie Friends[14] advising unrepresented litigants in ways that 'promote powerful social myths that support gender inequality and violence against women, and deny children's rights'.[15] Melville's concern derives from the frequency with which McKenzie Friends are associated with fathers' rights groups and she gives a concise summary of the profusion of research tracing the influ-

[11] In the case of fathers, the perception of bias was predominantly (though not exclusively) related to the feeling that residence is automatically awarded to women. Mothers on the other hand tended to perceive a pro-contact bias that trivialises child welfare concerns.

[12] In Smart's study men were overwhelming likely to be the 'contact' parent, while women/mothers were correspondingly more likely to be the 'resident' parent or main carer. These patterns are, of course, in line with general post-separation parenting norms.

[13] For reports of practitioners expressing these concerns, see Tickle (2018) and various posts on barrister Lucy Reed's 'Pink Tape' blog: www.pinktape.co.uk.

[14] In England and Wales, litigants who are unrepresented have a rebuttable right to be accompanied in court by a lay supporter, known as a 'McKenzie Friend'. Some individuals act as McKenzie Friends repeatedly, charging a fee for their support. Their role tends to encompass the giving of advice prior to attending court. Many, though not all, have associations with fathers' rights groups. For research on the work of McKenzie Friends see Smith, Hitchings and Sefton (2017).

[15] Similar concerns about how fathers' lobbying groups might influence litigants in person through social support groups that they have set up are noted in Trinder et al (2014) and Smith, Hitchings and Sefton (2017).

ence of fathers' rights groups on family justice over time (ibid: 150–52). Online discussion forums create a window through which the unfolding of group norms pertaining to family justice might be viewed, potentially leading to a better understanding of how and why conceptualisations of family justice vary.

III. THE POWER OF ONLINE DISCUSSION FORUMS

Thus far it has been suggested that online discussion forums can give us access and insight into social exchanges and processes that are usually hidden but highly important in the context of family dispute resolution. However, this is not the only reason that they are worthy of attention. In this section I continue to draw on insights from social psychology and suggest that online forums also have an intrinsic capacity to shape views and behaviours in a uniquely powerful way. I advance two reasons for this argument. The first is that the influence of groups in shaping views and actions is likely to be intensified through online communities. The second is that the very act of contributing to an online discussion is likely to increase trust in the information shared in that discussion.

A. Group Identities and Norms in Online Discussion Forums

Online discussion forums represent a new site for the formation of connections between individuals who might share membership of a particular group but would not necessarily encounter each other in the real world. It has been observed that, 'One of the most valuable features of [online] information pools is that they enable widely dispersed and diverse users to seek out and interact with others who are different from the people they may encounter regularly offline' (Flanagin, Hocivar and Samavito, 2014: 683–84).

The reference to 'information pools' in the above quote merits some explanation. The authors use the term to describe online resources containing user-generated content that is both consumed and created by a large number of users. These resources include online discussion forums.[16] The terminology should prompt a realisation that not everyone who accesses an online discussion forum related to family dispute resolution will do so for social reasons, and neither is it inevitable that they will be attracted to the forum because of its function as a community. Many will have a more instrumental purpose, namely the seeking of information about how to resolve their dispute. In England and Wales reliance on self-help strategies to support family dispute resolution has increased since such disputes were almost completely withdrawn

[16] The authors classify a diverse range of other online resource types as 'information pools', including user-generated encyclopaedias (such as Wikipedia), and user-ratings sites (such as Trip Advisor).

from the scope of legal aid following the Legal Aid Sentencing and Punishment of Offenders Act (LASPO) 2012.[17] The *Legal Problem and Resolutions Survey* found that 46% of those who had recently experienced a family problem used the internet, either alone or in combination with another source of advice, to find information and advice on how to solve the problem (Franklyn et al, 2017: 81). Although that Survey does not contain more granular information about what types of internet source people use, it is clear to anyone who cares to look that online discussion forums are among them.[18]

Given that online discussion forums are probably perceived as an information source by many, we should be cautious about leaping to the assumption that they represent an extension of the informal social interactions and social groups that can shape views of family justice. Interestingly, however, some research suggests that, 'people often come to view online information pools as communities … which can incite among users a sense of group identification or shared identity' (Flanagin et al, 2014: 684).[19] In the context of online forums focusing on issues such as mental health and marginal environmental lifestyle decisions (such as using non-disposable nappies), research has found that: 'Most people joining forums are not very attuned to the community-building utility of forum membership; they are more interested in its instrumental value as a site of information transfer between members' (Pendry and Salvatore, 2015: 216).[20] Instrumental users of forums initially express low levels of identification with other forum users. However, because most users are not expecting to derive social benefits from engagement with the forum, their social expectations are often quickly exceeded. This is important because it appears that having had *social,* rather than instrumental, expectations met or exceeded is the strongest predictor of high identification with other forum users (ibid: 217). Applying this finding to the context of family disputes, it is likely that the initial purpose of many who engage with online discussion forums is to seek information about how to solve their dispute, rather than social support. But there is a strong possibility that what they initially saw as an 'information pool' will become a community of experience with which they identify.

The significance of this lies in the fact that research has also demonstrated that the tenets of social identity theory hold true in online communities; identification with particular groups will shape both views and behaviour. The evidence is summed up by Flanagin et al (2014: 692–3):

[17] Exceptions do exist. The post-LASPO scheme allows for legal aid to be awarded, subject to qualifying criteria, to the victims of domestic abuse and in 'exceptional' cases in which human rights might be breached if legal aid is not made available.

[18] This is reinforced by several qualitative studies from England and Wales that have found incidental evidence that research participants used online forums to discuss their family problems. See eg, Trinder et al, (2014); Smith, Hitchings and M Sefton (2017).

[19] Flanagin et al also cite other research in support of this position: Cho, Chen, and Chung (2010); Kim, Zheng, and Gupta (2011).

[20] Pendry and Salvatore's finding that information seeking is the most common reason for joining a forum held true across different types of forum: (2015) 215.

> people tend to be more motivated to contribute information to online pools when they believe that the others who will view and benefit from this information are similar to themselves. People also tend to find information contributed by similar others to be more credible and are also more likely to indicate that they will act on this information.

So, an antecedent of active participation in information exchange through online discussion forums is high identification with the members of the forum. But, in a sort of vortex effect, identification can increase from low to high levels as a result of the intrinsically social nature of online forums, meaning that the forum itself draws visitors to invest in it.

In light of this, my earlier observation that identity-based online forums relevant to family disputes appear to be considerably more active than those hosted by solution-focused websites is unsurprising. As Flanagin et al (2014: 692) conclude:

> Information pools, then, may actually form and sustain themselves best as communities comprising similar people with similar views. This supports a conceptualisation of information pools not only as communities or groups but more specifically as groups of similar users.[21]

This statement reflects one of the findings from Paechter's analysis of how a community of support for divorcing individuals developed through chat forums in the months following the launch of Wikivorce in 2007.[22] She observed in some discussion threads that, 'a collective refusal to consider alternative positions … excluding all those who disagreed with their perspective, thus threatened to lead some people to consolidate maladaptive belief systems about, for example, the fairness of the legal process' (Paechter, 2012b: 398). It is particularly interesting that this trend was evident on Wikivorce, which is a platform aimed at all those experiencing divorce and is likely to have a quite a diverse user-base. It begins to look as though online discussion forums could be more potent distillers of divergent group perspectives and influence than ordinary social relationships and interactions. Those of us who have an interest in family justice and effective family dispute resolution should be keen to explore the potential ramifications of this.

The potential significance of online forums is reinforced by elements of existing research that highlight a link between high identification with forum participants and behaviour. Flanagin et al (2014) found that forum users indicated intentions to act on the information they accessed through the forum. Meanwhile Pendry and Salvatore's research (2015) goes further, demonstrating a link between identification with a particular online discussion group and relevant offline activism. Their findings perhaps have a counterpart in research suggesting that some individuals who interact with online fathers groups while

[21] An embedded citation has been omitted from this quote.
[22] See n 5 above on Wikivorce.

they are experiencing a family dispute are subsequently motivated to contribute to local support meetings, or even act as McKenzie Friends (Smith, Hitchings and Sefton, 2017).[23] The step between online group participation and offline activism is a strong signifier of the capacity of online communities to influence and motivate the behaviour of individuals who have engaged with them.

B. Online Communities as Influential Information Sources

We have seen how the social character of online communities can boost individuals' identification with forum members, prompting them to place high levels of trust in the information shared in the communities, and to take certain actions. We turn now to consider another consequence of the social character of online communities. Studies combining the insights of social and cognitive psychology tell us that the very act of participating is likely to increase the value attached to information distributed through an online discussion forum.

The underlying concept here is known as cognitive elaboration. Cognitive elaboration occurs when a person actively engages with information, processing it in new ways to increase their understanding of how it might relate to their wider knowledge or experience. The idea that cognitive elaboration increases receptiveness to ideas and absorption of information should not be new to those of us who teach in a higher education setting. Pedagogy is infused with discussion of the value of cognitive elaboration, and promotion of the importance of students actively using information to improve their mastery of it lies behind many standard interactive teaching (or 'active learning') methods.[24]

Importantly, for pedagogical purposes cognitive elaboration and collaborative learning through interactions with other students go hand in hand, and have almost become synonymous. This is because it has been found that cognitive elaboration is best facilitated through interaction with others. Thus Laurillard (2000: 137) argues that engagement with both peers and instructors is a necessary condition for the development of real understanding.[25] Others have argued more specifically that the most effective cognitive elaboration tool, in terms of impact on learning, is explaining an issue to a peer and receiving and responding to their feedback on the information (Wittrock, 1977; Slavin, 2012).

In addition to the positive impact that social interaction has on learning by aiding cognitive elaboration, it seems that there are benefits to be gained from the social nature of exploring a topic in groups. Some research indicates that working in groups to solve a problem collaboratively results in higher performance

[23] See n 14 above for a definition of McKenzie Friends.

[24] For example, the rationale of the almost ubiquitous small group tutorial, in which students actively discuss, apply, critique and elaborate on ideas, hails from understanding that active engagement with information is a precursor to learning. See Anderson (2007).

[25] See also Slavin (2012).

because motivation increases, aided by a sense of 'team spirit' or 'cohesiveness' (Slavin, 2012).[26] All of this has led to widespread use of online peer-to-peer discussions in different education contexts, including distance learning courses and virtual learning environments designed to complement face-to-face learning (Rovai, 2007; Thomas, 2002).

In many ways, online discussion forums that form outside of the education context are a good natural proxy for the benefits of cognitive elaboration through collaborative learning that are espoused by pedagogues. As we have seen, they are frequently used by those who, like learners in education, are seeking to increase their knowledge or understanding of a topic. Participants tend to apply their knowledge or experience to different situations outlined by others, articulate and expand on ideas, give explanations to each other, and make judgements about the contributions of other forum users.

The latter point, about contributors to online community users having to make credibility judgements, prompted Westerman et al (2014) to test how the theory of cognitive elaboration plays out in the context of online communications. His work recognises the important role that social media play as influential tools of information transmission:

> Social media are a general category of channels and applications that highlight collaboration and working together to create and distribute content. This collaboration not only consists of creating content together, but also discussing the content in an attempt to improve it collaboratively and to come to a shared understanding of it. (ibid: 172).

The second part of the quote could almost be a description of the approach to cognitive elaboration that is promoted in education, making clear that in the process of participating in an online forum, people become invested co-producers of knowledge and ideas.[27] Importantly, Westerman et al's research indicates that, in addition to aiding information absorption, cognitive elaboration is a strong mediating factor in determining the credibility that people attach to information consumed on social media. In other words, the higher the level of participation, the higher the level of trust the participant is likely to place in the source. In a reinforcement of the work of Flanagin et al (2014) and Pendry and Salvatore (2015) that was discussed above, Westerman et al also found that cognitive elaboration in relation to different types of social media increases in line with the sense of shared identity that is generated by many online information pools.

To recap, we have seen that even those who start out seeking information are often sucked into participation in online communities precisely because of their social character. In turn, participation in an online forum is likely to

[26] This provides much of the rationale for Problem-Based Learning (PBL) methods, on which see Dolmans and Schmidt (2006).

[27] Westerman et al's focus was on social media, which is broader than but inclusive of the types of online community that have been focused on here. The particular study referenced explored the impact of engagement with threads on Twitter.

heighten the levels of trust individuals place in the information shared there as a result of both cognitive elaboration and the affective impact of social interaction, which leads to high identification with forum users. To all this could be added further magnetic functions of online communities that I have not explored. For example, there is evidence to suggest that the recent or contemporaneous updating of information that is frequently seen in online networks can also seduce people into higher levels of participation (or cognitive elaboration) than intended (Westerman, Spence and Van der Heide, 2014: 178).[28] This further reinforces the potential significance of my observation that there is more activity (and therefore, one assumes, more contemporaneous updating of information) in online forums built around identity than in those built around experience (eg, of relationship breakdown or separation). All in all, there is good reason for supposing that online communities might exert a considerable influence on those who choose to engage with them while they are navigating the resolution of family dispute.

C. The Potential of Online Communities

Thus far I have outlined two reasons for supposing that online discussion forums could be highly influential. The first looks concerning, given the potential for longstanding factional agendas, particularly in relation to fathers' rights, to become more widespread and entrenched through online communities. Consequently, it is tempting also to consider the potential of online communities as effective sources of information transfer to be negative; it does after all threaten to compound the increased influence of particular groups. Though the concern is a valid one, it is my contention that we should resist the temptation to focus only on the negatives here. In this section I want to adjust the tone slightly, by considering whether online discussion forums could serve a *useful* purpose as a result of both their instrumental and social functions.

Let us take the instrumental function of online communities as distributors of information first. In England and Wales, the need for accessible and useful information about family justice is acute post-LASPO. Information provision has arguably formed a key plank of government strategy in relation to meeting legal need. As a substitute for funding professional legal advice for private family disputes, resources have been invested in the development of information provision. For example, a 'Sorting Out Separation' web app has been designed (Department for Work and Pensions, 2014) and a series of other online guides has been piloted, including one for those trying to sort out arrangements for

[28] Westerman et al (2014) also suggest that the recency of posts can intensify trust, but that finding was reached in the context of online communications about news events, in which it is obvious that currency of information might be seen as a proxy for quality. It is less clear that this would apply in online discussions on less time sensitive issues.

their children.[29] This strategy has generated much criticism, with particular concerns being expressed about the ability of individuals to access and navigate information and about the deficiency of information that is generic and not tailored to the individual problem (Maclean, 2016; Marjoribanks, 2015, Trinder et al, 2014). It nonetheless remains central to the most recently published action plan for providing legal support to those with certain problems including family disputes (Ministry of Justice, 2019).[30]

Of course, this reality does not in itself make the case for championing the user-generated information provided through online communities. Indeed, the instinctive response might be that efforts should be made to warn those experiencing family problems *against* use of such information sources as part of a purposeful strategy to increase information literacy. But there are a couple of reasons for suggesting that such an approach would be shortsighted. For one thing, as we saw above, research from the education context tells us that online discussions can be a very effective tool for boosting absorption of information and understanding of an issue. This might explain why researchers have found that 'online forums are perceived by their users as an exceedingly successful means of information transfer' (Pendry and Salvatore, 2015: 216). Another potential advantage of online communities stems from the fact that personal narratives are used as a device for eliciting information which, as a consequence, is to some extent tailored to individual circumstances. It is easy to understand how someone seeking information about a child arrangements dispute might derive greater benefit and reassurance from accounts of their options based on similar experiences than from the generic information, such as that contained in the guide produced by the Ministry of Justice.[31]

On the face of it, the established effectiveness of peer-to-peer learning, combined with recognition of the potential for individuals to seek out information tailored to their specific circumstances, makes a good case for open-mindedness about the potential of online forums. The obvious retort is that information is useless if it is not accurate and online communities, populated by anonymous individuals with no legal training, are more likely to function as channels of misinformation than effective legal education. In fact, inaccurate information that is pertinent, memorable and generates a high degree of trust is arguably worse than useless.

[29] https://helpwithchildarrangements.service.justice.gov.uk. See Ministry of Justice Digital and Technology (2017) for other examples.

[30] Ministry of Justice, Legal Support: the way ahead. An action plan to deliver better support for those experiencing legal problems (January 2019). Although there is much talk of developing and expanding 'complementary legal support' (ie, support that does not come from a professionally qualified lawyer), it is clear that most of what is considered falls into the information giving category. Services that are referenced – such as the Personal Support Units and Citizens Advice – generally classify their services as falling on the information side of the information/advice continuum. Some funding for services that offer more direct forms of support has been made available. See Department for Work and Pensions (2013 and 2015).

[31] See n 29 above.

Having conducted some exploratory analysis of information about the law pertaining to family disputes shared in online forums I have some sympathy with this view. But, again, interesting lessons might be learned from research in the healthcare arena. Although the picture is mixed, several studies have found a far higher level of accuracy than expected in the information about medical conditions shared on online forums. For example, following a large-scale study in which professionals rated the information in online discussion forum posts for quality, completeness and usefulness, Cole et al (2016) concluded that,

> the health information found in discussion forums is of reasonably good quality and only rarely does it contain information that is very inaccurate and which … may lead someone to act in a way that may put their health at risk.[32]

In some cases it has even been suggested that lay individuals can become quite expert at collating and distributing information to online contacts (Ferguson, 2000). Given that 'peer-to-peer learning' and 'peer-to-peer healthcare' (Fox, 2011; Sillence, 2013 and 2014a) are terms that appear now to have good currency in their respective fields, it might well be time to consider the possibility that peer-to-peer legal support could hold some value.

Moving on, there is good reason to suppose that the social dimension of online communities enables them to serve a second useful purpose, namely that of empowering and boosting the well-being of users. It is well known that social support generally increases the ability of individuals to cope with stressful situations, improves well-being and even aids recovery time from illnesses (Jettan, Haslam and Haslam, 2012).[33] Volumes of healthcare research have found that these same benefits can be derived from the social interactions of those who engage in online communities (eg, Rodgers and Chen, 2005; Baum, 2004). Although there is some evidence to suggest that high use of online social media and social networks might function differently, to increase isolation and depressive symptoms (Turkle, 2012; Kraut et al, 1998), such evidence has often been refuted in later studies (Kraut et al, 2002) and it certainly does not appear to hold true in all circumstances (Pendry and Salvatore, 2015: 217).

In particular situations it has been found that engagement with online communities can have a very positive impact. For example, it has been observed that, 'getting involved in online groups can be of huge benefit to those with somewhat depleted offline social resources' (Pendry and Salvatore, 2015: 212).[34] Offline social resources might be inadequate in general terms as a result of circumstances that limit an individual's freedom to build or sustain social networks. For example, in the case of parents caring for children with special

[32] Other examples of studies reporting unexpectedly high levels of quality in information shared on online forums include Ferguson (2000), Sillence and Mo (2014b); Hoch, Norris, Lester and Marcus (1999).

[33] Pendry and Salvatore (2015) and Chung (2014) cite numerous other examples of studies providing evidence on this point.

[34] Pendry and Salvatore refer to the supporting findings of McKenna and Bargh's (1998) prior work on this point.

healthcare needs, Baum (2004) found that internet-based parent support groups not only improved parent-carer well-being, but led to improved relationships between the parent-carer and the child. This led to the recommendation that healthcare professionals should advocate the use of internet support groups as an appropriate intervention for this group. Meanwhile Fox (2013) describes the unique advantages of using online communities for people with chronic health conditions who might not easily find opportunities to meet other individuals with the same conditions.

Offline social resources might be thin in a more situational sense in relation to stigmatising or embarrassing issues that individuals do not feel comfortable discussing openly, or in relation to issues that a person's social contacts might struggle to relate to. Thus online social support groups have been found to have a positive influence on well-being in the case of people with mental health issues (Kummervold et al, 2002, Pendry and Salvatore, 2015, Rideout and Fox, 2018) and certain medical conditions, such as breast and prostate cancer (Sillence, 2013; Rogers and Chen, 2015). In each of these situations there is some indication that the improvement to the individual's well-being can empower the individual to make more active and constructive choices about managing their condition.

Returning to the context of people experiencing family disputes, it does not seem too much of a leap to suppose that the social functions of online communities might be similarly valuable notwithstanding that in this field we do not have a research base that proves it yet. We know that family disputes, and family justice processes, can be stressful and isolating. It is easy to imagine that individuals embroiled in high conflict family disputes, or even family justice processes might feel some embarrassment discussing their situation with their usual social contacts. It also seems likely that they might struggle to find people in their social circle who are able fully to understand what they are going through. And the lifestyle changes that are often incurred by a separation, such as changes in living arrangements and childcare responsibilities, might also lead to elevated levels of social isolation for some, if only temporarily. So a similar situational depletion of social resources that has been found to be a precursor to constructive use of online communities in healthcare might underpin use of online communities in the context of family disputes.

What of the difference that improved well-being could make, should it manifest as a result of online social interactions in relation to family disputes? An abundance of evidence points towards the stress that accompanies family disputes (Franklyn et al, 2017: 30) as well as the experience of navigating the family courts, particularly without representation (Trinder et al, 2014, Smart et al, 2005). So there is plenty of scope for improving well-being. And there are grounds for hypothesising that doing so could make a substantive difference to dispute resolution outcomes. Barlow et al have found that the 'emotional readiness' of parties to a dispute to engage in different types of dispute resolution, such as mediation, has an impact on the likelihood of a positive outcome (Barlow, Hunter, Smithson and Ewing, 2017). Hitchings and Miles (2014) have similarly observed that the emotional stress of separation can hamper parties' efforts to make decisions about their finances after separation before they are emotionally ready. So processes that have potential to help people progress through the distress and trauma of a relationship breakdown might well improve capacity to resolve disputes.

The words of Greiner et al (2017: 1173) seem pertinent here. Summarising the importance of attending to the emotional and confidence struggles of unrepresented litigants, they have warned that, 'the recipe for solving the legal problems of human beings has four-parts psychology for every one-part formal law'. If there is a possibility that online communities might serve a therapeutic purpose in relation to the emotional and psychological dimensions of family disputes, we should think very carefully before rejecting them out of hand.

IV. CONCLUSION

My purpose in writing this chapter has been to mount a convincing case for the representations of family justice that take place in online communities to be treated as an important feature of shifts in family dispute resolution that are heralded by the digital age. The chapter began by explaining that representations of family justice in online communities could be extremely revealing in terms of content relating to perceptions of family law, approaches to family dispute resolution and acceptance or rejection of particular perspectives. However, the discussion developed to show that the import of online communities is not limited to their function as an accessible version of the social exchanges about family justice that have always taken place. Rather, there is a good chance that they have a unique power to influence the views and actions of users. In this respect, a repeated refrain has been the potential for online communities to serve as a catalyst for the proliferation of partisan views of family justice, particularly in relation to gender. It is important that this prospect is not ignored. Neither, however, should it be permitted to mark the beginning and end of the discussion, and to stymie further debate and discovery.

Another recurring theme of the chapter has been the extent to which the inherently social nature of online communities lends them much of their power and significance. The importance of this social character cannot be over-estimated. In the healthcare context, Susannah Fox (2014) has described health information as acquiring 'a social life' since the advent of the internet.[35] In all likelihood, that same 'social life' applies mutatis mutandis to the context of family disputes, which – like health issues – are something that people have always included in

[35] Fox goes on to refer to powerful elements of online social communications that have not been covered here. She notes that they fuse two powerful forces: the instinct to seek and share information about health and the ability to do so at internet speed and scale.

their social exchanges. It may even constitute a paradigm-shift in the way that some people access and relate to information about family disputes. Meanwhile, all our talk of the digital sphere and family justice relates to such issues as how artificial intelligence might inform sophisticated online dispute resolution tools, creating traditional information portals and building user-friendly interfaces for engaging with aspects of the justice process. Worthwhile as these endeavours are, there is a risk that we are focusing on a side-show while the real drama happens elsewhere.

We do not know that for sure, of course. In constructing the arguments above, I have drawn on insights from research conducted almost entirely in other fields. The studies and theories I have used are rigorous, numerous and, to some extent and in varying ways, relate to topics that are analogous with the challenges of family dispute resolution. However, while they make a prima facie case for the significance of online communities to family dispute resolution, one of my concluding messages is that they are no substitute for tailored research that would show precisely how those communities are relevant. It is disappointing to have found that such research barely exists at present. With the exception of Paechter's study (2012) of how a single online community was established for divorcing individuals in 2007, the ramifications of online communities for family dispute resolution have been considered only tangentially. What's more, the tendency has been to approach them with suspicion (Melville, 2017) and to characterise them as problems (Tickle, 2018). This situation is in marked contrast to the open-mindedness and curiosity that characterises the expanse of research on online communities that exists in education, and healthcare in particular.

In this piece, I have only scratched the surface of that research. It moves from examinations of the scale of use of peer-to-peer healthcare, through identification of factors that incline users to be more or less influenced by online social exchanges and of why people select particular online communities over others, to understanding how participation in online communities impacts on individuals. The result is a profusion of evidence and, critically, much discussion of how the power and appeal of online communities might be harnessed through the creation of effective support resources. Ferguson (2000), for example, has outlined the prospect of 'patient-helpers' and healthcare professionals working in partnership to provide high-quality and accessible online support. In the education context, Rovai (2007) and Thomas (2002) have suggested that obstacles to effective student use of online discussion forums might be surmounted by instructors establishing a purposeful social presence to support the functioning of the student community.

Given the potential risks of individuals seeking information and support from peers in online communities, it might feel hard to countenance solution-focused approaches, which tacitly accept – maybe even encourage – a continued role for that practice. But Greiner et al (2017: 1172) have suggested that there is a need for methods of supporting unrepresented litigants that are 'subversive of the existing [United States] legal order, which continues to justify itself on the idea (perhaps the fiction) that addressing legal problems requires professional judgment'. Drawing on the tenets of cognitive psychology (much as I have done here), they argue that many of the challenges of resolving legal problems 'have little to do with formal law' and that 'thinking like a nonlawyer' in devising support is essential. Embracing the potential, or at the very least trying to address the power, of online social communities focused on family disputes is a perfect example of a subversive strategy that might well serve the needs of real people. In any event, the irreversible social life that the digital sphere has breathed into information about family dispute resolution means it is something that we cannot ignore.

REFERENCES

Anderson, C (1997) 'Enabling and shaping understanding through tutorials' in F Martin, D Hounsell, and N Entwistle (eds), *The Experience of Learning* (Edinburgh, Scottish Universities Press) 184–95.

Barlow, A, Duncan, S, James, G and Park, A (2005) *Cohabitation, Marriage and the Law: Social Change and Legal Reform in the 21st Century* (Oxford, Hart Publishing).

Barlow, A, Hunter, R, Smithson, J and Ewing, J (2017) *Mapping Paths to Family Justice: Resolving Family Disputes in Neoliberal Times* (London, Palgrave Macmillan).

Baum, L (2004) 'Internet parent support groups for primary caregivers of a child with special health care needs', *Pediatric Nursing* 30(5), 381.

Benkler, Y (2006) *The Wealth of Networks: How Social Production Transforms Markets and Freedom* (New Haven, Yale University Press).

Blader, S and Tyler, TR (2003) 'A four component model of procedural justice: Defining the meaning of a "fair" process', *Personality and Social Psychology Bulletin* 29, 747–58.

Bryson, C, Ellman, IM, McKay, S and Miles, J (2015) *Child maintenance: how would the British public calculate what the State should require parents to pay?* (London Nuffield Foundation).

Cho, H, Chen, M and Chung, S (2010) 'Testing an integrative theoretical model of knowledge-sharing behavior in the context of Wikipedia', *Journal of the American Society for Information Science and Technology* 61(6), 1198–1212.

Chung, J (2014) 'Social Networking in Online Support Groups for Health: How Online Social Networking Benefits Patients', *Journal of Health Communication* 19(6), 639–59.

Cole, J, Watkins, C and Kleine, D (2016) 'Health advice from internet discussion forums: how bad is dangerous?', *Journal of Medical Internet Research* 18(1), e4.

Davis, G (1988) *Partisans and Mediators: The Resolution of Divorce Disputes* (Oxford, Oxford University Press).

Department for Work and Pensions and The Rt Hon Steve Webb (2013) *Press Release: Government funds new innovative support for separated parents* 10 April 2013: www.gov.uk/government/news/government-funds-new-innovative-support-for-separated-parents.

Department for Work and Pensions and The Rt Hon Steve Webb (2015) *Press Release: New cash for innovative family support projects* 8 March 2015: www.gov.uk/government/news/new-cash-for-innovative-family-support-projects.

Department for Work and Pensions (2014) *Sorting Out Separation Web App: Evaluation of Effectiveness. Research Report No 863* (Department for Work and Pensions).
Dewar, J (1998) 'The Normal Chaos of Family Law', *Modern Law Review* 61(4), 467–85.
Diduck, A (2013) 'Autonomy and Vulnerability in Family Law: The Missing Link' in Wallbank, J and Herring, J (eds) *Vulnerabilities, Care and Family Law* (Abingdon, Routledge) 95–114.
Dolmans, D and Schmidt, H (2006) 'What Do We Know About Cognitive and Motivational Effects of Small Group Tutorials in Problem-Based Learning?', *Advances in Health Sciences Education* 11, 321–36.
Family Justice Review Panel (2011) *Family Justice Review: Final Report* (London, Ministry of Justice).
Ferguson, T (2000) 'Online patient-helpers and physicians working together: a new partnership for high quality health care', *British Medical Journal* 1129–32.
Flanagin, A, Hocevar, K and Samahito, S (2014) 'Connecting with the user-generated Web: how group identification impacts online information sharing and evaluation', *Information, Communication and Society* 17(6), 683–94.
Fox, S (2011) *Peer-to-peer healthcare* (Report from the Pew Research Center: Internet & American Life Project).
Fox, S (2013) 'After Dr Google: Peer-to-peer healthcare', *Pediatrics* Supplement 4 131(4), S221–S225.
Fox, S (2014) *The Social Life of Health Information* (Pew Research Centre FactTank post): www.pewresearch.org/fact-tank/2014/01/15/the-social-life-of-health-information/.
Franklyn, R, Budd, T, Verrill, R and Willoughby, M (2017) *Findings from the Legal Problem and Resolution Survey 2014–15* (Ministry of Justice Analytical Series).
Greiner, JD, Jiminez, D and Lupica, L (2017) 'Self-Help Reimagined', *Indiana Law Journal* 92(3), 1119–73.
Hitchings, E, Miles, J and Woodward, H (2013) *Assembling the jigsaw puzzle: Financial settlement on divorce* (Bristol, University of Bristol).
Hoch, D, Norris, D, Lester, J and Marcus, A (1999) 'Information exchange in an epilepsy forum on the World Wide Web', *Seizure* 8, 30-4.
Hu, Y and Sundar, S (2010) 'Effects of Online Health Sources on Credibility and Behavioural Intentions', *Communication Research* 37(1), 105–32.
Jetten, J, Haslam, C and Haslam, SA (eds) (2012) *The social cure: Identity, health and well-being* (Hove, England, Psychology Press).
Kent, C, Laslo, E and Rafaeli, S (2016) 'Interactivity in online discussions and learning outcomes', *Computers and Education* 97, 116–28.
Kim, H, Zheng, JR, and Gupta, S (2011) 'Examining knowledge contribution from the perspective of an online identity in blogging communities', *Computers in Human Behavior* 27, 1760–70.
Kraut, R, Kiesler, S, Boneva, B, Cummings, J, Helgeson, V and Crawford, A (2002) 'Internet paradox revisited', *Journal of Social Issues* 58, 49–74.
Kraut, R, Patterson, M, Lundmark, V, Kiesler, S, Mukhopadhyay, T and Scherlis, W (1998) 'Internet paradox: a social technology that reduces social involvement and psychological well-being?', *American Psychologist* 53(9), 1017–31.
Laurillard, D (2000) 'New technologies and the curriculum' in Scott, P (ed) *Higher Education Re-formed* (London, Falmer Press) 133–53.
Lind, E and Tyler, T (1988) *The Social Psychology of Procedural Justice* (New York, Plenun).

Maclean, M (2015) 'New Ways to Seek Legal Information and Advice on Family Matters in England and Wales: From Professional Legal Services to Google and Private Ordering' in M Maclean, J Eekelaar, J and B Bastard (eds), *Delivering Family Justice in the 21st Century* (Oxford, Hart Publishing) 323–39.
Marjoribanks, D (2015) *Breaking up is hard to do* (London, Relate).
McKenna, KYA ad Bargh, JA (1998) 'Coming out in the age of the Internet: Identity "demarginalization" through virtual group participation', *Journal of Personality and Social Psychology* 75(3), 681–94.
Melville, A (2017) '"Giving Hope to Fathers": Discursive Constructions of Families and Family Law by McKenzie Friends Associated With Fathers' Rights Groups', *International Journal of Law, Policy and the Family* 31, 147–73.
Ministry of Justice Digital and Technology (2017) Family Separation: What's GOV got to do with it? (Ministry of Justice Digital and Technology Blog: https://mojdigital.blog.gov.uk/2017/01/30/family-separation-whats-gov-got-to-do-with-it/).
Ministry of Justice (2019) *Legal Support: The Way Ahead. An action plan to deliver better support to people experiencing legal problems.*
Mnookin, R and Kornhauser, L (1979) 'Bargaining in the shadow of the law: the case of divorce', *Yale Law Journal* 88(5), 950–97.
Moorhead, R and Sefton, M (2008) *Just Satisfaction: what drives public and participant satisfaction with courts and tribunals?* (Ministry of Justice Research Series 5/08).
Paechter C (2012a) 'Researching sensitive issues online: implications of a hybrid insider/outsider position in a retrospective ethnographic study', *Qualitative Research* 13(1), 71–86.
Paechter, C (2012b) Online Learning in Divorce: how the formation of a community of practice in a divorce support website enables and inhibits learning', *E-learning and Digital Media* 9(4), 392–405.
Pendry, L and Salvatore, J (2015) 'Individuals and Social benefits of online discussion forums', *Computers in Human Behaviour* 50, 211–20.
Rideout, V and Fox, S (2018) *Digital Health Practices, Social Media Use, and Mental Well-Being Among Teens and Young Adults in the U.S.* A National Survey Sponsored by HopeLab and Well-Being Trust: www.hopelab.org/reports/pdf/a-national-survey-by-hopelab-and-well-being-trust-2018.pdf.
Rovai, A (2007) 'Facilitating Online Discussions Effectively', *The Internet and Higher Education* 10(1), 77–88.
Sillence, E (2013) 'Giving and Receiving Peer Advice in an Online Breast Cancer Support Group', *Cyberpsychology, Behavior, and Social Networking* 16(6), 480–85.
Sillence, E, Hardy, C, Harris, P and Briggs P (2014a) 'Modelling patient engagement in peer-to-peer healthcare' in *Proceedings of the 23rd International Conference on World Wide Web Companion* (New York, Association for Computing Machinery) 481–86.
Sillence, E and Mo, P (2014b) 'Communicating Health Decisions: an Analysis of messages posted to online prostate cancer forums', *Health Expectations* 17(2), 244–53.
Slavin, R (2012) 'Cooperative Learning and achievement: theory and research' in Weiner, I, Reynolds, W and Miller, G (eds), *Handbook of Psychology, Volume 7 Educational Psychology*, 2nd edn (Wiley) 179–98.
Smart, C, May, V, Wade, A and Furniss, J (2005) *Residence and Contact Disputes in Court Volume 2* (Department for Constitutional Affairs Research Series4/05).

Smith, HJ, Tyler, T, Huo, YJ, Ortiz, DJ and Lind, EA (1998) 'The self-relevant implications of the group-value model: Group membership, self-worth, and procedural justice', *Journal of Experimental Social Psychology* 34, 470–93.

Smith, L, Hitchings, E and Sefton, M (2017) *Fee-charging McKenzie Friends in Private Family Law Cases* (London, The Bar Council).

Tajfel, H and Turner, J (1979) 'An integrative theory of intergroup conflict' in Austin, WG and Worchel, S (eds), *The social psychology of intergroup relations* (Monterey CA, Brooks Cole) 33–47.

Thomas, M (2002) 'Learning within incoherent structures: the space of online discussion forums', *Journal of Computer Assisted Learning* 18(2), 351–66.

Tickle, L (2018) *How information technology and modern communications are affecting journalism and family law*. The Bridget Lindley Annual Memorial Lecture (Family Justice Council): www.judiciary.uk/wp-content/uploads/2018/03/transcript-of-bridget-lindley-annual-memorial-lecture-2018.pdf.

Trinder, L, Hunter, R, Hitchings, E, Miles, J, Moorhead, R, Smith, L, Sefton M, Hinchly, V, Bader, K and Pearce, J (2014) *Litigants in Person in Private Family Cases* (Ministry of Justice).

Turkle, S (2012) *Alone together: Why we expect more from technology and less from each other* (USA, Basic Books).

Turner, J (1991) *Social influence* (Milton Keynes, Oxford University Press).

Tyler, T (2009) 'Procedural Justice, identity and deference to the law: what shapes rule-following in a period of transition?', *Australian Journal of Psychology* 69(1), 32–39.

Westerman, D, Spence, P and Van Der Heide, B (2014) 'Social Media as Information Source: Recency of Updates and Credibility of Information', *Journal of Computer Mediated Communication* 9, 171–83.

Wittrock, M (1974) 'Learning as a generative process', *Educational Psychologist* 11, 87–95.

10

Digital Pathways in Australian Family Law: An Initial Snapshot

BELINDA FEHLBERG AND BRUCE SMYTH

I. INTRODUCTION

OVER THE PAST 18 months, the Australian family law system has been under comprehensive review by the Australian Law Reform Commission (ALRC), with a final report and recommendations released in March 2019.[1] Throughout the review, digital innovation did not feature strongly. Rather, stakeholder and ALRC preference appeared to be to utilise digital avenues in quite a limited way to support separated families – primarily through the provision of information, rather than advice or dispute resolution services – while maintaining non-digital avenues of assistance:

> To further enhance accessibility, submissions suggested that information should be provided in a range of formats, including websites and through telephone lines and web-chats, as well as in non-digital forms for people with limited digital literacy or access to computers or smart phones (Australian Government, Australian Law Reform Commission, 2018).

As regards new contexts within the system for possible use of digital technologies, the ALRC proposed at Discussion Paper stage only that '[t]he Australian Government should work with state and territory governments to explore the use of digital technologies to support the assessment of client needs, including their safety, support and advice needs' (ibid, Proposal 4-2: xv-xvi) within community-based 'Families Hubs', which the ALRC proposes be established 'to provide separating families and their children with a visible entry point for accessing a range of legal and support services' (ibid: Proposal 4-1: xv). This proposal did not ultimately become a recommendation, or a subject of discussion, in the Final Report.

[1] Australian Law Reform Commission, *Review of the family law system: Final Report* (ALRC Report 135 (2019)).

The ALRC's approach is highly consistent with the more general pattern we have seen in the sector of interest yet caution regarding digital innovation. This has encouraged continuing digital evolution, rather than revolution, underpinned by an emphasis on better catering for families with diverse needs, through a more accessible and integrated system.

These emphases were also central in 2001, in another major report on the Australian family law system produced by the Family Law Pathways Advisory Group (FLPAG). The FLPAG was appointed by the federal Minister for Family and Community Services and the Attorney-General to advise the government on how to achieve the government's vision of 'An integrated family law system that is flexible and builds individual and community capacity to achieve the best possible outcomes for families' (Family Law Pathways Advisory Group, 2001: Terms of Reference: v). Its report emphasised the complexity and fragmentation of the existing family law system (ibid: 16), and recommended an integrated approach (or 'service delivery system') based on three pathways: the 'self help', 'supported' and 'litigation' pathways (the Pathways model) (ibid: vxiii). At that point in time, digital technologies were largely absent in the family law area and, while mentioned, were not the focus of the *Out of the Maze* report. Although much has changed since then, we think the Pathways Model remains helpful for thinking about how digital technologies might come into play in various parts of what is still a complex system.

In this chapter, and in an ever-changing modern world, we draw on the Pathways model to consider the extent to which Australia has seen increasing interest in and commitment to the development and use of online family law resources available to separating parents for little or no financial cost. In summary, our sense is that most of the focus has been on the 'self help' pathway, especially the provision of online information (or e-resources). There has been much less emphasis, although some early work, in relation to the 'supported' pathway, through nascent development of online advice and dispute resolution options. Recent shifts in the 'litigation' pathway to online divorce and online court orders may suggest that the position is gradually shifting towards increased use of Online Dispute Resolution (ODR), but these mechanisms are directed at improving court administrative process, rather than playing a decision-making function. In the end, the picture as we see it is one of uneven and uncoordinated digital resources across and within each of the pathways. Given this, the ALRC's approach to digital family justice to date, as just outlined, appears consistent with existing patterns.

II. THE BROADER AUSTRALIAN CONTEXT

In contrast to the backdrop just outlined, the broader context to our chapter is that Australia, like many countries, has seen increasing and overwhelming uptake of digital technologies. For example, Australia remains at the forefront of smartphone ownership, with 89% of Australians owning one in 2018.[2] In 2016–17, 86% of households had access to the internet at home (Thomas et al, 2018):

> Desktop or laptop computers are used by 91% of connected households. Similarly, mobile or smart phones are also used by 91% of connected households. Tablets were the next most popular type of device used by 66% of households to connect to the internet. Internet connected TVs had the largest increase in usage by households, from 27% in 2014–15 to 42% in 2016–17.[3]

A total of 97% of households with children under age 15 had access to the internet, with an average of 7.8 devices per household.[4]

Accompanying this, Australia has seen the development of a significant array of internet resources provided by governments, non-government organisations, private providers, and individuals, aimed at informing and assisting separated families. These resources have burgeoned in recent years due to technological advances and increasing bandwidth (although internet speed is still slower than the global average[5] and access is still not available to all – as discussed below), combined in the family law context and more broadly with growing commitment to supporting people to resolving disputes privately without going to court. As elsewhere, the economic constraints of a tight fiscal environment are also evident in Australia (eg, non-availability of Legal Aid to all but the poorest in the community).[6] There has been significant monetary investment by government in developing internet resources, and growing government commitment to encouraging movement to online communication and service use (evidenced, eg, by the creation of the federal Digital Transformation Agency in 2015, and development of e-government services including myGov to access government services online, and currently My Health Record – with mixed reception for reasons including the digital divide).[7] The justification for government encouragement of online resources is generally expressed in terms of improvement of services, rather than cost-saving to government.[8]

[2] Deloitte, *Mobile Consumer Survey 2018 – The Australian Cut* (2017): www2.deloitte.com/au/mobile-consumer-survey.

[3] Australian Bureau of Statistics (ABS), *Cat No 8146.0 – Household Use of Information Technology, Australia, 2016–17*: www.abs.gov.au/ausstats/abs@.nsf/mf/8146.0.

[4] ibid.

[5] J Duke, 'Australia's Broadband is Slower than Kazakhstan's', *The Sydney Morning Herald*, 8 January 2018: www.smh.com.au/business/consumer-affairs/australia-s-broadband-slower-than-kazakhstan-20180108-p4yyb1.html.

[6] eg in Victoria: Victoria Legal Aid, *VLA Handbook for Lawyers*, 12- Means Test, handbook.vla.vic.gov.au/handbook/12-means-test.

[7] EJ Smith, 'My Health Record 'overlooked' Australians Without Internet Access, Says a Rural Health Worker' (ABC Kimberley, 12 November 2018): www.abc.net.au/news/2018-11-12/did-my-health-record-overlook-australians-without-internet/10482284.

[8] eg Australian Government, myGov: my.gov.au/mygov/content/html/about.html.

However, there is also much talk of the fact that not everyone has access to the internet, or to digital technology. Digital 'have-nots' in Australia typically include: the elderly, the poor, the homeless, migrants and others with low levels of English literacy or education, those with a disability, and those who live in regional or remote areas (Denvir, Balmer and Pleasence, 2014; Gauld, Goldfinch and Horsburgh, 2010; Sourdin, 2004). A recent analysis of Australian census data showed that '44 per cent of state or territory housing authority tenants across the country did not access the internet from their home on any device'.[9] A recent Australian news report emphasised '[t]he daily struggle' of people living in some regional areas of Australia to access the internet and enjoy mobile phone reception.[10] To sum up: digital resources remain inaccessible by some of the most vulnerable people in our community, who are also increasingly users of the Australian family law system and related services (Kaspiew et al, 2009; Kaspiew et al, 2015).

III. FAMILY LAW PATHWAYS

As noted in our Introduction, the FLPAG's *Out of the Maze* report, published in 2001 (Family Law Pathways Advisory Group, 2001), emphasised the complexity and fragmentation of the Australian family law system. In this section, we elaborate on key aspects of that report relevant to this chapter.

Specifically, the FLPAG likened the Australian family law system to a 'maze' with a series of 'random' entry points that had a 'disproportionate influence on the path taken' and recommending an integrated approach (Family Law Pathways Advisory Group, 2001: 16). To address this, the report recommended changes in each of the three (often overlapping) key pathways identified in the report (ibid, p xviii, and elaborated on from 55–76):

(1) self-help pathways, for parents reaching their own agreements with minimal or no outside help (xxviii), to involve provision of information, education, relevant advice and legal assistance;
(2) supported pathways, for parents who require support to reach their own decisions without resorting to litigation (xxviii) to involve the provision of information, education, counselling, mediation, financial advice, employment services, and unbundled legal services; and
(3) litigation pathways, where an urgent response is needed to protect a parent or child, or as a last resort (xxviii), to involve provision of information, education, legal advice, legal representation, and court processes (Family Law Pathways Advisory Group, 2001: xiv).

[9] Duke, above n 5.
[10] K Diss and M Bennett, 'Country mobile phone and internet bandwidth forces residents online in the middle of the night' (ABC News, 6 May 2018): www.abc.net.au/news/2018-05-06/country-towns-fight-for-good-internet-mobile-phone-bandwidth/9719946.

Research by the Australian Institute of Family Studies (AIFS) suggests that the first group is the largest, followed by the second and third groups, but that the third group consumes an inordinate amount of resources, time and energy given the small but significant size of this group (Kaspiew et al, 2009; Kaspiew at al, 2015).

The *Out of the Maze* report began a process leading to the establishment of a suite of initiatives in 2006 designed to establish and support these pathways (including Family Relationship Centres[11] and the Family Relationships Online[12]). However, the burgeoning development and use of digital technology could not have been anticipated in 2000, so we only see fleeting references to the internet in the report.

A. Digital Pathways

In this section, we take each of the three pathways described in the *Out of the Maze* report and consider the nature and extent of digital initiatives within each in recent years. This allows us to focus more clearly on digital innovation across the broader family law system. It also offers a coherent way of thinking about developments overall. Our focus is on access to online family law system resources – that is, resources about family law and process that are relevant to working out parenting and financial (child support, property and maintenance) arrangements, rather than the much broader range of services that may well be sought on or after separation, and which are beyond the scope of this chapter (eg, mental health, drug and alcohol, housing, and financial services).

In summary, there appears to be a significant amount of information available online for those in each of the three pathways, although more so for parenting and child support than for property. Most information appears to be designed for the self-help group. By contrast, far less is available for those who are in intractable, complex disputes (particularly where allegations of family violence or child abuse have been made) that require the involvement of lawyers and courts. This is not surprising given that the self-help group is the easiest to assist, and the group whom online resources are most likely to assist. The irony here is that much effort has been spent on assisting the group most likely to be able to help themselves.

B. Self-help Pathway

The self-help pathway is predicated on the idea that access to the right resources at the right time is likely to meet the needs of those who can manage independently to reach agreement after separation. Key developments since the *Out of the Maze*

[11] Australian Government, Family Relationships Online, Family Relationship Centres: www.familyrelationships.gov.au/talk-someone/centres.

[12] Australian Government, Family Relationships Online: www.familyrelationships.gov.au/.

Report are the rise of websites followed by apps, as mechanisms for communicating information and thus facilitating self-help for this group, and indeed the separating population more broadly. This is consistent with the Report's inclusion of 'Information' and 'Education' in each of the three pathways.

C. Websites

Websites are operated by most of the major providers of Australian family law system services[13] and provide a key means of communicating information about family law and process, as well as the particular organisation's services. However, the information provided across these websites often overlaps and does not appear to be integrated. One exception is Family law@australia.gov.au – a federal government website which is designed to help users '[f]ind government information about Australia's family law system, the family courts and help for families with relationship issues'.[14] It includes links to key information about Australian family law, child support, parenting orders, the Commonwealth Courts Portal, the family law courts, Family Relationships Online (see next paragraph), and key internet links on family law. However, whether this website is readily located depends on the search terms used. For example, when 'Australian family law' is used as the Google search term it appears third, but when the term 'parental separation' is used, the website does not appear until page three of the search results.[15]

Family Relationships Online,[16] as just mentioned, is one of a range of resources funded by the federal government as part of the Family Relationships Services Programme (FRSP).[17] Family Relationships Online is a website that 'provides all families (whether together or separated) with access to information about family relationship issues, ranging from building better relationships to dispute resolution. It also allows families to find out about a range of services that can assist them to manage relationship issues, including agreeing on appropriate arrangements for children after parents separate'.[18] Anticipated end users

[13] eg, the Family Court of Australia (www.familycourt.gov.au/wps/wcm/connect/fcoaweb/home), Child Support (www.humanservices.gov.au/individuals/child-support), state legal aid commissions (eg, Victoria Legal Aid: www.legalaid.vic.gov.au/), community legal services (including Community Legal Centres (www.fclc.org.au/) and state Women's Legal Services (eg, in Victoria: womenslegal.org.au/about-us.html), Family Relationship Centres (above n 11), and NGOs (eg, Relationships Australia: www.relationships.org.au/), as do many professionals (eg, in Victoria, Forte Family Lawyers: www.fortefamilylawyers.com.au/) and others (eg, DIY Family Law: www.diyfamilylawaustralia.com/).

[14] Australian Government, Australia.gov.au, Family Law: www.australia.gov.au/information-and-services/public-safety-and-law/family-law.

[15] As at 26 November 2018.

[16] Australian Government, Family Relationships Online, above n 12.

[17] Australian Government, Attorney-General's Department, Family Relationship Services Programme: www.ag.gov.au/FamiliesAndMarriage/Families/FamilyRelationshipServices/Pages/default.aspx.

[18] ibid.

included those in remote and rural areas, who would not be able to access the Family Relationship Centres established at the same time. However, without knowing the name of the website, it is not an easy one to find. A further issue, as noted earlier, is limited internet access in some remote and rural areas.

The federal government also funds the Family Law Pathways Network, 'a national program for professionals working with families who are separating, or have separated … The aim is to support practitioners to work collaboratively, maintain strong working relationships and develop appropriate referral mechanisms, across the broader Family Law system'.[19] However, the various state and territory Networks have developed unevenly, including in their online offerings.

The first port of call on child support matters for parents and family law professionals is Child Support, within the federal Department of Human Services, whose services are not fee-based and are available online or by phone, but not face to face.[20] Child Support offers a sophisticated website, including a significant amount of information for parents[21] and an online calculator that is widely used, due to the increased complexity of the new child formula introduced in 2008.[22] Application for child support and payment of child support can be made online.[23] However, we are not aware of any data about the extent to which these options are used, as opposed to phone applications.

D. Apps

Still more recently, with significant and increasing smartphone uptake, a corresponding array of apps has become available in Australia to help parents to manage post-separation parenting. One example is the MyMob app,[24] an initiative of several NGOs,[25] which encourages positive communication to help build a stronger family and family connection. It is designed to be used by a wide range of families, including separated families.

In a recent analysis (Smyth and Fehlberg, 2019) we found that the number and various features of apps relevant to managing post-separation parenting was significant and bewildering. Our small purposive sample of 35 participants' email responses to two questions about smartphone use to assist with post-separation parenting also conveyed that use of smartphones was not universal

[19] Australian Government, Family Law Pathways Network: www.familylawpathways.com.au/.

[20] Australian Government, Department of Human Services, Child Support: www.humanservices.gov.au/individuals/child-support.

[21] Australian Government, Department of Human Services, Parent's Guide to Child Support: www.humanservices.gov.au/individuals/subjects/parents-guide-child-support.

[22] Australian Government, Department of Human Services, Child Support Estimator, processing: csa.gov.au/estimator/About.aspx.

[23] Australian Government, Department of Human Services, Child Support, above n 20.

[24] mymob.com/.

[25] Drummond St Services, Interrelate & Stepfamilies Australia.

and that where smartphones were used, a limited array of features was likely to be accessed, particularly email and text options, with cooperative parents also reporting use of shared calendars. A minority considered using apps but no one said they had so far used one specifically designed for separated parenting (though some had heard of friends using these apps, such as *2Houses*, and *Shared Care*). Ongoing high parental conflict and discomfort with the use of digital technology generally or in this context were main factors discouraging use. Respondents' suggestions for apps that would help them frequently referred to features of apps that already existed – as identified in our app mapping exercise – suggesting an underlying lack of awareness regarding available options.

E. Supported Pathway

For those who need free or low-cost legal assistance outside the courts, there are relatively few digital options, in addition to the options already discussed for the self-help group, which may also be relevant to this group and to those on the litigation pathway.

Interestingly, modest use by professionals of technology was indicated by recent AIFS research on 'how professionals in the child, youth and family sectors are using digital technology in their work. This includes apps, social media services, and any other online services that you use to share information with clients and colleagues'. Of the 365 respondents, 68% used digital technology and of these 81% used it every day or almost every day. The main form of digital technology used was social media. Digital technology was used mainly to share information with colleagues, keep up to date, and communicate with clients (Smart, 2017). Consistent with this, while federal and state governments fund organisations to provide limited but free legal advice and assistance through the state legal aid commissions and Community Legal Centres around the country (including Women's Legal Services), these services are available face to face or by phone – not online.

As regards ODR for those seeking to resolve post-separation disputes without going to court,[26] recent initiatives include the Australian Mediation Association's new online service that will allow mediation to take place no matter where the parties are. Within the academy, initiatives include the University of Melbourne's Network Society Institute[27] and at the Australian National University, Scott Chamberlain's research agenda that brings together blockchain, smart contracts and Artificial Intelligence, and their potential to change how lawyers do their work and improve the delivery of justice by removing the human risks

[26] For a recent discussion, see eg, Program on Negotiation–Harvard Law School Staff, 'Using E-Mediation and Online Mediation Techniques for Conflict Resolution', Harvard Law School Program on Mediation, Daily Blog, 18 April 2019: www.pon.harvard.edu/daily/mediation/dispute-resolution-using-online-mediation/.

[27] networkedsociety.unimelb.edu.au/.

arising from, for example, trust accounts and conveyancing.[28] Within the family law profession, Settify is a recent Australian online initiative aimed at reducing costs of accessing family lawyers for clients, most obviously by doing a lot of the work involved for lawyers in taking instructions from a client.[29] Portable, an Australian technology company, has designed several platforms of relevance to ODR in family law matters: Settle (an AI model to help make decisions that seeks to mimic judicial decision making by analysing data from reported family law cases to make recommendations).[30]

A challenge for the development of online digital justice is the fundamental position in Australia that legal advice can only be given by a legal practitioner, that is, a person admitted to legal practice who has a current practising certificate.[31] Section 24 of the Legal Profession Practice Act 2007 (uniform legislation governing the Australian legal profession through the adoption of Model Laws in each state) says that without a practising certificate it is an offence to engage in legal practice. Engaging in legal practice is not defined in the Act but by the common law and will generally include giving legal advice. Significant difficulty surrounds the distinction between the provision of legal information and legal advice, with a recent report suggesting that 'the need to revisit the legal information/legal advice distinction. This may actually prove the greatest of the challenges identified, raising large questions about the public interest, access to justice, and the potentially disruptive role not just of technology but of legal services regulation itself.'[32]

F. Litigation Pathway

The Australian family law courts (that is, the Family Court of Australia, the Federal Circuit Court of Australia and the Family Court of Western Australia) have been under-resourced for many years,[33] with significant waiting times in some registries between filing and final orders being made (Federal Circuit Court of Australia, 2018: 50; Family Court of Australia, 2018: 30) There is clearly a need to reduce the significant delay and cost encountered by families in this context.

As noted in the previous section, ODR is still in its infancy in Australia. Family law courts have increasingly utilised digital technology to achieve greater administrative efficiency rather than to contribute to the decision-making process itself. In addition to websites providing significant amounts of information about family law and court processes (see earlier), the family law courts

[28] Scott Chamberlain, 'The Clockwork Society': www.youtube.com/watch?v=rM1i7pn0eoM.

[29] www.settify.com.au/.

[30] settletech.com.au.

[31] See further Maclean and Eekelaar (2016).

[32] J Bennett, T Miller, J Webb, R Bosua, A Lodders, and S Chamberlain, *Current State of Automated Legal Advice Tools* (Networked Society Institute Discussion Paper 1, April 2018) 36.

[33] Robyn Powell, 'Family Court Underfunded, Letting People Down, Chief Justice Says', ABC News, 1 May 2017: www.abc.net.au/news/2017-04-30/family-court-letting-families-down-chief-justice-says/8483858.

are gradually offering more online and e-filing services, specifically: live chat, the Commonwealth Courts Portal (which 'provides users with secure web-based access to information about their file and access to electronically file (eFile) a range of applications and supporting documents',[34] online payments for hearing and conference fees, proof of divorce, a law term finder (plain language translation tool of the most common terminology used in family law)[35] and since 1 January 2018, digital orders (orders are no longer posted to parties, apart from consent orders and appeals).[36] Family law courts also use Twitter (@FedCctCourtAU – 1,709 followers at 19 May 2019) and YouTube (an American, video-sharing website[37] which includes videos on e-filing, seeing a family consultant (designed for children), a court tour, and what to expect from mediation).

In summary, family law courts are using online mechanisms in relation to information sharing and process, not ODR. While the shift towards digital information provision will be a positive one for some families considering or in court proceedings, our sense is that it is likely to be bewildering for many others, and out of reach of those without access to the internet, a scanner and a printer for sending and receiving court documents.

As noted earlier, the legal aid commissions and Community Legal Centres (which are funded by state and federal governments to provide free or means tested legal services) use their websites to offer information about how free legal information and advice might be obtained from them, rather than providing individualised advice or other online dispute resolution services.[38] However, in 2016 Victoria Legal Aid took an interest in the Dutch Rechtwijzer technology.[39] More recently, the Commonwealth Attorney-General's Department has provided seed funding to investigate the introduction of an Online Dispute Resolution System (ODRS) for separating couples in Australia for children and property matters.[40] In broader terms, the project (which is being managed by the Legal Services Commission of South Australia) aims to: assist couples to resolve disputes with less reliance on formal pathways; provide users with critical information, empower them and offer guided pathways of assistance; and assist those who may not qualify for legal aid but cannot afford legal assistance:

[34] Family Court of Australia, 'Commonwealth Courts Portal': www.familycourt.gov.au/wps/wcm/connect/fcoaweb/reports-and-publications/publications/ccp/commonwealth-courts-portal.

[35] Family Court of Australia, Online Services, Digital Court Program: www.familycourt.gov.au/wps/wcm/connect/fcoaweb/online-services/dcp/dcp.

[36] Family Court of Australia, About the Court, Accessing Your Orders: www.familycourt.gov.au/wps/wcm/connect/fcoaweb/about/news/accessing-your-court-orders.

[37] www.youtube.com/user/familycourtAU.

[38] eg, in Victoria, Legal Aid Victoria (www.legalaid.vic.gov.au/get-legal-services-and-advice); Fitzroy Legal Service (www.fitzroy-legal.org.au/free_legal_advice_service); Women's Legal Service Victoria (www.womenslegal.org.au/our-services.html).

[39] Rachael Brown, 'Robot lawyers could make time-consuming, expensive court conflict thing of the past', ABC News, 6 July 2016: www.abc.net.au/news/2016-07-06/robot-lawyers-dutch-conflict-resolution-technology-on-its-way/7572488.

[40] Private email communication, David Mazzone, CEO, Legal Services Commission of South Australia to Belinda Fehlberg, 5 December 2017.

> For example, the technology provides users with templates highlighting parenting agreements that have worked for other couples. The Artificial Intelligence software can also assess previous family law court decisions to show couples how judges generally treat disputes that are similar to theirs. … Technology, including so-called robot lawyers, is not designed to replace lawyers and cannot resolve all types of family law disagreements. But it can empower couples to reduce the areas of dispute. That can only be a good thing.[41]

The project has engaged with users and stakeholders to identify key requirements and priorities for an ODRS. Qualitative research with potential users has been undertaken by a market research company to determine whether a market exists for ODRS in Australia and, if so: who the market is and what user needs and requirements are; how the ODRS needs to be accessed; and communication strategies to ensure ODRS is found by users. This research found that there is a market, a need, and a strong appetite for an ODRS, but that any system needs to accommodate a range of users with tailored ODR for different groups of users. Portable Australia (mentioned earlier) has been engaged to assist in the development of an ODRS for property matters. The prototype includes development of an AI model to propose an equitable property division to users on the basis of prior Australian Family Court cases.[42]

IV. DISCUSSION AND CONCLUDING THOUGHTS

Our brief summary suggests that the development of online resources for separating parents in Australia continues to be largely ad hoc. The result is an apparent potpourri of online family law resources. We can see the need for greater coordination of digital efforts to reduce overlap, reduce confusion, and ensure that online resources are trustworthy, of high quality and up to date. There is also a need to improve accessibility. However, we can also see that rapid technological developments provide many challenges in this complex and challenging space.

It also seems at present that that while there is much free online *information* available to separating parents, free or inexpensive legal *advice* is much harder to obtain. There is some interest in ODR, but the work remains embryonic. Overall, Australian initiatives seem consistent with the view that there is value in developing online resources and services that improve access to information and increase administrative efficiency of family law professionals, rather than providing advice or dispute resolution services.

[41] Gabrielle Canny, quoted in 'SA selected for digital divorce disputes project', Adelaide, Legal Services Commission of South Australia, Media Release, 9 August 2017.

[42] Private email communication, Jacob Bonnici, Manager, Program Management Office, Legal Services Commission of South Australia to Belinda Fehlberg, 7 September 2018.

The current position is reflective of the reality that internet use in Australia although widespread, is not universal and that the so-called 'digital divide' remains a major barrier to access. Given this, caution is rightly exercised in the development of resources that are not available to vulnerable families, who number significantly among key end-users.

REFERENCES

Australian Law Reform Commission, *Review of the family law system: Final Report* (ALRC Report 135, 2019).

Australian Government, Australian Law Reform Commission (2018) *Review of the Family Law System*, Discussion Paper No 86 (Brisbane, ALRC, 14 September 2018).

Denvir, C, Balmer, NJ and Pleasence, P (2014) 'Portal or pot hole? Exploring how older people use the 'information superhighway' for advice relating to problems with a legal dimension', *Ageing & Society* 34, 670.

Family Court of Australia (2018) *Annual Report 2017–2018* (Canberra, Commonwealth of Australia).

Family Law Pathways Advisory Group (2001) *Out of the Maze: Pathways to the Future for Families Experiencing Separation: Report of the Family Law Pathways Advisory Group ('Pathways Report')* (Canberra, Commonwealth of Australia).

Federal Circuit Court of Australia (2018) *Annual Report 2017–2018* (Canberra, Commonwealth of Australia).

Gauld, R, Goldfinch, S and Horsburgh, S (2010) 'Do they want it? Do they use it? The 'Demand-Side' of e-Government in Australia and New Zealand', *Government information quarterly* 27, 177.

Kaspiew, R, Gray, M, Weston, R, Moloney, L, Hand, K, Qu, L and the Family Law Evaluation Team (2009), *Evaluation of the 2006 Family Law Reforms* (Melbourne, Australian Institute of Family Studies).

Kaspiew, R, Carson, R, Dunstan, J, Qu, L, Horsfall, B, De Maio, J, Moore, S, Moloney, L, Coulson M and Tayton, S (2015) *Evaluation of the 2012 Family Violence Amendments: Synthesis Report* (Melbourne, Australian Institute of Family Studies).

Maclean, M and Eekelaar, J (2016) *Lawyers and Mediators: The Brave New World of Services for Separated Families* (Oxford and Portland, Oregon, Hart Publishing).

Program on Negotiation – Harvard Law School Staff, 'Using E-Mediation and Online Mediation Techniques for Conflict Resolution', Harvard Law School Program on Mediation, Daily Blog, 18 April 2019: www.pon.harvard.edu/daily/mediation/dispute-resolution-using-online-mediation/.

Smart, J (2017) 'Digital technology in the child, youth and family sectors', Paper presented at the FRSA Conference (Melbourne, November 2017).

Smyth, B and Fehlberg, B (2019) 'Australian Post-Separation Parenting on the Smartphone: What's 'App-ening?', *Journal of Social Welfare and Family Law* 41, 53.

Sourdin, T (2004) 'ODR – an Australian perspective on the digital divide', paper presented at the Third Annual UN Forum on Online Dispute Resolution (Melbourne, 2004, unpan1.un.org/intradoc/groups/public/documents/apcity/unpan046580.pdf.

Thomas, J, Barraket, J, Wilson, CK, Cook, K, Louie, YM, Holcombe-James, I, Ewing, S and MacDonald, T (2018) *Measuring Australia's Digital Divide: The Australian Digital Inclusion Index 2018* (Melbourne, RMIT University, for Telstra).

Part C

The Way Ahead

11

The Online Divorce Resolution Tool 'Rechtwijzer uit Elkaar' Examined

BREGJE DIJKSTERHUIS

> The focus in the legal system should be which solution enables parties to continue with their lives and not who is right; on standardizing and innovation in a world that has stayed the same for decades. We have something good in our hands with Rechtwijzer. (Legal Aid Board 2015)

I. INTRODUCTION

ONLINE DISPUTE RESOLUTION (ODR) has recently attracted a great deal of attention in the Netherlands and elsewhere. The online divorce self-help tools or platforms are a prominent example. It is not surprising that the internet revolution should leave its mark in the field of divorce law. After all, this is an area consisting of a large number of legal cases, often simple with regard to legal issues, but psychologically complicated with far-reaching consequences for (former) partners and their children in a divorce situation. New developments in dispute resolution, which might offer an answer to the complex family issues in a divorce, are therefore eagerly tried and welcomed by some experts, legal practitioners and social scientists.

For a few years the Netherlands was a leader in online (divorce) dispute resolution, through the introduction of the Rechtwijzer, which can be translated as the Roadmap to Justice. (Legal Aid Board, 2017: 8) This was an online self-help tool, designed for people who were having a range of legal problems, including getting a divorce, and developed through cooperation between government, science and business (Smith, Roger and Paterson, 2014). It received a mixed response from both the legal profession and (socio-legal) scientists. For the supporters, in the Netherlands as well as in other countries such as the United Kingdom[1] and Canada (with the introduction of MyLawBC[2]), the Rechtwijzer was thought to provide the answer to the seemingly insoluble problems of the divorce process. The critics however considered the online tool as potentially dangerous for (vulnerable) people in a divorce, and a potential cause of even more problems arising from the divorce.

Rechtwijzer is not a single tool; it has gone through many changes, and the first version of the Rechtwijzer from 2007 is very different from the last version which was terminated in 2017. The latest version 2.0, called Rechtwijzer uit Elkaar, is the main focus of this chapter as it contained the most far-reaching elements of online dispute resolution and self-help. Rechtwijzer 2.0 cannot be considered separately from the earlier 1.0 version; they are intertwined and based on the same assumptions, theories and vision about dealing with legal issues online. It is important to analyse why an online divorce tool that started as such a promising development, at least in the view of many policymakers and some scholars, ended so abruptly. As Smith writes: 'The Rechtwijzer was – and remains – an important project whose one-time global eminence and now demise merits a good deal of contemplation.' (Smith, 2017)

Though not a member of the development team, the author was involved with the Rechtwijzer several times. First as a researcher: in 2013 an evaluative research was conducted with other researchers on one aspect of Rechtwijzer 1.0: an online self-help tool for alimony/child support payment. (Dijksterhuis and Van Duijvenvoorde, 2013) Secondly as a (critical) person involved in the development/review: from 2016 to 2017 the author was a member of the editorial board of the online divorce tool or platform Rechtwijzer uit Elkaar. In addition the author was an adviser in one of the so called 'Scrum' meetings of the product developers to assist in writing legal texts for Rechtwijzer uit Elkaar. And thirdly, the author was present as an observer at theme meetings organised by The Hague Institute for Innovation of Law (HIIL), including the 2016 annual Global ODR conference in the Peace Palace in The Hague.[3] Thus the author had a close-up view of the beginning and the course of the Rechtwijzer, from a largely independent position. This chapter examines what policymakers and socio-legal scientists might learn from the experience of the Rechtwijzer. Three questions are adressed: what was the Rechtwijzer (uit Elkaar)? Why did the Rechtwijzer (uit Elkaar) not work out as intended? What were the positive aspects of this online self- help tool?

II. WHAT WAS THE RECHTWIJZER (UIT ELKAAR)?

The first version of Rechtwijzer (1.0), which went online in 2007, was developed by the Legal Aid Board and Tilburg University with the involvement of Professor

[1] Advocates of online dispute resolution in the UK were not discouraged after Rechtwijzer ended. See eg: www.lawgazette.co.uk/practice/online-court-wont-repeat-failure-of-dutch-model-mor-claims/5061641.article.

[2] www.mylawbc.com/paths/family.

[3] 'Can ODR Really Help Courts and Improve Access to Justice?': www.20160dr.wordpress.com.

Maurits Barendrecht and Corry van Zeeland.[4] It was not initially an online dispute resolution tool, and could be used by just one (ex)partner in a divorce. It did not offer a service only for divorce, but was aimed at a broad range of frequent legal conflicts such as consumer, tenant, and debt issues. Moreover it had modest ambitions: Rechtwijzer 1.0 had the prime function of signposting users towards the resolution of their problems (Smith, 2015; Peters et al, 2009: 27). Or as researchers Bickel, Van Dijk and Giebels (2015) wrote: 'The Legal Aid Board developed Rechtwijzer to improve access to justice and legal information. Its primary goal is to encourage self-reliance by improving control over the conflict process and understanding of your own and the other party's positions and motivations in the conflict. It is designed to assist parties in solving legal conflicts on their own where possible, and finding the right kind of help where needed.'

It is important to note that the intention of Rechtwijzer and the different online tools was not to give people concrete legal advice for their particular situation on what to do or their legal rights or obligations, as that was not part of the (statutory) task of the central office of the Legal Aid Board, but of the online and geographically distributed offline Legal Services Counters 'Juridische Loketten': 'The Legal Services Counters act as what is commonly known as the "front office" (primary help) where legal matters are being clarified to clients and information and advice given.' (Legal Aid Board 2017: 8,11.) Thus in that sense there was limited room for manoeuvre for Tilburg University while developing the tool. But on the other hand Tilburg University could experiment with applying their theories through a concrete and practical instrument for people, for which considerable public funding was available from the Ministry and the Legal Aid Board. The project initially cost (for the 1.0 version) €2.3M (Smith and Paterson, 2014). The theory behind Rechtwijzer 1.0 focused on conflict resolution and access to justice in civil law (see for an explanation in depth: Tilburg Institute of Interdisciplinairy Studies of Civil Law and Conflict Resolution Systems (ed), 2010). The initators of Rechtwijzer built on empirical research and theory, especially the socio-legal studies on how people deal with problems with legal aspects and potential legal disputes, including Hazel Genn's *Paths to Justice* (Genn and Beinart, 1999; Genn and Paterson, 2001). The so-called conflict resolution Delta was built on that basis (Voert, 2004; Velthoven and Voert, 2013). Rechtwijzer aimed at increasing self-reliance and lowering the threshold of access to justice.

This corresponded with the reforms and/or cuts in legal aid by the then Ministry of Security and Justice (later on: Ministry of Justice and Security). Adjustments were made in the Legal Aid Reform of 2009 in the so called 'Besluit eigen bijdrage rechtsbijstand' (about user contribution to legal aid[5]) and 'Besluit vergoedingen

[4] www.rechtwijzer.nl/door-wie-is-rechtwijzer-ontwikkeld.

[5] The Dutch legal aid system does not provide for full coverage of legal aid by the state in principle (there are some exceptions), therefore every applicant has to pay an own contribution, of which the amount is dependent on income. (Barendrecht et al, 2015: 32). In 2019 this own contribution for family law was between €345 and €862: www.rechtsbijstand.nl/over-mediation-en-rechtsbijstand/hoeveel-moet-ik-zelf-betalen/inkomensnormen.

Rechtsbijstand' (the legal fees for legal aid lawyers).[6] In 2013 this was followed by another increase in the user contribution, and the abolition of special arrangements which gave a reduction in user contribution when people applied for legal aid in multiple cases within a certain period (Voert, 2015: 4). The aim of the increased contribution for people and reduced compensation for legal aid lawyers was mainly to cut the costs[7] of government financed legal aid. In 2015–16 more legal aid cuts were proposed (NOVA, 2015: 11). The Rechtwijzer is mentioned by the Ministry of Justice as one of the alternative ways[8] to decrease pressure on the legal aid system: 'In the case of legal aid, the purpose is to have as many practical tools as possible, such as Rechtwijzer, so that people can solve their legal problems or conflicts themselves in an efficient and effective way. This development offers possibilities of using the system (of legal aid) only in those cases when it is really necessary and self–reliance cannot be expected. The system of legal aid offers (just) a safety net' (translation).[9] As HIIL states in a comparative study commissioned by the Research and Documentation Centre of the Ministry of Justice and Security on legal aid: 'The fifth trend is to provide online platforms supporting dispute resolution and access to justice. These trends are seen as promising by experts because they can reduce costs of access to justice and improve quality.' (Barendrecht et al, 2014: 102.)

III. HOW DID RECHTWIJZER WORK?

Via www.rechtwijzer.nl people in a legal conflict situation could fill in a questionaire on different topics relating to their legal problem. Rechtwijzer aimed to make people aware of the different possibilities in a situation of legal conflict, especially by referring them to (legal) experts, relevant websites and by offering checklists, films and interactive online self-help tools such as the divorce and parenting plan and an online self-help tool for the calculation of child support (Combrink-Kuiters, 2014: 29,30).[10] These latter two online self-help tools, which are especially relevant with regard to the development of Rechtwijzer uit Elkaar, will be examined briefly.

The divorce and parenting plan ('Echtscheidings- en Ouderschapsplan') was a part of Rechtwijzer and an 'online application for the law (translation)' (Raad

[6] Besluit eigen bijdrage rechtsbijstand (Stb., 2009,46); Verzamelbesluit rechtsbijstand 2009 (Stb, 2009, 353); Wijzigingswet Wet op de rechtsbijstand (herijking verlening rechtsbijstand) (Stb, 2009, 4).

[7] Because there was less budget for legal aid available by the Ministry of Security and Justice, and plans to decrease the budget more (Barendrecht et al, 2015: 8; NOVA, 2015:11).

[8] Since 1 July 2011 the 'Diagnose and triage' method was introduced by legislation: people received a reduction in their own contribution when they first visited the legal services counters who afterwards refered them to a lawyer: Wijzigingsbesluit Besluit eigen bijdrage rechtsbijstand, enz. (stimuleren verlening [...] lid, of artikel 8, tweede lid, Wet op de rechtsbijstand (Stb., 2011, 322); See also: NOVA (2015: 17,18).

[9] www.sociaalverhaal.com/wp-content/uploads/Wetsvoorstel-Juridisch-Loket-als-poortwachter-1.pdf.

[10] See also: www.rvr.org/nieuws/2011/april/steeds-meer-mogelijkheden-met-rechtwijzer.html.

voor Rechtsbijstand, 2010). The Legal Aid Board offered this online application or tool to their clients from 2010 onwards. The immediate cause was that from 2009 onwards, for parents who wanted to divorce it became a legal requirement to make a parenting plan, called 'Ouderschapsplan' together, with agreements on the division of care for the children, education and child support.[11] Without an 'ouderschapsplan', people could not go ahead with their divorce, a few exceptions aside. Thus the online, interactive divorce and parenting from the Legal Aid Board plan was meant to support people in a divorce situation to make this legally required plan. Moreover it offered the possibility to make some other agreements on money and proporty, such as dividing assets. The main target audience were mediators and lawyers. Therefore there was an explanation for the mediators and lawyers on how it worked in a small booklet as a practical signpost ('praktische wegwijzer') (Raad voor Rechtsbijstand, 2010) and on the website of the Legal Aid Board.[12] As mentioned in the introduction to the booklet: 'This practical signpost is written for everyone who professionally needs to deal with people who are getting a divorce, such as mediators, lawyers, employees of the Law Counters ("Juridische Loketten") that offers information and self-help assistance, and for social workers and family doctors.' (Raad voor Rechtsbijstand, 2010.) As stated on the website at that time: 'Not all people who decide to separate do preparatory work. By referring clients to the divorce and parenting plan, you (mediators and lawyers) can already enable them to think about possible agreements with regard to division of childcare, costs for the children, primary residence etc. Then it will also be clear on which subjects your clients cannot yet reach agreement. Such an overview saves you (mediator, lawyer etc.) a great deal of time' (translation).[13]

Following the launch of Rechtwijzer 2.0 it was not possible to open a new file after 15 October 2014. According to the Legal Aid Board 7,071 files were created in 2014 through the echtscheidingsplan.nl. In 2013 the total had been 8,908. In 2014 about half of the files were only used on the day of the creation (69% in 2013). According to the Legal Aid Board from this it can be deduced that people do not fully use this 'functionality' (Combrink-Kuiters, 2014: 32). This is indeed significant, as the Legal Aid Board also remarked, because this might mean that people started, but perhaps did not finish it, and did not use it to come to agreements with their (former) spouse, in order to prepare for the divorce process with the mediator or lawyer.

The Online Alimony Calculation Tool (Kinder Alimentatie Reken Tool or KART) was part of Rechtwijzer and is still recommended by the Legal Aid Board.[14] The tool calculates the amount of child support in each divorce case. The tool is a guideline; it is not obligatory. According to Dutch legislation, when

[11] Wet bevordering voortgezet ouderschap en zorgvuldige scheiding (Stb. 2008, 500).
[12] www.rvr.org/nieuws/2010/maart/echtscheidings--en-ouderschapsplan-online.html.
[13] www.rvr.org/nieuws/2010/maart/echtscheidings--en-ouderschapsplan-online.html.
[14] www.rechtwijzer.nl/uit-elkaar.

determining the alimony (child and spousal support) amount, the only criteria are the capacity 'draagkracht' of the party obliged to make alimony payments and the need 'behoefte' of the one who has the right to receive alimony. As explained above, the amount of child support was one of the aspects people in a divorce situation had to agree on in the legally required parenting plan. Therefore the Legal Aid Board developed a formula in 2010 with a corresponding calculation system: the KART-tool.[15] The aim was and is: to reduce high procedural costs for divorce law cases, improve the willingness of people who are obliged to pay maintenance allowances to comply with judges' decisions, in this way increasing access to justice, and promoting self-help through mediation.

Especially when using digital self-help tools, these kinds of simple rules or formulae were considered by some as helpful or even neccessary. As Smith (2013) pointed out: 'Self-help and the operation of digital forms of resolution work better when judicial decisions are predictable; there are clear rules on such matters as maintenance; and minimal discretion'.[16] This online alimony calculation tool was also recommended in a legislative proposal by Recourt and Van der Steur (members of the Second Chamber) whose aim was to realise a simpler and fairer calculation system for child support (Dijksterhuis and Van Duijvenvoorde, 2013: 17). It worked according to five steps: people had to fill in: (1) names and number of children, (2) the total income of both parents, (3) the home address of the child, (4) how many nights are spent at the other parent's house, and (5) who pays the main expenses (school, insurance, sports etc).[17] Then the system calculates the (non-obligatory) amount of child support and gives an indication of when an amount of child support that is agreed between partners is unreasonable (see also Dijksterhuis and Van Duijvenvoorde, 2013: 24–6).

On the request of and commissioned by the Legal Aid Board and the National Support and Maintenance Agency, 'LBIO', quantitative (questionnaire) and qualitative (interview based) research was conducted on this child support tool. A questionnaire was linked to the website of the online alimony calculation Tool. Thus after people received the result of the calculation, namely

[15] www.rvr.org/nieuws/2010/september/kinderalimentatierekentool-kart.html.

[16] Actually this calculation system for child support, developed by the Legal Aid Board, was not generally used by the legal professions. From 1975 onwards a Commission of Judges drafted alimony guidelines that gave judges something to refer to when calculating the amount of alimony in order to limit the role of discretion and therefore to increase the uniformity of judicial decisions. (The development and functioning of these alimony guidelines were the subject of the author's PhD thesis: Dijksterhuis, 2008.) These guidelines are still in force and used in all courts and by (almost) all lawyers. The (more than 100) alimony guidelines are quite complex as the judges prefered comprehensive, custom made guidelines to a broad system, such as a formula. For the application of these comprehensive alimony guidelines lawyers and judges are needed, and they do not offer (ex-)partners the opportunity to calculate the amount of alimony themselves (Dijksterhuis, 2008: 223, 224). The Legal Aid Board chose to develop and recommend a different calculation system. Because this system or tool is partly based on criteria other than the judicial alimony guidelines, the amount of alimony in similar cases can differ depending on using the one or other calculation system, though no research is yet published that examines when and to what extent this happens.

[17] www.rechtwijzer.nl/uit-elkaar/kinderen/kinderalimentatie-berekenen.

the 'amount of child support', they were asked to fill in the questionnaire. 292 users responded. Afterwards we conducted 34 semi-structured interviews with some of those (292) users, who had agreed to participate in this evaluative research. The aspects that were measured were: user-friendliness, transparency/ comprehensability, justice (in procedure and outcome), and empowerment/ self-help (See Dijksterhuis and Van Duijvenvoorde, 2013: 19) The replies used a scale of 1–10: for user-friendliness people gave a 7.9 grade (alimony debtor) or 7.2 (the alimony creditor); for comprehensibility 7.6 grade (the alimony debtor) or 6.9 (the alimony creditor) and justice a 7.2 grade (the alimony debtor) and 5.9 (alimony creditor) (ibid: 7–10). Thus the conclusion was that people were in general content to help themselves: they considered the system to be user-friendly and transparent. But there was some difference between the opinions of the people who had to pay and the people who wanted to receive child support, especially with regard to how they viewed the level of justice.[18] In interviews people explained that the online tool was simple and therefore easy to use. With regard to transparency people remarked that they expected that willingness to pay the obliged amount of child support would increase when the calculation (for example the different items that were considered as relevant by the system) was transparent (ibid: 8). In the context of legal aid policy, however, it should be noted that these respondents had a relatively higher education and a higher income. Thus the group that is entitled to receive legal aid was somewhat under-represented (ibid: 28).

Evaluative research was also carried out on the Rechtwijzer as a whole. In 2015 researchers of the University of Twente, Department Psychology of Conflict, Risk & Safety, published the results of a research project on 'online Interventions in legal conflicts' (Bickel, Van Dijk and Giebels, 2015)[19] which focused on people who had visited the Dutch website Rechtwijzer (and some of whom had used the online applications such as the online Child Support Tool and the Divorce and Parenting plan). The version of Rechtwijzer.nl tested in that report was launched in October 2012. The longitudinal research project measured participants' experiences and reactions at three points: 'at the outset of the divorce (1), one to five weeks later (2) and another three or six months later. (…)' The researchers used a control group of people going through the same conflicts but who did not use Rechtwijzer, to enable the researchers to draw conclusions about the effect of use (ibid: 11). By answering digital questionnaires, 1,553

[18] www.hva.nl/content/nieuws/persberichten/2013/09/burgers-berekenen-zelf-binnenkort-hun-kinderalimentatie.html; B Dijksterhuis, 'Users' Opinion about Online Self-Help Tools on Alimony Payment', Paper to Legal Profession Group Meeting of the Research Committee on the Sociology of Law, International Sociological Association, Frauenchiemsee, July 2014 (see also: Maclean and Eekelaar (2015) 66, annotation 8).

[19] M. van Dijk also made a contribution as a researcher at the Legal Aid Board to the development of Rechtwijzer 1.0 and later on and started her PhD thesis at Twente University on the topic of the evaluation of Rechtwijzer.

respondents (467 respondents going through a divorce and 1086 respondents dealing with a consumer conflict) participated in the research.

According to the researchers, these people were dealing with complex issues with high stakes (ibid: 2). The different levels of education and the categories of income were fairly evenly distributed across the respondents (ibid: 13, 14). Rechtwijzer users who had gone through a divorce gave an overall quite positive grade (7.51 on a scale of 1–10) and were inclined to use the website again or recommend it to others (an average answer was 5.26 on a scale of 1 to 7). Almost half of the respondents indicated they would use the divorce and parenthood plan again (ibid: 22, 23). Moreover, people who used Rechtwijzer reported that they felt more capable after using Rechtwijzer. But the researchers could not find a difference in reported self-reliance before and after using Rechtwijzer (ibid: 36) The researchers found that people who used Rechtwijzer were dealing with a moderate amount of stress, and some were experiencing high levels of stress with escalation (ibid: 34). Moreover, the divorce conflicts were often characterised by dependence asymmetry; women felt more dependent on their (ex-)partner than vice versa. Many people also had concerns about debts and especially an impending fall in income (ibid: 28). Furthermore, the researchers found that Rechtwijzer users were at a relatively early stage in their case, and that the tool might be especially useful for orientation and gaining information about the conflict process (ibid: 2,19).

What was remarkable was that the need for 'empowering help' depended on whether the respondent had taken the initiative for the divorce. Respondents who were taking the initiative themselves experienced significantly less need for this type of help than respondents whose (ex)- partners were taking the initiative. When the respondents took the initiative themselves and wanted to get a divorce, they also experienced significantly less need for social-emotional help than when they did not want to separate, but their (ex-)partner was taking the initiative (average answer of 4.67). Furthermore, having additional concerns besides the divorce seemed to increase the need for both problem-focused empowering help and social-emotional help (ibid: 32). It was also found in separate research that financially dependent (ex-partners) needed more problem-focused empowering help (Dijk, Giebels and Zebel, 2016).[20] In a review Smith (2015: 32) remarked: 'it is not clear from the research why Rechtwijzer should be a source of legal aid support for those on low incomes, save from the logical fact that nothing else may exist'. Furthermore he stressed the importance of finding out 'what proportion of the population (particularly those who had been historically eligible for publicly funded legal aid) can be shown to derive benefit from website-based provision (ie how many are excluded by reasons of lack of access and adequate skills such as literacy?' (ibid: 28).

[20] See more on this subject of financial insuffiency of (ex-)partners after divorce and the role of gender, as this concerns mostly women; also Dijksterhuis (2013) and Treloar in ch 2 of this book.

IV. RECHTWIJZER UIT ELKAAR (2.0)

Between 2007 and 2015 there were some changes in Rechtwijzer, but the major reform was the introduction of the second version (2.0), also called Rechtwijzer uit Elkaar in 2015 (Annual Report Dutch Legal Aid Council, 2015). HIIL was involved with Maurits Barendrecht, who as well as being a professor at Tilburg University, was a director of HIIL, and Jin Ho Verdonschot, the designer and architect of Rechtwijzer uit Elkaar at HIIL as leaders, and HIIL's CEO, Sam Muller, in the background as an advocate for access to justice, innovation and ODR (for their vision on dispute resolution see Barendrecht et al, 2015, 2016; Muller et al, 2014; Verdonschot, 2013, 2015 and 2016). HIIL was a strong advocate of online dispute resolution as is illustrated in their 2016 'Trend Report': 'This report illustrates how ODR can end the administrative frustrations of the courts and the disillusionment of citizens. It can help to standardise, simplify and humanise legal procedures, empowering people seeking access to justice to negotiate, mediate and submit any unresolved issues to courts. The user experience can become that of a fully integrated justice journey.' (HIIL, 2016.)

Rechtwijzer uit Elkaar (or 2.0) was a self-help online dispute resolution tool for partners who get divorced; a combination of self-help and online assistance on request by (legal) professionals. As Smith (2015) writes: 'Rechtwijzer 2.0 does inherently a different job from the first version: it was designed to go beyond signposting (like Rechtwijzer 1.0) and provided a means of resolution itself.' HIIL often called Rechtwijzer uit Elkaar a dispute resolution platform, which was consistent with their vision on ODR and dispute resolution in civil cases. It was an initiative of the Dutch Legal Aid Board, Tilburg University and the Hague Institute for Innovation of Law (HILL). Modria was responsible for the ICT implementation. Peter van den Biggelaar, the director of the Legal Aid Board, was a fervent supporter of the idea behind Online self-help in general and Rechtwijzer uit Elkaar in particular. There was close cooperation between HIIL and the Legal Aid Board, which was illustrated by HIIL's prominent role at the conference of the Legal Aid Board to celebrate the Board's 20th anniversary.[21]

The aim of HIIL and the Dutch Legal Aid Board was for people in a divorce to be able to make their own agreements on the division of care for the children and on financial matters in a harmonious negotiation. The target users were all people involved in a divorce, regardless of sex, income, educational level and ethnic background. It was meant for both simple and complex divorce cases. The tool was, compared to a regular divorce procedure, relatively cheap: a fixed minimum price of between €100 and €300 per person (Scheltema, 2016) with some extra costs (a few hundred € per service) when one needed the help of an expert in decision making when (ex-) partners disagreed. Rechtwijzer was a tool

[21] www.rvr.org/nieuws/2014/mei/verslag-miniconferentie-twintig-jaar-wrb.html.

which could be used on a voluntary basis: it was not intended as a replacement (or front office) for the 'traditional' legal process: people in a divorce had normal access to a judge. There was moreover no pressure from the governement nor the judiciary to use Rechtwijzer, though on their website the Dutch Legal Aid Board referred clients to it. HIIL though had high expectations and aimed to be suitable for approximately 80% of the 'divorce market'.

Because Rechtwijzer uit Elkaar was intended as an almost complete do-it-yourself online divorce tool, the starting point was the cooperation of both (ex-) partners.[22] It consisted partly of self-help by both (ex-)partners and partly of assistance from lawyers, mediators and other experts. It started with so called Diagnose and Triage. According to the Dutch Legal Aid Board these two so called services were part of the so called screening function 'zeeffunctie', which were related to the legal aid reforms/cuts mentioned above.[23] Diagnose meant determining what the problem is, what people had already done for themselves and what they still can do; triage meant determining what steps can be taken to solve the problem. People should be able to find information about their legal rights and obligations. The next step following Diagnosis and Triage was to negotiate with their (ex-partner), call in assistance from a third party when needed, make agreements, and ask for them to be reviewed. It ended with the follow up and after care.

The initiators of Rechtwijzer uit Elkaar had a clear vision of the divorce process: 'managing the process and desired outcome in their own home, using their own words and at their own pace' (LinkedIn Page Jin Ho Verdonschot). But HIIL was not completely neutral or unbiased concerning the way the divorce process should take place, especially with regard to the relationship between partners. People in a divorce were to be nudged by Rechtwijzer towards a certain degree of harmony. On their website the Dutch Legal Aid Board mentioned that it stimulated online solutions, and supported the self reliance of people with legal problems. The website Rechtwijzer.nl informed citizens about the pathway through the law that they could follow in case of legal problems. Rechtwijzer uit Elkaar was one prominent example, supported by the Legal Aid Board.

The transcript of Rechtwijzer uit Elkaar gave a good overview of how the tool or platform worked:

> manage your divorce yourself. Make a clear and complete divorce plan online, step by step with your partner. With legal help when needed. You log in with DigiD. Next you describe in the answer to some questions how you look at different aspects: communication, children, housing, finances/ income/property. Following the line of related themes and with illustrations, we help you to express your thoughts. After payment you can invite your partner to join online (translation) so that he or she can express thoughts on the agreements that need to be made. After that you can work together

[22] www.rechtwijzer.nl/binaries/content/assets/rechtwijzer/visie-rechtwijzer-2017-2019-versie-1.0.pdf: 2.

[23] www.rvr.org/nieuws/2011/april/steeds-meer-mogelijkheden-met-rechtwijzer.html.

> on your divorce plan, with the help of model texts. You can make proposals to each other and chat online. Rechtwijzer assists you with additional information, relevant tools and a clear structure. The contact centre helps you. If you do not succeed in reaching agreements, there is online professional help through mediation ('bemiddeling') and an external decision maker/adjudication ('beslisser'). For an extra payment this person will help you to reach agreements. When all arrangements are made and affirmed by your (ex)partner, then the first version of your divorce plan is ready. Next an independent divorce expert/lawyer, the so called 'reviewer', will check the arrangements to see if the agreements are fair, complete and legally correct. After some corrections or additions your divorce plan is ready for the last step. You sign the plan and the divorce expert sends it to the court. After the hearing in and decision from the court, you receive a so called 'akte van berusting, which means that both partners declare that they will not appeal. After signing the 'akte van berusting' and submitting it to your municipality, the divorce is official.[24]

A lawyer explained her work as a reviewer as follows: 'I receive an e-mail with the request to answer within three working days. I log in the system, access the (personal) data and check if there might be a barrier to handle the case, for example a conflict of interest. Next I contact the people and tell them I am their reviewer at this office: I will look at your divorce plan and how you have come to agreements. As a reviewer you see both the divorce plan and the position that had been were adopted.' (translation) (Scheltema, 2016). It is remarkable to see how the role of the (legal) professions changed; mediators became 'adjudicators' or 'decision makers' and lawyers became 'reviewers'.

Early in 2017 the initiators 'pulled the plug' on Rechtwijzer uit Elkaar: from 30 March 2017 onwards it would no longer be possible to start an online divorce plan through Rechtwijzer uit Elkaar. From 25 June 2017 onwards it would no longer be possible to work on the plan. According to HIIL, 813 couples had made a parenting plan since the start of Rechtwijzer uit Elkaar. And according to them in a questionnaire half a year after completion of the divorce, respondents reported a level of satisfaction on average of 7.7 (on a scale of 1 to 10).[25] This means that satisfaction with the website among people in a divorce who where using Rechtwijzer uit Elkaar, was quite high.

In 2017 the Rechtwijzer uit Elkaar restarted in a commercial version, 'Uit Elkaar'. The initiator and director, Kaspar Scheltema, had been an adviser involved with the Rechtwijzer. According to the company it directly removed some 'bugs' in the system that did not work in Rechtwijzer uit Elkaar and it used a different digital platform.[26] The tool in its new form is still recommended by the Legal Aid Board on their website. Moreover there is a special arrangement

[24] www.rechtwijzer.nl/uit-elkaar/transscript-rechtwijzer-uit-elkaar. See also for an explanation: Combrink-Kuiters 2014: 33.

[25] www.rechtwijzer.nl/uit-elkaar/meer-informatie/rechtwijzer-uit-elkaar-door-in-vernieuwde-vorm.

[26] www.mr-online.nl/online-scheiden-weer.

through legislation that users of Uit Elkaar get legal aid.[27] The online text of Uit Elkaar is: 'Arrange your divorce online, step by step and in consultation with each other. At Uitelkaar.nl people receive personal assistence and you pay a fixed price.(translation)'[28] The CEO, Kaspar Scheltema, was interviewed about the company on the Dutch radio programme BNR on 21 November 2018. According to him there are a few changes with regard to Rechtwijzer uit Elkaar: Uit Elkaar.nl is more forcused on the Dutch market; there is a case manager people can contact when they cannot continue. Some changes were made in Uit Elkaar.nl a year after the launch: it offers also offline mediation; thus the service is now more comprehensive than just an online dispute resolution platform. Some aspects stayed the same; the programme seems to consist of basically the same architecture. Scheltema asserted that people who make agreements independently of (legal) experts comply better with these. Scheltema stated that business was going quite well, between 100–150 people per month used the online tool, but there were two problems: finding good ways of marketing and distinguishing oneself from the competition.[29]

There are indeed many online divorce services (tens or perhaps hundreds): some examples (in 2019) are: scheiden-online.nl, netjesscheiden.nl, Scheidingsprofs.nl, Rocketlawyer.nl. Behind many online divorce services, the initiators are lawyers (Scheltema, 2016). And furthermore they often offer this service and also provide traditional forms of assistance. For example, the renowned lawyer, Teurlings, was one of the first to offer an online divorce tool 20 years ago: his approach is different: the conditions for an online divorce are that people agree on the fact that there will be a divorce application; that the people have already made agreements in a 'reasonable and equal dialogue, that the finances are already divided and agreed by both and there are already provisions with regard to arrangements on care division and child support'.[30]

What has happened with Rechtwijzer 1.0 since Rechtwijzer 2.0/uit Elkaar was terminated? Rechtwijzer 1.0 as an interactive platform still exists in a 'lite' version with regard to legal fields other than divorce.[31] The explanation of the Legal Aid Board on their website is: 'There is the longer term need for "smaller" government and more self-help and responsibility for individuals. Rechtwijzer offers the opportunity to choose the right approach for themselves through a digital process' (translation).[32] For consumer and tenant issues, one can still fill in a questionnaire and get some general (legal) advice or a plan for what to do

[27] This is for the extra costs of the decisionmaker/mediator 'bemiddelaar/adviseur' and for the costs of the reviewer: Subsidieregeling uitelkaar.nl (Staatscourant 2017, 61460); See also: www.uitelkaar.nl/kosten-uitelkaar.nl/kosten-scheiding/subsidie.

[28] www.uitelkaar.nl.

[29] www.bnr.nl/programmas/zakendoen/10361294/in-goed-overleg-met-elkaar-uit-elkaar.

[30] www.teurlingsadvocaten.nl/nl/echtscheiding-online-aanvragen/.

[31] www.rechtwijzer.nl.

[32] www.rvr.org/Informatie-over-de-raad/organisatie/taken-van-de-raad.html.

next. One does not receive advice that is specific to the particular situation of the person with the legal problem. But in general it is quite similar to the Canadian MyLawBC. For divorces or relationship break ups though, there is just a 'static' version, information without interaction. The remaining online interactive element is an online self-help tool only for calculating the alimony payment.[33] For more interactive self-help for divorce the Legal Aid Board chose to refer to Uitelkaar.nl, the online (now commercial) tool they co-developed themselves.

V. WHY DID RECHTWIJZER UIT ELKAAR NOT WORK OUT?

'The Dutch Rechtwijzer, the poster child of the internet revolution in legal advice and online dispute resolution, has proved financially unsustainable.' (Roger Smith)[34] The number of divorces using the online platform Rechtwijzer uit Elkaar fell short; it was insufficient for the platform to be sustainable in the current partnership.[35] The cause of this financial issue according to HIIL was at first the lack of readiness of the legal institutions: 'We learned that getting to a mutually reinforcing partnership with the traditional justice institutions to scale up a platform like Rechtwijzer is difficult.'[36] The word 'tradition' illustrates the argument. Later on Barendrecht added some other explanations. (Barendrecht 2017). This section will examine three possible explanations.

The first explanation was resistance by (tradition) legal institutions. One aspect was the reaction from the NOVA: the Netherlands Bar which is the professional organisation of the lawyers. The NOVA draws up regulations and rules for the legal profession. The adoption thereof is done by the board of representatives of the Bar ('College van afgevaardigden').[37] The Netherlands Bar was part of the advisory board of Rechtwijzer uit Elkaar, but apparently this was not an endorsement. According to an article by the editors of the Advocatenblad, the legal magazine for lawyers, the main argument was that the Rechtwijzer was 'under fire' by the Netherlands Bar (translation): The Netherlands Bar was critical on three points: the so called 'Vergewisplicht', 'Zorgplicht' en 'Geheimhouding'.[38] The 'Vergewisplicht' means the obligation for the lawyer/attorney to *ascertain the identity* of the client: ie that the lawyer/attorney knows for certain that it was indeed ('vergewissen') that specific person who filled in the elements in the online tool and therefore agreed to settlements about their family matters in the divorce covenant.

That identity was not secured by Rechtwijzer uit Elkaar according to the NOVA: a neighbour or a family member, or even the former spouse could have

[33] www.rechtwijzer.nl/uit-elkaar.
[34] www.law-tech-a2j.org/advice/goodbye-rechtwijzer-hello-justice42.
[35] www.mr-online.nl/scheidingssite-stopt-ermee.
[36] See n 34.
[37] www.advocatenorde.nl/english.
[38] www.advocatenorde.nl/nieuws/nova-signaleert-knelpunten-bij-rechtwijzer-uit-elkaar.

filled in the elements of the divorce covenant; the lawyer/attorney cannot find out who sat behind the computer screen; the 'zorgplicht', duty of care, means that the lawyer/attorney needs to *inform the clients of their legal position/* their rights and is obliged to ascertain that the clients understand the agreements. In Rechtwijzer uit Elkaar, the lawyer is only involved at the end of the process, when the agreements between partners have already been made. The Dutch internal code for lawyers requested physical contact (at least via skype) according to the Netherlands Bar. One indeed needed to see a lawyer before signing a legal divorce covenant with agreements. The 'Geheimhoudingsplicht' aims at lawyer/attorney confidentiality. Because also other people, such as a staff member of Rechtwijzer uit Elkaar, could see the information, including personal information, the answer to the questions and agreements filled in on the online system Rechtwijzer uit Elkaar by people, attorney confidentiality was infringed. Because of the criticism by the Bar, the Dutch Legal Aid Board finally announced just a few months before the end of Rechtwijzer that it would change some aspects of the architecture of Rechtwijzer, especially with regard to the duty of care 'zorgplicht'. HIIL and the Legal Aid Board promised to make some concessions: Rechtwijzer uit Elkaar would improve with regard to the contact with the lawyer at the end: and there would be at least some form of physical contact through skype.

It is entirely possible though that the resistance from the NOVA was not solely based on their professional attitude and conformity to the legal requirements (especially legal internal rules for attorneys). There might have been other interests at stake: the threat of competition, fear of losing work, loss of their familiar way of working and of their autonomy, being replaced by computers in at least part of their work (see also Dijksterhuis, 2008[39]). Moreover the connection that was frequently made by the Ministry of Security and Justice and the Legal Aid Board between Rechtwijzer and the legal aid reforms/cuts might have played a role.[40] Rechtwijzer uit elkaar was not a formal part of the judicial procedure, using it was voluntary, which made it harder to enter this field as a newcomer. Judges or lawyers who were not involved did not refer people in a divorce situation to the Rechtwijzer uit elkaar, as they were used to doing with regard to mediation. There was hardly any collaboration from the legal profession, especially the society of lawyers. Rechtwijzer uit elkaar moreover received critical reviews in legal magazines such as the Magazine for Laywers *Advocatenblad*.

On the other hand this could not be the sole or even most important explanation for the failure of Rechtwijzer uit Elkaar: first, not all of the legal

[39] The author's PhD thesis investigated these aspects when the legal profession feels threatened by new developments such as digital innovation and the need for standardisation.

[40] See eg a critical lawyer/mediator: www.sarahkoller.nl/scheiden-goedkoop-en-snel and a mediator: www.lianaderuiter.nl/online-scheiden.

profession was opposed to the introduction of Rechtwijzer. Regarding the introduction of Rechtwijzer 1.0, the more modest version, Smith (2013) noticed: 'The initial reaction of lawyers showed some hostility but, as time goes on, they are adapting.' And also the more ambitious 2.0 or Uit Elkaar was not vilified by the legal professionals: there were lawyers/attorneys who wanted to be part of Rechtwijzer uit Elkaar and collaborated as reviewers. For example one lawyer/ and attorney and reviewer of Rechtwijzer uit Elkaar stated in an article in the lawyers' magazine: 'It is 2016! It is important that we as the legal profession work with innovative instruments that are connected to the digitised world.'[41] Moreover the legal professions did not forbid the online divorce tool. The Bar asked for a few requirements to comply to legislation and internal rules, but it did not seem impossible to implement them, as they would increase the costs of Rechtwijzer uit Elkaar.

The *second* explanation might be that there had not been enough attention to the needs of people in a divorce situation. There was a lot of focus on science, innovation and (international) expansion. The initiators seemed to be more focused on promoting the online service to the outside world than to the Dutch (potential) clients: people who were getting a divorce. There were worldwide conferences, for example HIIL organised a world wide conference on ODR.[42] HIIL and the Dutch Legal Aid Board were 'selling' the idea to other jurisdictions: including England and Canada. The project gained worldwide attention and even (European) nominations and prizes. 'The Rechtwijzer was accompanied by a major promotional effort that sent members of the support team, largely from HIIL, around the globe to proselytise for its approach. Maurits (Barendrecht, director of HIIL) noted the degree of international interest and it was extraordinary. For example, HIIL team members presented both to conferences of the International Legal Aid Group (multiple times) and the Legal Services Corporation Technical Initiative Grants programme' (Smith, 2017).

HIIL, the Legal Aid Board, and also the Ministry of Justice seemed to expect too much from online divorce with regard to solving the complex problems of divorce. In a sense it it is similar to the promotion, especially by governments, of mediation in divorce. (See for example Maclean and Eekelaar, 2016: 14–16, Chin-A-Fat, 2004; Treloar in chapter one of this book.) There seemed to be insufficient insight into the needs of people who were getting a divorce. One aspect is that the initiators lacked knowledge about the specific characteristics of divorce law. There was no expertise in the developing team regarding the legal divorce aspects. The focus was on dispute resolution in general; or as HIIL called it: 'online supported resolution' (Barendrecht, 2017). The researchers at Tilburg University explained their methods as follows: 'Taking a bottom-up approach,

[41] www.advocatenblad.nl/2016/10/07/klik-door-om-te-scheiden-rechtwijzer-uit-elkaar-vraagt-om-harmonieuze-aanpak.

[42] 'Can ODR Really Help Courts and Improve Access to Justice?': www.20160dr.wordpress.com.

TISCO members develop, integrate, and apply insights from negotiation theory, conflict research, dispute system design, (comparative) legal research, network theory, behavioural law, and law and economics in their research in order to connect and extend the body of knowledge on building, maintaining and (constructively) ending horizontal relationships in which people and businesses are involved.' (Smith 2015: 63; quote from Tilburg University Website.)

The team treated divorce almost as a private contract. Also there was a lack of knowledge about the mental state people are in when getting a divorce: some people are involved in an acrimonious divorce, thus in a crisis situation; whereas to use Rechtwijzer uit Elkaar, both partners had first to agree on using the platform at all. It is easy to see the similarity with mediation, which is doomed to fail when one of the partners does not want to cooperate. (Chin a Fat, 2004, Maclean and Eekelaar, 2016, Treloar in chapter one of this book.) Secondly, (former) partners needed to agree on the division of care for the children and the financial aspects; The developers in the Scrum-meetings did not seem to have a sufficient connection with the people who were getting a divorce, especially not the more economically deprived ones who needed Legal Aid.

There were also differences of opinion between the wishes of HIlL on the one hand and the priorities of the Legal Aid Board. First, there were restrictions because of the restricted legal task of the Legal Aid Board: giving specific online legal advice was not permitted. Secondly, the main focus of the Legal Aid Board was helping their clients with lower incomes (often with a more practical, less theoretical education) or stay-at-home parents and people from non-Western ethnic backgrounds. Rechtwijzer on the other hand was more suitable as a self-help tool for people who are able to be self-reliant: for financially vulnerable people, in other words the clients of the Legal Aid Board, there were barriers, such as the Digid code, a lot of (complicated) texts, and few images /films, no app. Moreover there was of course the (minimum) price of a few hundred euros for a (former) couple, which might have been too much for some people for this product, especially because the other (online) services of the legal aid board were free of charge or were available for a very low price (under €100).

In the report on the self-reliance of people, the Scientific Council for Government Policy was sceptical about the ability of people to be self-reliant, especially in stressful situations (with legal aspects). The Council mentioned divorce as a prominant example, among dismissal from a job, illness, debt. Making the right decisions in such life events was hard for people, because of acute and extreme stress; and people tended to make decisions that would not promote their well being in the long-term (Wetenschappelijke Raad voor het Regeringsbeleid, 2017). Furthermore there seemed to be some omissions in the preparation of Rechtwijzer uit Elkaar from the viewpoint of a (commercial) service: no market research was conducted before the development and design to identify what people who are getting a divorce want or need; furthermore there was no dummy/show model available for lawyers, mediators or other interested people or organisations, or cycles of testing (such as test design in the market or review of design) as are often used in the business world when developing a new product.

The developers of Rechtwijzer used only focus groups instead of market research. Initially there was a great deal of public funding by the government so in that context it was not important how many clients actually used Rechtwijzer uit Elkaar. But after a certain period for development, the Rechtwijzer uit Elkaar had to be a financially sustainable platform and that was apparently not possible; the Rechtwijzer was not profitable or even able to cover their costs. Also Barendrecht himself mentioned the lack of marketing as a reason why Rechtwijzer uit Elkaar could not succeed. But he mentioned specifically the lack of marketing (and funding for it) by the Ministry of Justice and Security and the Legal Aid Board (Barendrecht, 2017). Moreover, neither the Legal Aid Board nor HIIL had experience with launching an innovative commercial product such as Rechtwijzer uit Elkaar in a very competitive, quite traditional, field. It was a cooperative venture by government and a social entrepeneur/scientific organisation. Moreover Rechtwijzer uit Elkaar received some unfortunate media attention because of competitors' failures. There was a television item on 7 May 2016 on online divorce in a programme on consumer affairs. There was quite strong criticism and although that was not specifically aimed at Rechtwijzer, the developer from the Legal Aid Board was present and therefore it was therefore not favourable marketing.[43]

A *third* explanation might lie in the ideas and concepts behind Rechtwijzer uit Elkaar. The general idea is that if you nudge people towards a harmonious divorce, people will not fight. Thus this online divorce tool was supposed to do something the traditional legal professions could not deliver: prevent people from having high-conflict divorces. This fits in with the broader view about the so-called tournament model 'tournooimodel', in an adversarial procedure with two lawyers involved, which could be a major cause of conflict for people in a divorce. Looking at the avaliable socio-legal research on this topic though, it does not seem that having two lawyers causes the conflicts between (ex)spouses. (See eg, Maclean and Eekelaar, 2016: 44–68). Furthermore, surely the people who use an online divorce tool such as Rechtwijzer are those who are already trying to divorce without severe conflict. Is it helpful therefore to compare the people who choose to divorce through Rechtwijzer uit Elkaar with the ones who both want their own advocate to represent their case or position before the judge?

What also seemed to be missing was a guarantee of fair arrangements (see also Smith, 2015). The website of Rechtwijzer uit Elkaar did not make clear what lawyers should do when they considered the agreements as very beneficial for one partner and very disadvantageous for the other. Or what to do when there was a situation of abuse and violence. Barendrecht stated that Rechtwijzer

[43] www.npostart.nl/is-online-scheiden-zo-snel-en-goedkoop-als-het-lijkt/07-05-2016/POMS_VARA_3863190.

uit Elkaar was suited to that kind of situation; but the lawyers who collaborated disagreed.[44] It was very much focussed on the prevention of conflicts. And thus it overlooked that there might be reasons why people in a divorce situation had conflicts; for example because one partner avoids paying a reasonable amount of child or spousal support or because a partner tries to prevent the other one from seeing their child. Furthermore the role of the experts was very different from the traditional role. Mediators were involved in the Rechtwijzer uit Elkaar, but it was not transparent who they were nor what their specific role was. The lawyer was only involved at the end, as a reviewer and people did not see the lawyer, either face to face or by Skype connection (although later on, just before the end of the Rechtwijzer uit Elkaar, the Legal Aid Board did agree to make that an obligatory step).

Rechtwijzer uit Elkaar might have been too innovative and therefore too uncertain for people in a divorce situation; it was perhaps a step too far to expect that huge numbers of people would go for it in such a short period, when in a stressful and unknown situation. The target audience was not ready for it; the legal professions were not – they needed to make too many changes with regard to their role. This online innovation or even online dispute resolution might become inevitably in the (near) future an alternative to going to court. But it is still an unknown; people do not trust it yet, especially in a complex family matter such as a divorce. They seem to prefer the safe and familiar route through lawyers. It may also have been a factor that the opportunity to have a publicly funded lawyer from the start of the procedure in the Netherlands is still intact.[45] It is moreover also mandatory to have a lawyer in the Netherlands in a divorce procedure. Thus the online divorce cannot replace the lawyer nor the judge in the Netherlands. But most of all Rechtwijzer uit Elkaar or Rechtwijzer 2.0 seemed a step too far; the more modest, less ambitious Rechtwijzer 1.0, with mainly the mediators and lawyers as target audiences, might have had more chance of succeeding, especially looking at the limited self-reliance of the people who needed legal aid and people in complex divorce situations.

VI. POSITIVE ASPECTS OF RECHTWIJZER UIT ELKAAR

First, Rechtwijzer uit Elkaar can be seen as a pioneer: it was a new combination of online self-help and assistance on request from experts; it fulfilled the need of a particular group of people in a divorce: the more self-reliant, who had a mutual wish to divorce in an orderly manner. Moreover there were strong, passionate

[44] www.advocatenblad.nl/2016/10/07/klik-door-om-te-scheiden-rechtwijzer-uit-elkaar-vraagt-om-harmonieuze-aanpak.

[45] Though there are fewer and fewer lawyers in divorce procedures who do legal aid cases, because of the low pay, due to the legal aid cuts.

leaders from both the Dutch Legal Aid Board and HIIL. Also the fact that this was a cooperation between government (Legal Aid Board), business and science was a major strength. This was an example of an innovative form of cooperation which resulted in international cooperation: it was so special that England and Canada were going to build on the concept; other countries such as Australia, Scotland and Ireland were interested; thus it was an international and interdisciplinary cooperation, which should be better than having every country reinventing the wheel over and over again.

Secondly, some of Rechtwijzer has been retained. The commercial follow up version of Rechtwijzer uit Elkaar is called Uit-Elkaar.nl and is still operating. Though the Legal Aid Board is not involved any longer as a partner, and therefore the focus on the group with less financial means has weakened, it may be useful for a certain group in society. Apparently the Legal Aid Board still supports the online divorce tool by referring to it as they consider the tool useful for their clients. Also Rechtwijzer as an online interactive tool still exists, though not for divorce. The Legal Aid Board still recommends Rechtwijzer to their clients as 'a preliminary provision that helps people find solutions for their legal problems in an interactive manner' (Legal Aid Board, 2017: 7, 8), before people go to the Legal Service Counters or ask for state-financed legal aid for legal advice and representation by a lawyer. Rechtwijzer uit Elkaar, Rechtwijzer 1.0 and the connected tools such as the child support calculation tool, moreover had quite good evaluations from people who used it. This may indicate that there is a need for those kind of services and people can experience satisfaction when using them, though it is not yet clear when and how these online tools help them in their conflict.

Thirdly, Rechtwijzer uit Elkaar and similar online dispute resolution tools offer a valuable opportunity to reflect on the role of the legal professions in the field of divorce. The lawyer's role changed – he became a reviewer. Mediators became adjudicators and so on.The critical attitude of the NOVA and the Dutch Bar meant that they were forced to explain why their contribution was crucial to help people in a divorce process.

REFERENCES

Barendrecht, M, Kistemaker, L, Scholten, HJ, Schrader, R, and Wrzesinska, M (HIIL) (2014) *Legal aid in Europe: Nine different ways to guarantee access to justice* (Den Haag, WODC).

Barendrecht, M, Piest, J, and Gramatikov, MA (2015) *De rechtvaardigheid van scheidingsprocedures* (Den Haag, HIIL Innovating Justice).

Barendrecht, M (2017) *Rechtwijzer: why online supported dispute resolution is hard to implement*.

Bickel, E, Dijk, M Van and Giebels, E (2015) *Online legal advice and conflict support: a Dutch experience* (Twente, Department Psychology of Conflict, Risk & Safety, Faculty of Behavioural, Management and Social Sciences University of Twente).

Chin-A-Fat, B (2004) *Scheiden: (ter)echter zonder echter? Een onderzoek naar de meerwaarde van scheidingsbemiddeling* (diss) (Den Haag, SDU).

Combrink-Kuiters, L, Van Gammeren-Zoeteweij, M and Peters, S (2014) *Monitor Gesubsidieerde Rechtsbijstand 2014*, (Utrecht/Den Haag/Oisterwijk, Wolf Legal Publishers/Raad voor Rechtsbijstand): www.rvr.org/binaries/content/assets/rvrorg/informatie-over-de-raad/monitor/monitor-2014-def.pdf.

Dijk, M (2015) 'Rechtwijzer 1.0 Research: A comment on Roger Smith's Review', *Digital Delivery of legal services to people on low incomes*, Quarterly Update, (The legal Foundation).

Dijk, M van, Giebels, E, and Zebel, S (2016) 'Building strength or Lending an ear in Legal Conflicts: Dependence and conflict Assymetry as Distinct Predictors of Needs for support', *Negotiation and Conflict Management Research* 9(1) (research supported by a grant from the Dutch Legal Aid Board).

Dijksterhuis, B (2008) *Rechters normeren de alimentatiehoogte, Een empirisch onderzoek naar rechterlijke samenwerking in de Werkgroep Alimentatienormen (1975–2007)* (Leiden, Leiden University Press).

Dijksterhuis, B and Duijvenvoorde, M van (2013) 'Kinderalimentatiesysteem Recourt/Van der Steur. Evaluatieonderzoek onder gescheiden burgers (samenvatting)' (Amsterdam/Rotterdam, HvA/LBIO).

Dijksterhuis, B (2013) 'Women judges in the Netherlands', in U Schultz and G Shaw (eds) *Gender and Judging* (Oxford, Hart Publishing).

Droogleever Fortuyn, S (2018) 'Rouvoet bepleit alternatieve procedures echtscheidingen', *Advocatenblad* 22 Februari.

Genn, H and Beinart, S (1999) *Paths to Justice: What People do and think about going to Law* (Oxford, Hart Publishing).

Genn, H and Paterson, A (2001) *Paths to Justice Scotland. What people in Scotland do and think about going to law*, (Oxford/Portland Oregon, Hart Publishing).

HIIL (2016) *ODR and the courts: the promise of 100% access to justice? Online dispute resolution 2016* (HIIL Trend report IV (Den Haag, HIIL).

Legal Aid Board, *Legal Aid in the Netherlands: a broad outline* (brochure) (2017, September) (Utrecht, Legal Aid Board).

Maclean, M and Eekelaar, J (2016) *Lawyers and Mediators. The Brave New World of Services for Separating Families*, (Oxford, Hart Publishing).

Muller, S, Barendrecht, M, Porter, R, De Wever, W and Pouwelse, E (2013) *Innovating justice: Developing new ways to bring fairness between people*. (Den Haag, HIIL).

NOVA (2015) *Eindrapport Commissie 'Duurzaam stelsel gefinancieerde rechtsbijstand* (Den Haag, APE/NOVA).

Peters, SL, Combrink-Kuiters, L and Van Gammeren-Zoeteweij, M (2009) *Monitor gesubsidieerde Rechtsbijstand 2009* (Den Haag, Boom Juridische uitgevers).

Raad voor Rechtsbijstand (2010), *Scheiden? Het kan anders! Praktische wegwijzer bij het Echtscheiding- en Ouderschapsplan* (Leeuwarden, Intermediately).

Raad voor de Rechtsbijstand (Dutch Legal Aid Council) (2015), *Jaarverslag 2015 (Annual report 2015): Voorbereid de toekomst in* (Utrecht, Raad voor de Rechtsbijstand).

Scheltema, T (2016) 'Klik door om te scheiden – Rechtwijzer uit elkaar vraagt om harmonieuze aanpak', *Advocatenblad* 16, 12–17.

Smith, R (2013) *I have seen the future and it works – maybe and in Dutch* (blog).

Smith, R and Paterson, A (2014) *Face to Face Legal Services and their Alternatives: Global Lessons from the Digital Revolution* (Glasgow, Strathprints).

Smith, R (2015) 'A review of Online Legal Advice and Conflict Support: a Dutch Experience' in E Bickel, M van Dijk and E Giebels, *Digital Delivery of legal services to people on low incomes* Quarterly Update (The Legal Foundation).
Smith, R, (2017) 'Classical Lessons from the Rechtwijzer: a conversation with Professor Barendrecht': https://law-tech-a2j.org/odr/classical-lessons-from-the-rechtwijzer-a-conversation-with-professor-barendrecht/, accessed 13 April 2019.
Tilburg Institute of Interdisciplinary Studies of Civil Law and Conflict Resolution Systems (ed) (2010), *A Handbook for measuring the costs and quality of access to justice* (Apeldoorn/Antwerpen/ Portland, Maklu).
Velthoven, B van and Voert, M ter (2013) 'Rechters in de delta: Over de rol van de rechtspraak in de beslechting van geschillen van Nederlandse burgers', *Rechtstreeks* 4.
Verdonschot, J-H (2013) *Sharing rules that work: Developing law as practical and concrete guidelines for fair sharing* (Oisterwijk, Wolf Legal Publishers (WLP)).
Verdonschot, J-H (2015) 'In the Netherlands, Online application helps divorcing couples in their own words, on their own time' *ABA Dispute Resolution Magazine* (Winter Edition).
Verdonschot, J-H (2016) 'Kei & ODR, hand in hand vooruit', *Recht der Werkelijkheid* 2.
Voert, M ter (2011) 'Hoe ontstaan en verlopen geschillen', *Recht van Onderop* (Nijmegen, Ars Aequi Libri).
Voert, M ter (2015) *Factsheet 2015-3. Ontwikking hoogte eigen bijdrage gesubsidieerde rechtsbijstand 2002–2014* (Den Haag, WODC).
Voert, M ter and Klein Haarhuis, C (2017) 'Waarom schakelen burgers (geen) rechtshulp in?', *Recht der Werkelijkheid* (Den Haag, Boom Juridische Uitgevers).
Wetenschappelijke Raad voor het Regeringsbeleid (Scientific Council for Government Policy) (2017) *Weten is nog geen doen. Een realistisch perspectief op redzaamheid* (Den Haag, Wetenschappelijke Raad voor het Regeringsbeleid/Amsterdam University Press).

12

The Digital Contribution to Reforming the Traditional Family Justice System in England and Wales: Reaching for the Best of Both Worlds?

MAVIS MACLEAN

I. INTRODUCTION

WE HAVE SEEN in this book how pressures on the family justice system in different jurisdictions have arisen for a variety of reasons, including a need to deal with increasing numbers of family cases, cuts in public spending under austerity, and policies of post- liberalism or other political change. ADR in the form of Family Mediation had been greeted with enthusiasm by policymakers in many jurisdictions some years ago as the most promising solution, offering value for money and at the same time encouraging development of individual responsibility. But it has not been received with the same kind of enthusiasm by the people with family matters to resolve. It has not replaced, though it may support, traditional courts and lawyers.

Then came the digital movement, as the next 'silver bullet' which might help to rescue family justice. The new technology is affecting all areas of life and has been greeted positively by policymakers across jurisdictions as a way of increasing the efficiency and decreasing the cost of providing many services, including family justice. This book has asked how digital technology is being used in family justice, what goes well and what becomes problematic. It is clear that there is much to be gained from using technology to support the efficient administration of the courts, and in helping parties to find information to manage their situation hopefully without any need for further help, or as a last resort by applying to the courts. But we are cautious about seeing digital justice as standing alone to provide a universal panacea from the user perspective. People come to the justice system because they have a problem, which has taken the form of a dispute which may merit legal intervention. Online information and application forms provide fast and low cost access to justice in the procedural sense. But they cannot yet offer individual personal help throughout the process in the way that a lawyer representing a client is required to do under a professional duty of care. In England and Wales the family lawyers in the public sector have often been characterised by critics as escalating conflict by fighting for their clients within an adversarial system. In our observational studies of family solicitors and the bar, however, we saw not warriors but representatives, gathering relevant information, organising the case and supporting the client to reach the best possible outcome with a first thought always for any children involved (Eekelaar, Maclean and Beinart, 2000; Maclean and Eekelaar, 2009). Indeed, one of the first findings of the Ministry of Justice Digital team reported below was that people are happy to receive information online if they are confident that they may talk to a human later.

This chapter offers some examples of recent digital policy developments in England and Wales, and asks what works well, what might work better, and how other 'green shoots' activity might perhaps work with the government's digital services to help resolve the crisis arising from increasing demand and decreasing resourcing in family justice.

II. THE INTERNATIONAL STARTING POINTS FOR THE EMERGENCE OF DIGITAL FAMILY JUSTICE

The Oñati Workshop from which the chapters in this book have developed arose from a sense of panic about the direction and speed of the digital journey family justice appeared to be taking. After the rapid rise of mediation to the top of the policymakers' agenda in the 1980s onwards, with little evaluation of what was to be gained, never mind what might be lost, in moving away from the traditional work of courts and lawyers in family matters, we were seeing an even more rapid change process, this time towards the application of digital technology. Of course this increase was not limited to the work of the justice system. Every area of life, from buying a pair of shoes to listening to music or sharing family news, was becoming digitised. It would be surprising if family justice remained outside the digital box.

The starting point for digital activity was taking different forms in the different jurisdictions represented in this book. For example, in France and Turkey the stimulus lay in the need to achieve more efficient management of an overburdened justice system, and progress is being made (see chapters three and seven). In Poland, ecourts are growing fast to deal with routine civil cases of debt, but are not being used for family matters in a society where family matters are private, and the current government is interested in upholding traditional family values and not wishing to facilitate family separation (see chapter two). In Canada, there are issues about moving away from traditional courts towards private ordering (see chapter one). And in the Netherlands, with its strong tradition of offering publicly funded support, the process had gone further and digital techniques were developed to reach to the very heart of the justice system, the resolution of individual conflict (see chapter eleven). The mighty Rechtwijzer (pathway to justice) appeared to offer separating couples a calm and constructive way of making their own post-separation arrangements and resolving their own difficulties, resorting to the legal system only for confirmation of decisions taken. Sadly, although this system was so technically advanced that through voice sensitivity it could identify when a conversation became heated and a pause was needed, it had a number of problems in relating to the legal system. For example, it could not satisfy the courts that the participants were who they claimed to be. Dijksterhuis has described how take-up remained low, and that the Rechtwijzer in its then form collapsed for lack of financial viability. It had been hoped that it would be able to help large numbers of former Legal Aid clients, but instead Legal Aid resources are now being cut back. In effect, it had worked best with well- informed computer-literate couples who had already made most of their important decisions about their post-separation financial and childcare arrangements.

At the same time, the earlier forms of ADR, notably family mediation, were not achieving widespread use either (see chapters five, six, and seven on Germany, Spain and France). As always the Scots are taking a different and more effective approach (see chapter eight), whereby separation is managed mainly by negotiating private contracts but with expert support. This seems to work well. It is not a highly digitised approach, but rather a form of facilitated private ordering within a traditional legal framework, where parties are not being ordered but instead enabled to take control of their lives by bargaining in the shadow of clearly defined legal objectives. We also see in chapters nine and ten how the use of digital technology is developing in the community, outside of the formal justice 'system', in England and Wales and Australia.

But before going further, we would do well to pause and ask the big question of how are we to assess effectiveness of such change? The cross-national examination of digital development in this book has reminded us of how important it is to identify what we want from a justice system before making any assessment of what is being achieved by all those who now work with separating families. These include not only the courts and lawyers but all the other professionals now involved – counsellors, mediators, accountants, tax advisers, child development specialists, pedagogues. And there are the non-professionals – the lay advisers, often volunteers, and of course the input from friends and family.

When family matters arise which cannot be resolved with the help of friends and family alone, what do we expect from a family justice system? Is the aim to solve problems? Or to resolve disputes? Is the main task to provide help, or might there be a preventative function to assist in avoiding the problems which may become disputes? Or is it to provide various methods of dispute resolution, including as a final resort adjudication and compliance? Is the policy priority to deliver sufficient Welfare Assistance, or is it to maintain Access to Justice and the Rule of Law? Do we have even higher aspirations to carry out social engineering, by asking family law to change individual behaviour, whether by discouraging parental separation, or by supporting cross-household parenting over time? Or do we simply want a good enough continuation of the existing system but with better value for money – that is, a quicker, cheaper and maybe better, family justice system?

These are emerging questions for future work. But they underlie this final chapter, which, through the exploration of recent developments in England and Wales, begins to try to consider where we stand. Some of the objectives described above are complementary, many are not. A cheaper system is seldom both quicker and better. And priorities change with changing circumstances.

III. RECENT DEVELOPMENTS IN FAMILY JUSTICE IN ENGLAND AND WALES

In London the government department concerned with legal matters has undergone a number of transformations, not only in title but in fundamental aims and methods. The Ministry of Justice was previously known as the Lord Chancellor's Department when it was a small group of lawyers supporting the work of the head of the judiciary, who was also a member of cabinet, and Speaker of the Upper House in Parliament. At that time the official statement of intent for family law in the 1980s and 1990s took a welfare based approach, aimed at 'Protecting the Vulnerable'. But the department grew in size and organisational responsibilities as it took over the court service, and eventually the offender management (ie, prison) service. At the same time the department was experiencing the constitutional changes of 2005[1] by which the Lord Chancellor became the Secretary of State for Justice and Lord Chancellor combined (recent incumbents have had to indicate which title they prefer to be addressed by), ceased to have an automatic seat in cabinet or act as Speaker of the Upper House, and responsibility for judicial appointments passed to the newly created Judicial Appointments Commission. Furthermore, the Law Lords, the highest court, had been retitled the Supreme Court and moved physically out of the House of Lords into their own building across Parliament Green. So while growing in size, the department for legal matters, by then the Department for Constitutional Affairs (DCA) and now the Ministry of Justice (MoJ) is thought to have lost both influence and status. While seeking to fulfil the aim of achieving separation of powers between the legislature, the executive and the judiciary, DCA became just another government department headed by just another politician. Charles Falconer presided with dignity over the change, but the first non-lawyer to be appointed 'Lord Chancellor' (Chris Grayling, 2012–15) was not regarded as successful, and he was followed in rapid succession by three appointees in three years.

[1] See the Constitutional Reform Act 2005.

With these developments came a new emphasis on 'family justice' meaning a 'family justice system', delivering justice rather than writing family law. Budgetary responsibilities grew, as did the level of supervision required. The new Public Service Agreements (PSAs), introduced by Tony Blair in 2001,[2] required each government department seeking money from the Treasury to define exactly the purpose of the grant, and account for how it was used. There was to be no more looking across departmental boundaries to see the impact of the work of one department on another. Silo management had arrived. There were clearly advantages in achieving clearer accountability, but also a frustrating lack of flexibility. A review of the family justice system was set up in 2010 under David Norgrove, who produced a far reaching and thoughtful analysis of how the system was working, and how it might improve (Ministry of Justice and Department for Education, 2011). At the same time the strapline for family justice changed from protection to 'promoting fair and informed settlement', which indicated the interest in ADR/mediation rather than courts and lawyers. An element of Value For Money across the justice system was appearing alongside the welfare-based thinking of the earlier version, hardly surprising in view of the financial crisis and the beginning of austerity policies across the public sector.

This was also the time when lawyers and courts were becoming a cause for concern in that public funding for Legal Aid in family matters was increasing rapidly. This was due not so much to lawyers working in an aggressive way in an adversarial system to maximise their income, but to the fact that the number and complexity of divorces had increased and thereby enhanced the Legal Aid bill. Policymakers thankfully embraced mediation as a possible low-cost way out of this funding crisis, as mediators often worked pro bono and when they did charge it was at a much lower rate than the lawyers. The overarching aim was to enable parties to avoid the need to use the courts for dispute resolution, and for courts to become the service of last resort used mainly for registering an order made by consent which could then be enforced if either party appeared to be failing to comply.

However, following the acute financial crisis of 2008–09 and the subsequent need to cut public spending, a more radical approach to family justice was required. Government began to plan the removal from the scope of Legal Aid of almost all private family law matters on the grounds that public money should not be spent on private quarrels. This culminated in the Legal Aid Sentencing and Punishment of Offenders Act 2012 (LASPO) recently reviewed (see Ministry of Justice, 2019). This did not result, however, in the increased use of mediation as government had hoped, nor in reduced court use. Instead it was followed by continuing high levels of applications to courts in divorce-related matters, but with parties often appearing as litigants in person without legal advice or representation, and the work of the judiciary became much more difficult. The family

[2] PSAs were abolished in 2010.

justice strap line changed again, and is currently 'protecting and advancing the principles of justice', a formulation with which it is hard to disagree, but which avoids commitment to any particular activity or form of help.

If we return to our wish to measure whether the family justice system is effective in England and Wales, we may safely assume that Value For Money remains high on the list of priorities. The LASPO review, published in February 2019, has now acknowledged that the legislation did achieve the desired levels of overall cuts in public expenditure, but that the outcomes were not as expected. The 200,000 cases removed from eligibility for Legal Aid did not turn to mediation (ibid: 609); instead mediation take-up fell by 60% (ibid: Fig 87) and the Review states that there may be people unable to pay for legal help who are now excluded from the scheme It cannot be concluded 'that equity has been achieved', nor that ADR was 'better value for the money for the taxpayer' (ibid: para 739). The report stresses that new thinking is required, and, although still hoping to persuade people to stay out of court (at an estimated cost to the state of £2,700 a day compared with the cost of a publicly funded mediation of £400), the Report asks for a new range of 'legal support' services, which need not all be provided by lawyers. Digital developments are welcomed, but while valuing innovation, the Review also observes that traditional ways of delivering legal services are important and emphasises the need for early legal advice, and that digital technology is the servant not the master in the process.

So what is the way forward? From the costs given above, mediation remains desirable for the policymaker, but it has not been possible in England and Wales, as elsewhere, to achieve large scale participation (see J Beck paper to MoJ HMCTS Public User Event 6 November 2019 Consultation on Modernising the Courts) who notes that even a small degree of diversion from court to mediation could cover the cost of recovering some of what was lost under the Legal Aid cuts, for example to offer legal help in cases where children are concerned, and support the setting up of a loan system in financial cases).

Government is currently engaged in a modernisation of the courts programme, with funding of £1 billion, which focuses on digital developments for applications to court, and video-enabled hearings, with assisted digital support to be provided through a contract with the Good Things Foundation. It includes 'tactical telephony with enhanced multi-channel customer experience', improved workflow management, performance management and the 'Human Voice of Justice', a telephone messaging system using 'The First Word' product bought by MoJ. The report of the HM Courts and Tribunal Service in September 2018 entitled 'Reform Update'[3] describes six Family Justice projects in progress: online divorce, online probate, streamlining of public law children cases, early work on adoption, the court of protection, and work is beginning on private law family matters.

[3] See HM Courts and Tribunals Service, Reform Update, Autumn 2018, Ministry of Justice, September 2018: https://assets.publishing.service.gov.uk/government/uploads/system/uploads/attachment_data/file/772549/Reform_Update_issue_2_September_2018.pdf.

The team are aiming to achieve 'seamless digital working in family public law', the use of online application forms with local authorities, and are testing a core document management system for family courts, financial remedy systems to enable solicitors to manage multiple cases, and systems and processes to enable family private law litigants to manage their cases online.

The response is mixed. The new President of the Family Division, Sir Andrew MacFarlane, the senior judicial member of the family justice system, has expressed concerns about any move towards video-based hearings in contested family cases involving children.[4] But the famous quotation from Henry Ford has been used when negative opinions are expressed: 'If I had asked the public what they wanted they would have said a faster horse'!

IV. GOVERNMENT ACTIVITY AND DIGITAL DEVELOPMENTS IN ENGLAND AND WALES

We turn now to look at how the digital movement has developed in England and Wales, and how it is now moving with care in a positive direction after a high speed but perhaps over ambitious start towards a more cautious approach involving careful consumer consultation. There follows an account of the setting up in 2016 of the MoJ Digital workstream on family justice and an account of two projects concerned with child contact cases. The first of these projects sets up a website to encourage out of court solutions in child arrangements cases. The second, a pilot for using online applications to court by separated parents, has been evaluated by Alexy Buck and Alejandra Diaz, of the Ministry of Justice, and is presented by the researchers as a case study in chapter thirteen. This chapter closes with a discussion of the way in which the now fully operational government online divorce application scheme benefitted from developmental work in the advice sector which contributed a new way of incorporating legal support within an interactive website, which it is suggested could be considered as a website with a duty of care.

A. Ministry of Justice Digital: Family work January–August 2016

In January 2016 work began in the MoJ department known as MoJ Digital to develop an Out of Court Pathway for family cases as part of the programme for Transforming our Justice System, to be launched by the then Lord Chancellor Liz Truss[5] in September 2016. There was a six-month 'discovery' period, during

[4] See *The Guardian* newspaper report, 12 December 2018.

[5] See Lord Chancellor, Lord Chief Justice and Senior President of Tribunals, *Transforming our Justice System* MoJ, September 2016: https://assets.publishing.service.gov.uk/government/uploads/system/uploads/attachment_data/file/553261/joint-vision-statement.pdf, last accessed 15 April 2019.

which members of the team examined relevant research findings, in this jurisdiction and abroad, and then showcased their progress to a meeting on 31 August 2016 of interested parties who were invited to share the information. They reported to us that there was currently no existing overarching service for potential court users, there were many concurrent changes, and that users were in emotionally difficult situations. They described how they had 'walked through a prototype', 'tested and refined hypotheses' about user needs, with a key finding that 'People will accept initial information through algorithms/online if they know they will be able to talk to a human later in the process.'

They decided that they would be able to provide users with a Personalised Action Plan when they were emotionally ready, and that the service providers would be able to 'stop people going to court unnecessarily, and to empower people to make their own decisions'. In addition, the team would be able to 'utilise information about users and their needs to facilitate more proactive interventions, develop information resources into nonlinear products that can surface where most appropriate to users, and create a platform for a range of products, services to be delivered and added to over time'. The plans set out a content strategy and landscape, proposals for measuring success, and a digital roadmap to give an overview of all the products. The Service Principles for the Separating parents pathway aimed 'to help these parents create better long term outcomes for their children and family and to reduce parental conflict, and the likelihood of recurrent problems, lowering any unnecessary financial burden on the government or third sector'. The headings run: 'just, fair affordable … easy to use, transparent'.

The next six months were to be spent building the project. The ongoing developments are described not as pilots but as 'experiments'. Information was to be given by the right person at the right time in the right place. The team would start from need … user preference … assessment and triage … and each user would have a Family Case adviser (no information was available about where these advisers would come from or what their skills would be). The current cost of a children case to final hearing was estimated as £1,500, or £800 to first hearing or FHDRA (First Hearing and Dispute Resolution Appointment).

The Out of Court Digital Pathway programme was developing with great energy and enthusiasm as part of the government-wide programme of using the new technology to maximise value for money, increase effectiveness and efficiency, and enable the user to have more control over the pathway through a particular situation. Two things happened, however, which brought the work not to a halt, but to a slower and less generously resourced way forward. The impact of austerity on departmental budgets led the MoJ to experience a 30% funding cut in 2015. MoJ Digital had been generously funded with technical experts brought in from outside the department on short-term contracts (the first Head of Digital Capability and Engagement has been paid £118k per annum). Budgets were now trimmed. Nevertheless, at the time of writing (March 2019), three of the proposed 'experiments' were in the process of completion or evaluation: an online tool 'Get help with child arrangements' aiming to 'nudge' people away from making court applications for child arrangements, piloting for online application in these cases using form C100 (setting out information and proposals concerning child arrangements), and online divorce application, now fully operational.

These 'experiments' indicate the range of activities being undertaken. The first development, described in the MoJ blog as 'Get help with child arrangements', was a guide placed on the government website GOV.UK and widely accessible to parents thinking about making or changing arrangements for their children after separation. This attempts to encourage people to keep out of court, on the basis that going to court could escalate existing conflict and be bad for the children concerned as well as costly for the government. The second is also concerned with children cases, aiming to make a procedure simpler and more accessible by enabling application for a child arrangement order online, though there might be concerns about making the process too easy and thus going against the approach of the digital tool 'Get help to stay away from courts'. The apparent success of the information giving digital 'nudge' exercise may be contrasted with the difficulties experienced by the CAFCASS (Children and Family Court Advisory and Support Service) pilot programme 'Support with Child Arrangements' in Manchester. This offered a tailored package, making arrangements quickly online to set up a SPIP,[6] mediation, supervised contact and a parenting plan meeting before a FHDRA in order to reduce court attendance. But this ended in August 2018 after six months, having achieved only a 15% reduction in court applications and at a considerable cost. Intervening with the intention of changing behaviour rather than expediting it is a challenging task.

The third area of work described is the development of online divorce application, to simplify and streamline a procedure which had become unnecessarily complex given the rarity of dispute about the change of legal status, though remaining of importance and not to be undertaken without serious consideration.

The progress and evaluation processes for these three projects will be described, and we are grateful to the MoJ for providing accounts of the work on child arrangements. This will also look beyond the digital work of government when considering the online divorce petition, where a private advice sector project known as COURTNAV had carried out ground-breaking developmental work which the MoJ was able to draw on. This will lead to final observations, examining not only the boundaries of digital intervention in general but specifically some of the differences between government and non-governmental digital intervention with a view to identifying areas for successful expansion, and working across the public and private sectors, including of course the third sector.

[6] Separated Parents Information Programme.

B. Arrangements for Children

In August 2018 Alejandra Diaz of the MoJ digital team published an account of digitally 'nudging' separated parents to agree arrangements for their children out of court.[7] In her role working with policymakers, she was involved in designing this experiment using nudge principles to design services that could lead to better outcomes for court users, working with experts in the Behavioural Insights team. She describes how, over the previous two years, drawing on the academic literature, she and her team had conducted research with 140 parents, and found that many were not aware of or did not understand the alternative services available when they began their court application. As a result, she says that they were not in the best position to make a decision about what alternative services were available to settle children disputes. So she has tried to identify relevant interactions, and, by making various touch points easy to use and simple to understand, and by guiding users to specific outcomes based on their journey so far, she is aiming to inform and guide behaviour so that more people who could benefit from out-of-court dispute resolution options are guided towards them.

For example, when making an application, the form now says: 'Before you continue with your application you should consider what the court process might involve and whether you need to go. The next section begins with the heading 'What happens at court?' and states that 'a judge must, by law, put the children first'. The court will decide on what it thinks is best for the children. 'If you apply to court you must be prepared to follow the court's decision even if you don't agree with it …'. 'If you consider challenging or enforcing an order', she stresses that 'A court order is not flexible. You'll need to apply to the court again if your situation changes'. Then the pros and cons of court orders are listed: 'Pros … legally binding order, a decision is made in the best interests of the children'; 'Cons …. It can be expensive, you may not feel in control, a judge makes the decision, it can be more stressful for you and the children, may increase conflict between you and the other person …'. ' … if you still communicate with the other person, and there are no concerns about domestic or child abuse, the cheaper and easier way to make arrangements is to negotiate with each other …'. Then information is given on professional mediation, lawyer negotiation, collaborative law and a Mediation Information and Assessment Meeting.

Alejandra Diaz adds: 'we also want to explore how we can make it easy to actually pursue the options once they learn about it. Amazon are kings of this with their one click ordering process. We will continue to explore how we can make out-of-court options easy to access so we can remove barriers and influence human behaviour in a positive way in the coming months'. Feedback was

[7] https://mojdigital.blog.gov.uk/2018/08/28/nudging-separated-parents-to-agree-arrangements-for-their-children.

requested: 'we have the digital tools to experiment with a number of options and we hope to affect people's behaviour in a positive way, so watch this space …'.

Although the 'nudge' project was aimed to make it easier to use out-of-court methods of reaching agreement, the MoJ accepts that some people will still need to go to court and has also promoted making application easier with the online C100 project described in chapter thirteen below.

C. Online Divorce

The third experiment, now fully operational, is for online divorce application, designed to deliver a national transformed end-to-end digital service for individuals and their legal representatives to make an application to end their marriage or civil partnership and resolve associated financial issues. The first stage, supporting applications for uncontested divorce and allowing digital upload of marriage certificates, was rolled out nationally from 30 April 2018, and 13,767online applications were received in the first six months. Fewer than 1% contained errors, whereas with the former paper-based application form, 40% were being returned to sender due to minor errors.[8] In addition, an online system is currently being tested to be used by legal representatives for Financial Remedy orders to be made by consent.[9]

There is a 'Special Procedure' for divorce which is basically administrative, allowing divorce to be granted on request if not contested, only requiring evidence that a marriage has taken place but has irretrievably broken down. This can be shown by reference to behavioural grounds, such as a statement that the other party has engaged in adultery or behaviour which the applicant finds it impossible to live with, or by living apart for two years with consent or five years without. Applicants must also show that they fall within the jurisdiction of the English courts. This is basic information, only a little more complex than used in the Polish civil debt cases.

The paper forms have changed over time. In 2009 the Oyez[10] forms were made up of a single large sheet of paper folded to give three pages. The cover states that this is a divorce petition between petitioner and respondent. On opening out, the first inside page is headed 'Prayer', listing what the petitioner seeks (dissolution of the marriage, and whether they may seek to be granted ancillary financial relief, or any order for the children) and names and addresses for service of papers. The third page opposite asks for details of any other proceedings, and choice of grounds, with a second blank page discreetly tucked behind

[8] The author experienced this problems when trying to help a friend with her petition, and having it returned because she wrote 'Borough of Camden' instead of 'London Borough of Camden' for place of marriage, and had to argue to avoid paying a second court fee of £300.

[9] See Practice Direction 36E.

[10] Oyez is a legal stationer.

the Prayer asking for details of any unacceptable conduct. There are also four pages of Notes for Guidance, which set out the information needed, explain that a solicitor or Citizens Advice Bureau could help, explain terms like 'residence', what to say in describing conduct, and advises that if you cross out ancillary relief you will have to ask the court's permission to apply if you change your mind later, and cannot do so after remarriage … and a reminder to sign and date. There is no mention of court fees, or of providing the marriage certificate.

By 2017 the Crown copyright form was set out with boxes to fill in, asking 'what do you want?', and for names and dates, details of marriage, jurisdiction. 'What do you want?' 'What documents are you supplying?' The current printed form looks much longer, and has explanatory notes on each page beside the information needed. The term 'Application', not 'Petition' is used, and the form is simpler but uses a lot of words. For example on page 2 it says: 'if you have a solicitor acting for you the courts will send all papers to their address; if there is no legal representation, to your home address, or you can provide a business address' and 'a copy will be sent to your spouse so if you do not want them to know your contact details do not enter them here'. It is quite challenging to understand how to do this and still get a reply!

The new online version is much briefer.[11] But it is a little 'clunky' to use, in the experience of the author. For example, the screen closed saying 'you can't use this you did not accept cookies', and then suddenly reopens. But there is a good checking service which provides a printable version of the information in three pages, including 'who you are divorcing, date of marriage, based in England and Wales, names and addresses, grounds, other proceedings, payment, declaration of truth'. That is all! There is no mention of children, but there is a reminder not to submit your application unless you can pay now. If not, you can give a number to be called on the next day to pay by card. The final option is to save and return later. This form, like the online C100, might make it easier to act in haste and repent at leisure. The move to make access to justice quick and simple is understandable, but does perhaps run counter to the aim of keeping people away from courts and lawyers. The message from government includes, as it must, both 'stay away' and 'this is how to get to court'.

The online divorce website raises the question whether it is possible to do more online? Might digital justice be better? As noted earlier, one of the first findings of the Digital Family Justice Reform team was that people are willing to accept information or advice online provided that they are confident that they will be able to talk to a human later. Given that this may be difficult to achieve, with neither government nor individuals finding it easy to meet the cost of lawyers, might we look again at how close to 'human' a website might become? What is it that is missing in an online interaction?

Before designing the online divorce application, the MoJ were fortunate in being able to benefit from talking to the RCJ CA (Royal Courts of Justice Citizens

[11] www.apply-divorce.service.gov.uk.

Advice) Family Advice team, who have been providing pro bono legal advice at the Central Family Court in London for many years. After LASPO came into effect in 2013 they were overwhelmed by the numbers of people seeking help, and wanted to make best use of their lawyers. With funding from Freshfields, a large city law firm, to cover the cost of technical support, and drawing on their own practical experience as legal advisers, they produced an interactive programme called COURTNAV (echoing the driver navigation system SATNAV) which can be used by an individual alone, or sitting with a frontline advice worker. Questions are asked in a simple way, and the information collected is checked by an online solicitor, agreed by the user, and then used to populate the actual divorce petition. For example, instead of complex questions about domicile and jurisdiction, COURTNAV Divorce asks: 'do you usually live in England and Wales?'. And instead of complex guidance notes, the programme uses pop-up boxes which make users aware of the consequences of the choices they are making. For example, when choosing the ground for divorce, the box advises you to think carefully. If you choose a behaviour ground you stay in control … if you choose a consent ground like separation, the other side can change their mind at any time. The website then points out that you don't have to say very much. For example you could say: 'we had financial problems and couldn't agree on how to deal with them'. When the programme asks about making a future financial application, the advice is very clear – to say yes to all the items listed to keep your options open. The tone of the advice is not aggressively pro the applicant, but does enable the programme to represent the user as a lawyer would represent a client with, in effect, a duty of care – ie accepting a responsibility to be aware of any steps which could be to the detriment of the user and to advise on how to avoid this. Using COURTNAV feels like having a friendly solicitor at your shoulder, saying 'take care'.

COURTNAV is in effect a website with a virtual duty of care. The solicitor has been inserted into the programme. This appears to work well, and have a major impact on user wellbeing. But when the MoJ drew on COURTNAV DIVORCE to prepare their own online form, they left out the majority of these kinds of notes. It may not be considered appropriate for a government service to appear to advise one side and not the other. But if a way could be found for government to offer a website which not only promises accuracy, but accepts a duty of care, this might go some way towards meeting the frequently expressed wish to talk to a human.

The COURTNAV team are now going even further with their development of Finding Legal Options for Women Survivors (FLOWS) in domestic abuse cases. This programme is still at the pilot stage, but is progressing well. It is designed for women who urgently need some form of protection, usually a non-molestation order, but cannot access a lawyer. The programme is designed to be used by the woman alone or with a trained frontline advice worker. Questions are asked about recent experience of abuse in such a way that, after checking by a pro bono solicitor and the user, the information provided can be used to write her statement to the court, ready for use. The woman is then screened for eligibility for Legal Aid, simply, and if she is eligible, the names of three solicitors who are contracted to do Legal Aid work and accredited for domestic violence will appear on screen. They will already have checked for potential conflict of interest by using the name and address, and so can confidently offer to represent her. This is not just clever digital design, but also the strategic development of a virtuous circle where everyone benefits – not only the woman but also the lawyer who is repaid for his or her voluntary work on the COURTNAV process by getting a client with guaranteed funding and half the work already completed! COURTNAV would like to extend the process even further so that the court could accept the application without requiring the woman to go to the court. But this is ambitious, and not yet within reach.

Might this kind of interaction between digital and non-digital ways of working become a productive part of developing access to family justice? FLOWS combines two vital new elements, both inserting the lawyer into the machine, and creating the virtuous circle, embracing and benefitting not only clients but also lawyers and lay advisers, paid and unpaid, working together. Other services working on this model using online and traditional forms of service to mutual advantage include CLOCK (Community Legal Outreach Collaboration Keele) at the University of Keele which provides training for students with local solicitors who can then use their help in working with clients, and the university can use the data from cases recorded on the CLOCK website for research purposes. Students perform better, the university adds to its research portfolio, lawyers can take on work which they would otherwise be unable to do, including legally aided cases, and most importantly people can receive the legal help they need but cannot afford. A further example lies in the development of legally enhanced support, where digital training and online access to second tier support for lay advice workers in various specialist areas of law enable legally assisted advice to be given more widely (see Kirwan, 2016). This has worked well in employment cases, but could be extended to family work where there is the similarity of an ongoing relationship to be considered plus unequal division of resources.

Perhaps it is time to stop fearing Digital Justice as an Express Train, but instead to welcome it as a magic box of tricks, and to understand that it can do more if the box is opened to extend and support traditional legal ways of working, and increase the possibility of offering to many what lawyers currently offer to a few, a personal service with a duty of care. The case study which follows closes this book with a clear description of what can be achieved through digital family justice.

REFERENCES

Eekelaar, J, Maclean, M and Beinart, S (2000) *Family Lawyers: The Divorce Work of Solicitors* (Oxford, Hart Publishing).

Kirwan, S (ed) (2016) *Advising in Austerity: Reflections on challenging times for advice agencies* (Bristol, Policy Press).

Maclean, M and Eekelaar, J (2009) *Family Law Advocacy: How Barristers help the Victims of Family Failure* (Oxford, Hart Publishing).
Ministry of Justice and Department for Education (2011) *Family Justice Review Final Report*, London, Ministry of Justice.
Ministry of Justice, *Post-Implementation Review of Part 1 of LASPO* (2019) CP 37, February 2019: https://assets.publishing.service.gov.uk/government/uploads/system/uploads/attachment_data/file/777038/post-implementation-review-of-part-1-of-laspo.pdf.

13

A Short Case Study: A Considered and Collaborative Approach to Digital Delivery in England and Wales

ALEXY BUCK, ALEJANDRA DIAZ AND KATE GREGORY-SMITH

I. INTRODUCTION: THE POLICY CONTEXT

THERE IS AN established policy goal in England and Wales of helping separating parents to avoid court hearings where appropriate, recognising that this can help families to resolve disputes in environments which do not exacerbate conflict and lead to poorer outcomes for children. Importantly, however, there is also a recognition that there is a real need for some cases to be in court. Policy thinking has been informed by evidence, financial context and digital possibilities. The overall aim is to develop user-centred digital and non-digital products to help support separating parents through the journey of making arrangements for their children. For new digital products, continuous feedback contributes to the wider policy work and facilitates a nuanced response when a new product is not yet fulfilling user needs. We present one specific example of the successful development and implementation of a digital tool: the digitised 'C100 application form'. This form, used to make applications to the court under section 8 of the Children Act 1989 to make child arrangements after separation, was previously in a long and complex paper format. The value of an interdisciplinary and collaborative approach – drawing on policy, digital and analytical expertise – is highlighted in this short chapter.

In England and Wales, the Legal Aid, Sentencing and Punishment of Offenders Act 2012 (LASPO) came into force in April 2013. LASPO removed a number of family, civil and administrative justice problems from the scope of Legal Aid. Whilst the category of private family law[1] was removed from the scope of Legal

[1] This chapter concentrates on the private family law system which deals with issues that may arise following the breakdown of a family. This ranges from divorce and finance through to arrangements for where children should live, as well as domestic violence. The public family law system deals with when local authorities apply to the courts to take children into care (public law).

Aid, it is still available for private family law cases where domestic violence or child abuse can be evidenced. Access to Legal Aid in these cases is subject to the domestic violence 'gateway'. Recognising that some people need help to resolve problems without going to court, means tested Legal Aid for mediation in private law cases also continues to be available.

Over a third of private family law disposals, that is the court's final determination of the case, now do not have legal representation.[2] This figure has risen from 28% in January–March 2014 up to 37% in July–September 2018, with over a third of disposals having no representation for the last two and a half years, stretching back to April 2016. The number of people using mediation to resolve disputes instead of going straight to court has fallen sharply over the last six years; it became evident that before LASPO's implementation solicitors had been referring clients to mediation if their dispute did not need to be heard by the family court. The number of mediation starts has dropped from a high of over 15,000 in April 2011–March 2012 to under 6,500 in April 2017–March 2018, a fall of 59%.[3] Lastly, there has been a recent and sustained increase in the volume of child arrangement applications made to court. In 2014 the number of child arrangement applications was around 58,000, which has risen to over 73,000 in 2017, a rise of 26%.[4] However, this has still not exceeded the peak of almost 80,000 in 2013.

Responsibility for the family justice system in England and Wales is complex and stretches across a number of government departments and agencies. In addition to the Ministry of Justice's responsibility in family justice, Her Majesty's Courts and Tribunal Service (HMCTS), the Legal Aid Agency (LAA), the Children and Families Court Advisory and Support Service (Cafcass) and its equivalent in Wales (Cafcass Cymru) are critical to delivering an efficient and effective court process. Across government, the Department for Education (DfE), the Department for Work and Pensions (DWP), the Ministry of Housing, Communities and Local Government and the Department of Health and Social Care lead on interconnected policy areas which impact on families more broadly, and which may in turn drive demand for family justice services.

With reform and complex cross-departmental responsibilities as backdrop, the Ministry of Justice has recently focused on a private family law development programme that aims to give better information about alternatives to court and reduce volumes of people going to court to settle private disputes on child arrangement cases *where appropriate*. This policy aim also recognises that avoiding court hearings might help families resolve disputes in environments which do not exacerbate conflict and potentially lead to poorer outcomes for children.

[2] Ministry of Justice, *Family Court Statistics Quarterly* Jul–Sep 2018 (Table 10).
[3] *Legal Aid Statistics* Jul–Sep 2018 (Table 7_2).
[4] *Ministry of Justice Family Court Statistics Quarterly* Jul–Sep 2018 (Table 3).

Research commissioned by the Ministry of Justice[5] shows how parents often see courts as the last resort, after all other options have been exhausted. Parents were also unaware of alternatives to court. Research has further consistently highlighted how parental conflict has an adverse impact on children. Yet more needs to be known about what outcomes alternative dispute arrangements lead to, relative to court, in terms of cost, time and quality of justice (in particular how (cost)-effective mediation is in family disputes); which groups face barriers to accessing justice services, including where access is through new digital forms of delivery; what family or parental characteristics indicate there may be difficulties in reaching amicable decisions regarding children and finances on separation, and whether these families are equipped to deal with conflicts by themselves; and how best to support litigants in person and unrepresented defendants to successfully navigate the family justice system.[6]

II. THE APPLICATION TO COURT TO MAKE CHILD ARRANGEMENTS (C100 FORM)

The C100 form is the form used to apply to the courts for Child Arrangements Orders. Before applying, separating couples are legally required to attend a meeting to discuss their suitability for mediation. This meeting is known as a MIAM (Mediation Information and Assessment Meeting). There are exceptions to the requirement to attend a mediation meeting in certain cases, for example if there is evidence of domestic abuse.

The pre-digitisation C100 form was 26 pages long and difficult for applicants to understand and complete correctly. Approximately, a third of applications were returned to applicants because of missing or incorrect information. This led to significant unnecessary administrative work for HMCTS and Cafcass chasing missing information and potentially creating delays. The overly technical legal language meant litigants in person were unclear about what information they needed to provide and why. Finally, the nature of the form as an application to court meant that it was difficult to highlight alternative ways of resolving disputes or emphasise the potential benefits of mandatory steps such as attendance to mediation before court.

In summary, digitising the C100 sought to achieve three main objectives:

1. *Gain additional insights about our users.* Putting the form online allows for the collection of new data about what users, in this case parents applying to make child arrangements in court, need, and to build a stronger evidence base to inform future private law reforms in the justice system.
2. *Guide users to safe Alternative Dispute Resolution (ADR).* Journeys can be tailored to users' circumstances enabling the Ministry of Justice to assess

[5] Ministry of Justice, *Varying Paths to Justice* (2015).
[6] See Ministry of Justice, *Areas of Research Interest* (2018).

their needs and, where appropriate, present information about the court process and ADR options and their benefits before they continue pursuing the court route.

3. *Benefit the wider business.* By enforcing mandatory steps in the journey such as the MIAM requirement, the aspiration is to save valuable court and Cafcass resources. By offering digital submission to the relevant court the aim is to improve the user journey and support people without representation with step-by-step guidance and clearer content that explains the court process.

III. WAYS OF WORKING: A COLLABORATIVE APPROACH

In the Ministry of Justice, officials from three different specialisms worked together to deliver the first phase of the digitisation of the C100 form. This comprised policy specialists leading on private family law reform, specialists from Ministry of Justice Digital and Technology[7] leading on the digital transformation, and social researchers from MoJ Analytical Services bringing their expertise to bear. Collaborative working included weekly meetings, co-location involving analysts and policy specialists sharing a work space, the co-production of internal documents and an openness and willingness to share ongoing work with the external research community. Throughout this process of the digitisation of the C100 form, further stakeholders such as the judiciary, lawyers and mediators have been consulted.

Given that the application to court to make child arrangements is such an important touchpoint in the user journey, it was a priority for the Ministry of Justice to adopt a considered, balanced and iterative approach.

A. Digital Delivery: Ongoing Development

The project started with a four-week discovery period of scoping and research to understand user needs, define the scope, agree the technical solution and confirm achievability of the digitised C100. The initial digital development phase created the C100 prototype in stages. Work was undertaken in partnership with HMCTS to ensure consistency between the design of the C100 project's output and the other reform service projects in development at HMCTS such as digital divorce,[8]

[7] Digital professionals are governed by the Data, Digital and Technology guidelines set up by the Government Digital Services (GDS) to set standards for digital delivery. GDS was set up in 2011 by the Cabinet Office in the UK with the responsibility for digitally transforming public services. The purpose of its creation was not only to save taxpayers money but to make transacting with government much simpler, cheaper and faster for citizens, businesses and users, many of who are going through a stressful time in their lives.

[8] In England and Wales, HMCTS reform programme included the development of online divorce application.

and that the courts could operationally adapt to a new format. During development, digital specialists completed fortnightly user testing sessions where parts of the form were tested, including information, language, design and flow of the form with parents trying to make child arrangements. The testing made it possible to see what worked, for example asking users to select topics that they wanted the court to consider (eg, arrange with whom the children live). It also helped to identify problems, for example users missed the text about the requirement to attend a MIAM and proceeded to complete subsequent pages of the form. This process helped to iterate the digital C100 prototype by refining the design principles and influencing decision-making upstream (ie, the process by which courts can enforce and collect additional information about the application was informed by parents' feedback).

The digital C100 pilot was launched at the end of March 2018 in the following court areas that included: Milton Keynes, Watford, Guildford and Reading courts. During an initial three-month period, further development was completed and by starting small, the digital team was able to iterate processes and train court staff.

A second phase of the pilot started after this initial period, including extending the digital C100 form to more court locations, allowing the submission of urgent applications, and introducing additional features such as electronic submission and 'save and return' based on users' feedback.

Expanding the pilot to additional court areas helped provide more data on the extent to which reduction of errors submitted on an application reduced processing time and cost for both Cafcass and HMCTS. It also helped better understand the context in which parents were making court applications and their expectations of the process. This informed further digital and operational changes to the service.

Qualitative and quantitative data collected through analytics on the digital tool as well as digital user surveys and follow up interviews were gathered through the pilot phase. Insights included:

- A strong suggestion to develop the ability for an applicant to check their answers before 'signing' the statement of truth and completing the application.
- For users who completed the service in one sitting, it took about an hour (52 minutes). The digital service also allowed users to save their progress and return. For every 10 users who began an application, three made use of the 'Save and Return' function. Almost half of users who saved their application went on to complete it.
- Out of 72 responses to the survey, nearly all respondents (97.2%) were 'Satisfied' or 'Very Satisfied' with their experience of the digital service.

In addition to digital experts doing testing and user research on the actual digital tool, Ministry of Justice social researchers have conducted in-depth qualitative interviews to understand how and why people are using the form within their wider family justice journey and experience of resolving issues/making child arrangements. This research indicated that the trigger point in a relationship for applying to court was either due to a slow deterioration of a previously amicable arrangement, or as a reaction to a recent specific event. The primary reason for previous attempted mediation failing was lack of engagement from the other parent (ie, the respondent). There was some evidence to suggest that respondents were much more likely to be content with the current child arrangements and this contributed to the lack of engagement in mediation.

The research also found that by the time the applicant started completing the C100 application form, they were rigid in their goals and unlikely to be influenced by alternative paths and 'nudges' towards these. However, as only a small sample of applicants interviewed did not complete the C100, it was unclear whether the nudge content was having greater influence than the interviewees reported.

Most applicants who completed the online C100 form found that it was user friendly. However, there were consistent requests for more information on what the court process would be like and what potential outcomes could be. This was sometimes stated whilst completing the form but more often retrospectively after the applicant had gone through the court experience and acknowledged how underprepared they were. The applicants who went to court had neutral or unsatisfactory outcomes possibly due to having unrealistic expectations about the outcome of court proceedings.

IV. CONCLUSIONS AND NEXT STEPS

This short chapter has described an interdisciplinary and nuanced approach to the successful development and implementation of a new digital product: the digitised C100 application form. This form is used to make applications to the court for child arrangements after separation. As we set out above, feedback from users of the form in now over 20 pilot areas has been overwhelmingly positive.

There is a clear appetite to build on the success in the pilot areas and roll the digitised C100 out nationally. The judiciary are also supportive of mainstreaming. HMCTS are now taking the next steps forward, including the funding of the work. HMCTS will also be integrating the form into its case management system upon handover. Work also continues on how this particular digital service can form an important component of the wider digital reform taking place across all HMCTS services.

A considered evaluation framework currently being developed for national roll-out will ensure that any further development work of the digitised C100 form will be based on evidence. The vision is that a nationally-rolled out digitised C100 form will be part of the wider private family justice service 'offer', improving the experience of parents and children during family breakdown.

Index

access to justice, 4, 5, 9, 11, 216–17
alternative dispute resolution, 22–23, 97–98, 141–42
inequalities, 44, 83–84
online dispute resolution, 39, 147, 215–16, 226
provision of information, 194–96, 201
austerity measures, impact of, 5, 25–26, 43
alternative business structures, 77
alternative dispute resolution (ADR), 2, 7–8, 217
arbitration, *see* arbitration
balance of power between parties, 21
collaborative family law, *see* collaborative family law
cost, 22–23, 38–39, 94–95, 100–1, 219–20
definition, 25
domestic violence, 21–22
lawyer-assisted negotiation, *see* lawyer-assisted negotiation
mediation, *see* mediation
online dispute resolution, *see* online dispute resolution
parenting coordinators, use of, *see* parenting coordinators
perceptions and experiences of ADR:
costs of justice, 25–27, 31
enforcement issues, 29
gendered expectations, 30–31
lack of accountability, 29–30
lack of empathy and support, 28
unnecessary prolongation of process, 27–28
settlement-driven nature, 25
apps, 9, 185–86
arbitration, 25
consumer matters, 97–98
Germany, 97–98
Scotland, 144–45, 146
Australia, 9, 217
apps, 185–86
digital divide, 181, 190
digital pathway, 183
digital technologies, use of, 180–81
lack of access, 182
Family Law Pathways Advisory Group:
accessible and integrated systems, 180
Pathways Model, 180
family law review, 179
digital innovation, 179–80
internet resources, availability of, 181
litigation pathway, 182, 187–89
online information, 182, 183–84
online dispute resolution, *see also* digital platforms:
moves towards, 180, 188–89
Pathways Model, 180
litigation pathway, 182
self-help pathway, 182
supported pathway, 182
self-help pathway, 182, 183–84
supported pathway, 182, 186–87
websites, 184–85

balance of power between parties:
alternative dispute resolution, 21
disadvantages the poorer party, 21
ethical issues, 21
inappropriate where domestic violence is involved, 21
women more likely to compromise, 21
British Columbia, Canada, 5–6, 216
alternative dispute resolution, 19–20
collaborative family law, 20
criticisms, 21
litigation, 21
mediation, 20
collaborative family law, 20
cost, 22, 24
client-led nature, 22
informed consent, 22
concerns, 22–23
core values, 22
family law legislative framework:
federal law, 18
state law, 18
internet for self-help, 32–33, 38
biased information, seeking, 33–34
face-to-face support compared, 36

MyLawBC, 34–35
neutral information, seeking, 33
online support groups, 33
websites of advocacy groups, 32–33
legal aid, 18–19
Legal Services Society, 19
mediation, 20
costs, 24
criticisms, 21
MyLawBC platform, 19, 34–35
online dispute resolution, 19, 34–35, 38–39
perceptions and experiences of ADR:
costs of justice, 25–27, 31
enforcement issues, 29
gendered expectations, 30–31
lack of accountability, 29–30
lack of empathy and support, 28
unnecessary prolongation of process, 27–28
privatisation of family law disputes, 23–25
proposed model of dispute resolution, 37
improved online information provision, 37–38
one-stop-shop service, 37
state funding of family law services:
redeployment, 19–20
internet for self-help, 32–34
MyLawBC, 34–35

Canada, *see* **British Columbia, Canada**
children:
acute conflict, 128
austerity measures, impact on, 24
centrality of children's interests, 28, 30, 69, 70, 143–44, 216
child protection, 60–61
child support arrangements, 56, 198–99, 201, 208
children with special needs, 170–71
co-parenting arrangements, 23
mutual consent arrangements, 130–31, 132
conflicts between parents and children, 51
cost of child hearings, 222
legal aid cuts, impact of, 230
McKenzie Friends, 162–63
mediation:
child support, 104, 121
childcare arrangements, 23, 56, 104, 106, 111–12, 121
excluded matters, 121
health and education of the child, 104, 121
use of family home, 104, 121
negotiation, 93–94
online dispute management, 188, 224
C100 form, 233–36
online forum/guidance, 157–58, 168–69, 184–85, 223
parenting plans, 197
peer mediation, 88, 91–92, 98–99
separation agreements and children, 150–51
video-based hearings, 221
clinical legal education, 7, 77–79
civil partnerships, 80, 81, 151, 225
collaborative family law, 20
assisted negotiation, 118
client-led nature, 22
collaborative practices, 116–17
concerns, 22–23
core values, 22
cost, 22, 24
different approaches, 116
informed consent, 22
Scotland, 151–52
Spain, 106, 110, 119–20
conciliation, 6, 89, 92, 95–96, 96–97, 146
civil cases, 96–97
success rates, 97
cost of justice, 25–27
alternative dispute resolution, 22–25, 25–27, 31, 38–39, 94–95, 100–1, 219–20, 233
court costs, 1, 2–3, 50, 215–16, 220, 223
mediation costs compared, 5–6, 220, 233
British Columbia, Canada, 5–6, 216
collaborative family law, 22, 24
mediation, 24
child hearings, 222
clinical legal education, 77
collaborative family law, 22–23, 24
legal aid, 141, 145, 196
see also legal aid
mediation, 94, 145, 220
British Columbia, Canada, 24
court costs compared, 5–6, 220, 233
English and Welsh justice system, 220
Germany, 94–95, 100–1
private family mediation, 121
online dispute resolution, 19, 34–35, 38–39
parenting coordinators, 109
Council of Europe Convention on preventing and combating violence against women and domestic violence (Istanbul Convention), 105
cross-border couples, 107, 134
cross-border disputes, 95, 98

digital platforms, *see also* **online dispute resolution, self-help (-tools),**
France, 134
MyLawBC (British Columbia), 5, 19, 34–35
Rechtwijzer (Netherlands), 194–96
domestic violence, 20, 30, 35, 37, 80, 92, 95, 227–28
Istanbul Convention, 105
legal aid, 231–32
mediation and, 20, 21–22, 62, 90, 104–5, 121, 233
victim/offender mediation, 90
see also gender violence

empowerment, 5, 17, 34–35, 83, 105–6, 131, 170–71, 188–89, 199, 200, 222
England, 8, 9, 217
financial crisis, 219–20
online social networks, 157–58, 161–63
cognitive elaboration, 166–67
collaborative learning, 166
distributors of information, 168–70
identity/experience-based forums, 167–68
identity-based forums, 165–66
online discussion forums, 163–6
risks, 172–73
social function, 170–72
sources of information, as, 166–68
support groups, 158–59
English and Welsh justice system, 217
adversarial divorce system, 215–16
children, arrangements for, 223, 224–25
C100 form, 233–36
mediation, 233
collaborative approach to digital delivery, 231–36
digitisation of C100 form, 233–36
costs, 220
digital developments:
children, arrangements for, 224–25
collaborative approach, 231–36
digitised C100 form, 233–36
MoJ Digital, 221–23
online divorce, 225–28
digitisation of C100 form:
aims, 233–34
evaluation, 235–36
extended roll-out, 235
pilot scheme, 235
prototype, 234–35
family justice system, 219
efficiency, 220
financial crisis, impact of, 219–20
legal aid reforms, 219, 231–32
impact, 220
mediation:
costs, 220
emphasis on, 219
Ministry of Justice, 10
reform, 218
family justice system, 219
alternative dispute mechanism, emphasis on, 219
mediation, emphasis on, 219
MoJ Digital, 221–23
modernisation of courts, 220–21
video-based hearing, 221
MoJ Digital, 221–22
children, arrangements for, 223
online divorce, 223
Out of Court Digital Pathway programme, 222–23
personalised action plans, 222
online divorce, 223
COURTNAV, 227–28
non-contested divorces, 225
Special Procedure, 225–26
responsible organisations, 232

fathers' rights groups, 32–33, 168
McKenzie Friends, 162–63
foreign courts:
recognition and enforcement of judgments, 60
foreign nationals:
cross-border couples,107, 134
cross-border disputes, 95, 98
France, 8, 216, 217
divorce without a judge:
children, 132, 134
conditions, 132
lawyers' attitudes to, 133
legislation, 132
nationality of couple, 134
notaries' role, 134
success, 133
mutual consent divorces, 130–31, 132, 133
online divorces, 134
online dispute resolution:
private online platforms, 134–35
privatisation of divorce, 137
divorce without a judge, 132–34
mediation, 131
mutual consent divorces, 130–31

online divorce, 134–35
simplification of divorce, 131–32
'uberisation' of divorce, 136
resource management developments, 127–28, 137
virtual private networks, 129, 130
transition to digital, 129
data protection concerns, 130
exchange of documents, 129
impact, 130
resource management developments, 127–28
virtual private networks, 129, 130
treatment of cases, 127–28
procedural reforms, 128
resource management developments, 127–28
streamlining, 128–29
transition to digital, 129
virtual private networks:
exchange of documents, 129

gender violence:
domestic violence, 20, 30, 35, 37, 80, 92, 95, 227–28
Istanbul Convention, 105
legal aid, 231–32
mediation and, 20, 21–22, 62, 90, 104–5, 121, 233
victim/offender mediation, 90
exclusion from mediation, 104–5
Istanbul Convention, 105
mandatory mediation, 21–22
Germany, 7, 217
arbitration, non-binding
consumer matters, 97–98
child care proceedings, 94
conciliation, 95–96, 96–97
civil cases, 96–97
success rates, 97
cross-agency cooperation, 94
cross-border disputes, 95
court-based mediation
civil law, 96–97
family law, 93–94
family courts, 92
family mediation, 92–96
Cochem model, 94–95
court-based mediation, 93–94
court proceedings compared, 92–93
imposed mediation, 94–95
independent from the courts, 94–96
legal aid, 92, 96
mediation as a condition for, 93–94
mediation
benefits, 99
challenges, 99–100
condition for legal aid, 93–94
cost, 94–95, 100–1
family mediation, 92–96
imposed mediation, 94–95
peer mediation, 91–92, 98–99
victim/offender mediation, 89–91
peer mediation
bullying, 91
evaluation, 98–99
school violence, 91
standards of practice, 91–92
victim/offender mediation, 89–91
enforcement of sanctions, 91
personal injury cases, 90–91

individual responsibility, 75–76, 215
Canada, 23–25
public expenditure cuts, impact of, 1–4
Scotland, 152–53
see also self-help
inequalities
balance of power between parties
disadvantages the poorer party, 21
ethical issues, 21
inappropriate where domestic violence is involved, 21
women more likely to compromise, 21
monetary barriers, 21, 26
see also gender violence
informal support, ***see*** **online social networks; social networks**
internet access to advice
face-to-face support compared, 36
MyLawBC (British Columbia), 34–35
Rechtwijzer, 194
alimony calculation tool, 197–99
divorce and parenting plan, 196–97
evaluation of users' experiences, 199–200
positive aspects, 210–11
purpose, 194–96
Rechtwijzer 2.0
commercialisation, 203–5
complete do-it-yourself divorce, 201–2
evaluation, 202–3
moving beyond signposting, 201
target users, 201

use of internet for self-help, 32–33
biased information, seeking, 33–34
neutral information, seeking, 33
online support groups, 33
websites of advocacy groups, 32–33

lawyer-assisted negotiation
collaborative family law, 118, 151–52
Scotland, 151–52
collaborative law, 151
separation agreements, 150–51
Spain, 118
see also collaborative family law
legal advice and legal information
conciliation, 96
distinction between, 3
England and Wales
clinical legal education, 77–78
family law clinics, 78–79
students, 76
non-lawyers v lawyers, 2, 121
online communities, 168–72
online dispute resolution, 187
online services and provision of advice, 36, 189, 220
MyLawBC (British Columbia), 34–35
Rechtwijzer tool, 195, 204–5
Rechtwijzer tool, 195, 204–5
students, 76, 83–84
legal aid
Australia, 181, 188
British Columbia, 5, 18–19, 24
Legal Services Society, 19
England and Wales, 7, 36, 75–79, 83, 163–64, 219–20, 228, 231–32
Legal Aid, Sentencing and Punishment of Offenders Act 2012 (LASPO), 75, 78, 163–64, 219–20, 227, 231–32
Germany, 92, 94
Netherlands, 9, 195–96, 199, 200, 206
Scotland, 141, 145
Turkey, 62
legal profession
alternative business structures, 77
changing role, 2–4, 37
England and Wales
France, 135, 136
Netherlands, 203, 205
mediation, 109–10
provision of legal advice, 187
see also professional roles

McKenzie Friends, 162–63
mediation, 1, 7, 8, 20, 87
balance of power between parties, 21
coercion elements of mediation, 21
disadvantages the poorer party, 21
inappropriate where domestic violence is involved, 21
women more likely to compromise, 21
British Columbia, 21–22
balance of power between parties, 21
coercion, 21
criticisms, 21
domestic violence, 21–22
ethical issues, 21
Comprehensive Accredited Lawyer Mediators, 151
court-based mediation, 88–89
civil law, 96–97
family law, 93–94
Germany
court-based mediation, 88–89, 93–94, 96–97
family mediation, 92–96
peer mediation, 88, 91–92, 98–99
victim/offender mediation, 89–91
family mediation
Cochem model, 94–95
court proceedings compared, 92–93
court-based mediation, 93–94
imposed mediation, 94–95
independent from the courts, 94–96
France, 131
Harvard concept, 87–88
lawyers, 109–10
peer mediation, 88
bullying, 91
evaluation, 98–99
school violence, 91
standards of practice, 91–92
Scotland, 144–45
legislative framework, 145
review of, 145
Turkey
growing importance, 63–64
legal aid, 62
legal framework, 62–63
victim/offender mediation, 89–91
aims, 89–91
enforcement of sanctions, 91
minimum standards for rights, support and victim protection, 89
personal injury cases, 90–91

mediators
accreditation, 8, 62
changing role, 2–4, 109–10, 203, 211
confidentiality, 115
cross-border disputes, 95
e-courts, 67–69
informal mediators, 64
lawyers as, 63, 110, 121
neutrality and impartiality, 21, 31, 99
peer-mediators, 91–92, 99
professionalisation, 109, 111–12, 131
registration, 62, 67, 112
training, 8, 21, 62, 109, 112, 115
mutual consent divorces, 93, 128, 130–31, 132, 133
online divorces, 134
see also uncontested divorce

nationality:
cross-border couples, 107, 134
cross-border disputes, 95, 98
Netherlands, 9, 216–17
access to justice, 195–196
legal aid cuts, 195–96
online dispute resolution, 193–194
divorce resolution, 193–94
Rechtwijzer, 194
reasons for failure of Rechtwijzer, 210
differences of opinion of developers, 208–9
financially unsustainable, 205
lack of attention to needs of users, 207–8
no guarantee of fairness, 209–10
resistance by legal institutions, 205–7
Rechtwijzer, 194
alimony calculation tool, 197–99
divorce and parenting plan, 196–97
evaluation of users' experiences, 199–200
positive aspects, 210–11
purpose, 194–96
Rechtwijzer 2.0:
commercialisation, 203–5
complete do-it-yourself divorce, 201–2
evaluation, 202–3
moving beyond signposting, 201
online self-help (tool), 196, 201
target users, 201
notaries, 8, 132, 134, 149–50

online dispute resolution (**ODR**), *see also* **digital platforms, self-help** (**-tools**), 7, 8
British Columbia, 32–34
MyLawBC, 34–35
cost, 38–39
face-to-face support compared, 36
France:
private online platforms, 134–35
internet for self-help, 32–33
biased information, seeking, 33–34
neutral information, seeking, 33
online support groups, 33
websites of advocacy groups, 32–33
MyLawBC, 34–35
Netherlands, 193, 205
Poland:
e-court, success of, 45–48, 55–56
e-justice, 45
Rechtwijzer, 193–94
Spain, 122
Turkey:
commercial and employment disputes, 68
e-court, 67–69
family law disputes, 68–69
online social networks, 157–58, 161–63
distributors of information, 168–70
online discussion forums, 163–5
identity-based forums, 165–66
risks, 172–73
sources of information, as, 166
cognitive elaboration, 166–67
collaborative learning, 166
identity/experience-based forums, 167–68
social function, 170–72
support groups, 158–59
British Columbia, 33
see also social networks

parenting coordinators, 25, 106, 108–9, 110, 122
parenting plans, 196–97, 198, 199, 203, 223
peer mediation, 88, 91–92, 98–99
personal responsibility, *see* **individual responsibility**
Poland, 6, 43, 216
courts, use of, 48–50
divorce, 44–45
politics, 56
religion, 53–55

e-court, success of, 45–46, 55–56
defendants' perspective, 46–47
plaintiffs' perspective, 46
socio-economic position of users, 47–48
e-justice:
e-court, 45
introduction of, 45
family disputes:
secrecy, 53–55
types, 50–51
willingness to use courts, 52–53
privatisation of family law disputes, 3
British Columbia, 19, 23–25
France, 137
divorce without a judge, 132–34
mediation, 131
mutual consent divorces, 130–31
online divorce, 134–35
simplification of divorce, 131–32
'uberisation' of divorce, 136
pro bono work, 76, 77–79, 83, 145, 226–27
mediators, 219
teaching family law for pro bono contexts, 79–82
public expenditure cuts, 1–3, 38–39, 215–16, 219–20, 222–23

rule of law:
access to justice, 4–5, 217–18

same-sex couples, *see* **civil partnerships**
Scotland, 217
access to justice, 140
alternative dispute resolution:
adjudication, 146
arbitration, 144–45, 146
collaborative law, 144–45
conciliation, 146
early neutral evaluation, 146
mediation, 144–45, 146
negotiation, 146
ombudsmen, 146
review of, 145
civil court statistics, 130
civil law reforms, 142
access to good quality information, 142
major review of civil courts, 142–43
collaborative law:
lawyer-led negotiation, 151–52
Comprehensive Accredited Lawyer Mediators, 141–42
negotiated settlements, 151
Digital Strategy for Justice in Scotland, 147
access to accurate, timely information, 147
making data work, 147, 148
provision of digitised systems, 147–48
divorce:
court-based resolution, 148–49
Ordinary/Simplified procedures, 149–50
system failure, 148
English law compared, 140–41
family dispute resolution:
bottom-up development, 141–42
lawyer-led negotiation, 150
collaborative law, 151
Comprehensive Accredited Lawyer Mediators, 151
separation agreements, 150–51
legal aid, 141
mediation, 144–45
legislative framework, 145
review of, 145
'modernisation and transformation', 139, 143–44
online dispute resolution, 8
personal autonomy principle, 152–53
separation agreements, 150
collaborative law, 151
Comprehensive Accredited Lawyer Mediators, 151
potential for digital modernisation, 153–54
registration of, 150–51
Simplified Procedure divorces:
non-cohabitation grounds, 149
statistics, 149–50
technological advances, 146–47
Digital Strategy, 147
self-help (- tools), *see also*: **online dispute resolution, digital platforms,** 32–33, 38
Australia, 182, 183–84
British Columbia, 32–33, 38
biased information, seeking, 33–34
face-to-face support compared, 36
MyLawBC, 34–35
neutral information, seeking, 33
online support groups, 33
websites of advocacy groups, 32–33
internet usage:
biased information, seeking, 33–34
face-to-face support compared, 36
neutral information, seeking, 33

online support groups, 33
websites of advocacy groups, 32–33
Poland, 49, 52, 53
Rechtwijzer, 194
alimony calculation tool, 197–99
divorce and parenting plan, 196–97
evaluation of users' experiences, 199–200
positive aspects, 210–11
purpose, 194–96
Rechtwijzer 2.0:
commercialisation, 203–5
complete do-it-yourself divorce, 201–2
evaluation, 202–3
moving beyond signposting, 201
target users, 201
see also online social networks; social networks
Spain, 8, 217
Basque region:
concerns, 115
mediation stages, 112–14
mediators, 112, 114–15
origins of family mediation, 111–12
out-of-court family mediation, 112
success of mediation, 114, 121
Catalonia, 106
analysis of implementation of mediation, 108
collaborative law, 110
concerns about mediation, 109–10
development of family mediation, 106
family law mediation framework, 106–7
parenting coordination, 108–9, 110
politics, 106–7
collaborative law, 106, 110, 119–20
family mediation, 120
Basque Region case study, 106, 121
Catalonia case study, 106
concerns about mediation, 109–10
equality between parties, 105–6
excluded matters, 104–5, 121
extra-judicial mediation, 104
gender violence, 104–5
intra-judicial mediation, 104
legal framework, 103–4
origins, 103
voluntary nature, 104, 120
gender violence:
equality between parties, 105–6
exclusion from mediation, 104–5
mediators, 112, 114–15
lawyers, relationship with, 121
online dispute resolution, 122
parenting coordinators, 106, 122
Catalonia, 108–9, 110
social networks, 217–18
family dispute resolution, importance for, 159–61
social identity theory, 161–62
see also online social networks
students:
pro bono family law schemes, 78–79
challenges, 83–84
diagnostic approach, 81–82
teaching syllabus, 79–81
triage method, 82–83

teaching family law, 79–81
diagnostic approach, 81–82
triage method, 82–83
Turkey, 6–7, 216
family, concept of, 59–60
family court system, 60, 61
rulings and measures taken, 60–61
procedural provisions, 61
family and religious guidance offices:
origins, 64–65
users, 65–66, 70
mediation:
growing importance, 63–64
legal aid, 62
legal framework, 62–63
online dispute resolution:
commercial and employment disputes, 68
e-court, 67–69
family law disputes, 68–69
politicisation of the family, 59–60, 70

uncontested divorce, 225
mutual consent divorces, 93, 128, 130–31, 132, 133
online divorces, 134

websites, 2–4, 66
advocacy groups, 32–33
law firms, 134–35
provision of information, 2–4, 32–33, 184–85, 188
women, *see* **domestic violence; gendered violence**

www.ingramcontent.com/pod-product-compliance
Ingram Content Group UK Ltd.
Pitfield, Milton Keynes, MK11 3LW, UK
UKHW021908150926
475560UK00003B/248